THE TRUMP TRILOGY

THE WAR FOR AMERICA'S SOUL + AMERICA IN
THE LAST DAYS + SPIRITUAL WAR TRUMPS
EVERYTHING

CHUCK MARUNDE, J.D.

Copyright Chuck Marunde 2024
Last Updated: 11-13-24, 11-27-24, 11-28-24, 11-30-24, 12-2- 24

Compare the most recent update here to the date of the version you purchased, because you get free Kindle version updates forever on Amazon. To learn how to get updates, see the instructions on BooksOnline.Club where you can also purchase this book, and where you can apply to become an affiliate and earn 30% on every sale. Need help funding your Youtube channel? Share the truth and become an affiliate.

All rights reserved. No part of this publication may be reproduced, stored in a retrieval system, or transmitted in any form or by any means, electronic, mechanical, photocopying, recording, or otherwise, without the prior written permission of the author. The author may be contacted by email directly at chuckmarunde@protonmail.com.

Cover Design by Chuck Marunde

CONTENTS: THE TRUMP TRILOGY

Preface to The Trilogy   7

THE WAR FOR AMERICA'S SOUL
THE DEEP STATE

Prologue   13

Introduction   15

1. We Were Created to Be Free   19
   Not Enslaved By Government

2. You Cannot Force Someone to Be Free   23
   Freedom Is A Personal Choice With Implications For The Whole Nation

3. Why There is No Turning Back   27
   Don't Believe Politicians Who Say Our Future Is Brighter Than Our Past

4. Four Trump Miracles to Save America   37
   The Greatest Disruptor in U.S. History

5. Puppets of Liberalism   49
   Main Street Media Exposed As The Ultimate Fake News

6. Liberals Own the Internet   57
   Google + Facebook + Amazon + Apple + Microsoft = Liberal Power

7. The Death of Truth   65
   And The Rise of Massive Lies, Misrepresentations, and Deception

8. When Facts Don't Matter   73
   Liberals Hate Facts That Contradict Their World View And Their Secret Agendas

9. The Turning Point in America   81
   God Gives Americans a Reprieve

10. The Kavanaugh Hearings   93
    Where Admissibility of Evidence, Weight of Evidence, and Credibility Are All Lost

11. Liberals Do Not Bargain   115
    Liberals Have No Intention of Compromising With Their Enemies

12. The Truth About Capitalism *And How Liberals Have Been Lying To An Entire Generation*	121
13. The Death of Privacy *How Americans Just Let It Happen*	125
14. The Boldest Liberal Misrepresentations *Liberal Politicians Do The Opposite Of What They Promise Their Constituents*	133
15. The 20 Rules of The Liberal Template *AKA: The Secrets Of Stalin, Zedong, Hitler, and Obama*	145
16. Liberalism and Christianity *Democrats Please Stop Saying You Are Christians! Your Behavior Is Anti-God!*	167
17. The Destructive Effect of Liberalism *America's Total Political, Economic, and Social Destruction*	179
18. Republicans Have Blood on Their Hands *They Continue To Compromise Our Most Sacred Rights*	187
19. Hope is Not a Strategy *Somebody Please Do Something To Save Our Country*	193
20. A Strategy *For The Salvation Of America*	201
Appendix: How Can People Be Blind to The Truth?	211

AMERICA IN THE LAST DAYS
THE SLAYING OF A GREAT NATION

Introduction	221
1. The Greatness of America *And The Precipice of Darkness*	231
2. America Is A Battlefield *With Dead and Wounded Everywhere*	237
3. The Psychology of Liberalism *You Are Their Mortal Enemy*	245
4. What God Says About Narcissism and Psychopathy *Old Illnesses, New Names*	263
5. Liberalism is Destroying America *Few Liberals Comprehend Their Destructive Role*	273
6. Liberals Murdered 66 Million Babies *They Celebrated Roe v. Wade*	281

7. LGBTQ+P and Sexual Perversion *Homosexuality, Transgenderism, Pedophilia and Human Trafficking Defines Liberals*	285
8. Liberals Destroyed Our Education System *From Kindergarten to Ivy League Universities*	289
9. Liberals Shredded the Constitution *Privacy is Completely Gone and They're Coming For Your Guns*	293
10. Liberals Destroyed The American Church *Their Hatred for Christianity and God is Legendary*	297
11. Liberals Destroyed The News Media *Their Evil Agendas Take Priority Over The Truth*	301
12. Liberals Destroyed The U.S. Government *They Have Infiltrated The Congress, The Senate, and Every Agency*	303
13. Liberals Destroyed The American Justice System *When Lies and Manipulation and Hidden Agendas Rule The Courts*	307
14. Liberals Destroyed Hollywood and Nashville *The Movie and Music Businesses All Fell to Liberalism*	311
15. Liberals Will Sink Their Own Ship to Defeat You *They Cannot Let You Win, Even If It Means Their Own Suicide*	315
16. The Trajectory of America's Final Days *What If You Knew The End Was Near?*	325
17. Defending America Against Liberalism *A Strategy for the 11th Hour*	345

SPIRITUAL WAR TRUMPS EVERYTHING
POLITICIANS ARE NOT YOUR SAVIOR

Introduction	351
Part I	355
1. The War of The Ages *The War That Lasts for Thousands of Years*	357
2. Satan's War Strategy *No Evil too Evil*	363
3. Satan's War Against God *No Stronger Hatred Exists*	369
4. Demons vs. Angels *The Invisible Raging War Around Us*	375

5. Angels Fight For Us and Minister to Us *Mighty Warriors to Our Aide*	381
6. Rewards To The Victors *What a Celebration There Will Be*	385
7. The Tribulation War Reaches an Eternal Apex *"For Then There Shall Be Great Tribulation."*	391
Part II	403
8. Preparing Our Weapons of War *The Ultimate and Only Source of True Power*	405
9. How To Use Weapons of War *The Victorious Soldier for Christ*	411
10. Wrong Weapons & Wrong Battlefields *Politicians Fail Us Because They Are Fighting The Wrong Enemies In The Wrong Arenas*	421
About the Author	429
Also by Chuck Marunde, J.D.	431

PREFACE TO THE TRILOGY
WHY READ THIS BOOK?

You and I just lived through an epic day in American history. If I may make some comparisons and pontificate with some hyperbole, I'm thinking of the volcanic eruption of Krakatoa in 1883 that was heard 3,000 kilometers away, the loudest explosion known in world history. I'm also thinking of the 1964 9.2 magnitude Alaska earthquake because I lived 340 miles from the epicenter. If you live in the South, perhaps you will think of Hurricane Katrina in 2005. These natural disasters changed a lot of lives.

Of course, the major event on my mind is the landslide victory that elected Donald J. Trump the 47th President of the United States! Granted, this is not in the nature of a natural disaster, but it was an act of God if we are to believe Romans 13:1, and it's impact will go down as one of history's epic events that changed the world forever.

President Trump's second term as President is almost certainly going to have greater long-term consequences for the world's population than any of the massive natural disasters mentioned above. Granted, natural disasters took lives and robbed people of their worldly possessions. Krakatoa officially killed 36,000 people, and the Alaska earthquake killed 136 people.

By comparison, the second term of Donald Trump will forever impact millions of lives in America and billions around the world. The world is about to experience a cataclysmic upheaval that will realign nations.

Never before has a single election held the power to disrupt and shape the fate of billions across every nation on Earth. Never has there been such a black-and-white contrast between good and evil exposed in the American government, a truly demonic agenda of a political party that captured and enslaved a nation for as long as the Democrat Party did in America. In real time, we are watching a nation get dramatically saved from the clutches of darkness with the single election of a President and his appointees.

No one would claim that Donald Trump is Jesus Christ or that he is a better communicator than President John F. Kennedy or Ronald Reagan. He is just a man. But great men throughout history whose legacy changed the world were also just men.

It only takes an ordinary man to accomplish extraordinary things if God appoints that man at the right time and place.

This book will prove why this election and this man have this unprecedented power to turn America around so dramatically. It will take three books to prove this, and that's why this is a Trilogy.

The War for America's Soul will articulate how we got to this place where Americans are no longer free but are enslaved to massive government power and a deep and dark network of institutions, corporations, and media.

America in The Last Days will carefully demonstrate why we are so close to the precipice of total annihilation by evil.

And **Spiritual War Trumps Everything** will not avoid the

spiritual realm and biblical prophesy as other books about America do, but details exactly what the Bible says about these times we live in and how America does or does not play a role.

We just crossed the tipping point, and there is no going back. Are you ready for what is to come? Do you understand the precarious nature of America's future? Do you understand what this means for your future and your children's future?

This election result is the equivalent of The Perfect Storm as multiple events and people and history come together like never before to create a devastating force against the darkness that has gripped our land. Unlike the movie in which George Clooney could not turn the boat around and get out of the darkness, will President Trump be able to turn America around?

Join me in a careful review of how we got here and the journey we are now embarking on with our 47th President. May God protect and guide President Donald J. Trump.

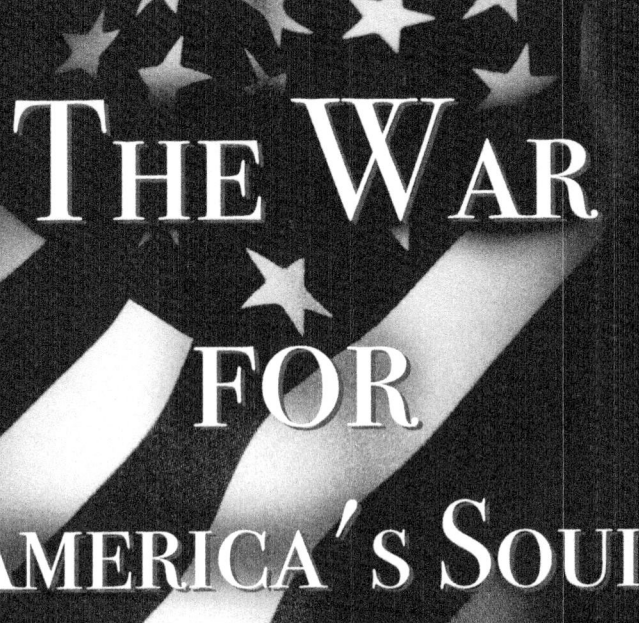

PROLOGUE

The War for America's Soul is a battle for the truth. It always has been. I'm not speaking metaphorically here. Literally, the battle is for the truth, and it has been from the beginning.

With all that is going on in the world today to take down America and consolidate control by the ruling elite worldwide, this book could not be more relevant.

It was a lie that destroyed a perfect world and began the long, painful fall of all of mankind. The battle for the truth started in the Garden of Eden when Lucifer lied to Eve. Then, Eve got Adam to accept the lie, and when God confronted him, Adam blamed Eve. Adam even blamed God to God's face when he said, "The woman you gave me . . ." is the one who caused me to sin.

Fast forward the clock thousands of years. In America today, we see an intense battle for the truth, and we see how lies, distortions, and misrepresentations dominate the discourse in America.

America is being ripped apart by lies. The battle for the truth is raging, and it rages in every corner of America on every subject and in every organization. It is personified by our own executive and legislative branches of government. The U.S. House and Senate are embarrassing institutions where lies dominate everything they do. The most powerful political body in the history of the world has become a laughing stock of lies and deception to the entire world.

This book explains precisely how America got to this point, who brought us to this place, and what we can do to fight for the truth and stand against the lies. This is an extremely practical book with real answers for the biggest problems America faces. Not only do I discuss political history that reveals how we got here, but I also include the wisdom of the ages, which is too often left out of the conversation entirely. What is that wisdom of the ages? It is the wisdom of God found in the bible.

> *It is no coincidence that Donald Trump coined the phrase "fake news," which has changed the entire landscape of false news and the issue of censorship. It is also no coincidence that this is the first President to proclaim that God is in charge, that Christians must and will have religious freedom and freedom of speech, and that it was God who saved his life in order to become the 47th President.*

INTRODUCTION

In 1966 Robert F. Kennedy delivered a speech in Cape Town, South Africa, in which he said, "There is a Chinese curse which says 'May he live in interesting times.' Like it or not, we live in interesting times. They are times of danger and uncertainty; but they are also the most creative of any time in the history of mankind."

It was only two years earlier when his brother, President John F. Kennedy, was assassinated, and it was two years later when Robert F. Kennedy would be assassinated. He was right about living in times of danger and uncertainty. 50 years after Robert Kennedy's assassination, his death and his brother's assassination are still clothed in mystery.

Since then, we have seen unbelievable political corruption, federal fraud, trillions of dollars disappear from our federal coffers, extraordinary behind-the-scenes compromises of American interests, the shredding of the United States Constitution and the Bill of Rights, and what appears to be a complete lack of accountability by criminals at the highest levels of government.

The United States has also been in a free fall when it comes to the moral fabric of the nation. Not only are bold-faced lies sold as absolute truth, but Americans can't seem to recognize the most obvious cases of lying, manipulating, and exaggerating.

We are living in interesting times, but life for many in America has turned into a nightmare that has become something akin to living in Sodom and Gomorrah. Chaos, hate, the politics of personal destruction, cheating, lying, sexual immorality, child trafficking and pedophilia, and the worst things you can possibly imagine, are no longer exceptions to the rule of life in America. They are life in America. They are not only accepted, they are proudly and aggressively promoted, and if you express a contrary opinion, you will be personally attacked viciously and relentlessly.

Our own congress and senate no longer work every day to take care of important business for the American people. Instead, they are constantly holding hearings and investigations on corruption and how to destroy their opponents and anyone who supports their opponents. The unbelievably vile attacks on Christians and conservatives in America have been facilitated by powerful agencies of the United States, including the IRS, the FBI, and the CIA.

We are not just talking about partisan politics hurting this country: We are talking about an intense form of personal destruction that was incomprehensible only a decade ago.

As one of my best friend's father used to say when I was a teenager, "This country is going to hell in a handbasket." How right he was, but in recent years this has accelerated, and the U.S. has come to the precipice of total disaster.

In this book, I will explain how we got to this place, and what we ought to do at this late stage of this country's demise. I've combined worldly wisdom with spiritual wisdom to understand current events and America's role in the last days.

My hope is that this book will help you understand the times in which we live, and better equip you for living and playing your part to make life better for your family and for all of us.

It is no coincidence that Robert F. Kennedy, Jr. nephew of President John F. Kennedy and son of Robert F. Kennedy, is going to play a major role in the Trump Administration.

CHAPTER 1
WE WERE CREATED TO BE FREE
NOT ENSLAVED BY GOVERNMENT

We hold these truths to be self-evident: that all men are created equal; that they are endowed by their Creator with certain unalienable rights; that among these are life, liberty, and the pursuit of happiness. Thomas Jefferson

We were created to be free. The desire to be free and to live free is at the core of who every human being is. Our hearts beat and our minds are excited out of a need to be creatively free and independent. Freedom is the driving force that makes us human and alive and productive. The exercise of freedom by honest and hard-working people is a powerful force for good.

This is the reason the United States became the greatest nation in the history of the world. We started as desperate people escaping slavery and running from governments that crushed freedom, infringed on the right to privacy, demeaned humanity, controlled religion, and deprived citizens of the right to own guns for self-defense. We escaped England, France, Germany, and Spain seeking freedom, and we found it in America.

The early settlers had little more than the clothing on their backs, but they were willing to work hard, to be creative, and to risk everything for the sake of freedom. They had no safe haven when they came to America. They faced uncertainty, dangers, and death. But they treasured freedom above all else, and they hated slavery, especially the kind fostered by self-serving politicians building government power. As a result, America became the greatest free nation on earth, and for two centuries, the power of individual pursuits built the greatest economy, the best inventions, and the most productive free people of any nation in the world. Even our most advanced military technologies are the result of the ingenuity of individual American inventors and private industry that contracted with the government. The U.S. government uses our tax dollars to buy the knowledge and equipment.

The idea that we were created to be free is not just a philosophical leaning--it is a spiritual truth. It is the way God created us. God abhors slavery, and He loves freedom. Some have called free enterprise God's economic system. If God had an economic system, it would be perfect, and free enterprise is not perfect. A man-made economic system of any kind will always fall short of a perfect system, but the free enterprise system created in America is the closest thing on earth to God's economic system.

This will infuriate Democrats, and it will entertain Republicans, but neither seem to understand the foundational importance of freedom in an economic and political system for every single human being. Talking points rule the discussions, and shallow debates between the political elite have captured the attention of the nation, but the discussions avoid an emphasis on the most fundamental of all human needs--the need to be free.

No people in history have ever said, "We want to be enslaved," or "We want to suffer under the hands of a cruel government." But they have said, "We want a king," and then suffered death and torture under his rule. They have said, "We yield to Royalty," never mind the dark dungeons and the witch hunts fostered by the religious leaders of the day. All over the world, they have said, "We bow down to a cruel dictator," and then suffered terribly for generations. They have said, "We willingly submit to a President, and we give him and Senators and Congressman authority to rule over us," and then suffered the loss of precious liberties.

Throughout history, the people could have stopped the King's murderous rule. They could have stopped the abuses of dictators, and they could have stopped liberalism in its tracks. But they did not . . . until the founders of America left England to start a new country. Even then, so determined were the liberals of England to expand government power over the people, they attacked us across an ocean.

The greed and reach of government always tend toward expansion and control. The naive assumption by many Americans that government is basically good goes against every example of every government in world history. No government has ever proven it is altruistic, self-sacrificing, loving and generous to all of its people. Not one. No government has proven it is all-wise. Not one. Government stands against personal freedom by definition. Governments do not set people free; they enslave them.

We were not created to be enslaved. We were created to be free. Every fiber of our humanity screams out, "I want to be free." Yet, this is not the topic of conversation today. Americans have been distracted by talking points, radical ideologies, and intellectual debates. Americans have lost their way. While they would acknowledge they do not want to be slaves, they consistently yield to government power and domination over their lives. In other words, while Americans claim to want to be free, they keep choosing the path to slavery.

When you make a wrong choice, even if you don't know it was a wrong choice at the time, later it begins to feel wrong, and as time passes, it feels more and more wrong. Throughout history, people have been short-sighted when it came to their rulers and elected leaders. Only after they lost most of their freedom and realized that their children and grandchildren were going to live in slavery did they begin to even ask questions about their leaders. By then, it is too late, as I'll explain in the chapter entitled *Why There Is No Turning Back*.

CHAPTER 2

YOU CANNOT FORCE SOMEONE TO BE FREE

FREEDOM IS A PERSONAL CHOICE WITH IMPLICATIONS FOR THE WHOLE NATION

The truth is not for all men, but only for those who seek it.
Ayn Rand

If you had the keys to the cell doors deep within the dungeon of a castle, but the slaves were afraid to come out of their dark cells into the light, you could not set them free. You could open the cell doors, but no matter how you coaxed them, no matter how you pleaded with them to recognize that freedom was theirs for the taking, if they refused to come out, they would remain slaves forever. You cannot set slaves free if they choose to remain slaves.

In America freedom is a choice. You choose to be free, or you choose to be a slave. There is no such thing as partly free. You are free or you are not. If you are not free, you cannot claim to be only partly enslaved. If you are enslaved at all, you are a slave. The question then becomes who or what is your master? To whom or to what do you bow down?

Consider the most fundamental of all freedoms--spiritual freedom. Jesus Christ came to set the captives free. The captives are all those who are not saved. Those who are saved are set free. You choose to believe by faith that Jesus is your savior, and you are given eternal salvation. All of this starts with a choice that you are free to make.

No one in all of history has ever been forced to become a Christian. Someone might be persuaded to say the right words, but freedom will not be fooled. Yielding to freedom must be genuine and it must come from deep within the heart and mind. As the author of freedom, God clearly has given everyone a choice to be free or to remain in slavery. This is true in the spiritual world, and it is true in our political world.

In the political realm, America has set more captives free around the world than any nation in history. This is our great heritage. America was able to do this because her people were free. America wove freedom into every fabric of its political, judicial, and economic systems. The freedom that built America into the greatest nation in world history has been the salvation of millions of people around the world for two centuries. Now that we've matured as a political system, how is freedom playing out in America today? There is a raging war in America, and the war might aptly be called "The War for America's Soul" or "The War for Freedom."

I would suggest the single most important word in American history is ***freedom***. America was founded upon the passionate desire and need of people to be free. The early colonists left England and many European countries because they sought one thing--freedom. They wanted to be free from bondage, free from slavery, and free from government domination. They abhorred the loss of their personal freedoms. They wanted their religious freedom. They wanted freedom from intrusions into their homes. They wanted the freedom to own guns and the freedom to defend their families and homes. They wanted freedom to express themselves without retaliation. They wanted freedom to associate with anyone of their choosing without condemnation. They wanted to be free from unreasonable arrests and unlawful imprisonment.

The Declaration of Independence is a declaration of freedom. The U.S. Constitution is the most powerful document ever drafted by a man promoting freedom under a government institution. The purpose of the Bill of Rights is the protection of personal freedoms. America's founding is all about freedom. Can there be any argument that the single most important word in American history is ***freedom***?

For thousands of years, people around the world have fought for freedom, have been enslaved by governments that stole their freedom, have died for freedom, have revolted for freedom, and have been enslaved again. Freedom and slavery are at the root of all wars and all revolutions. I think the most important word in American history is ***freedom***. Yet, there may be one other word more significant in the world—**truth**. Alexander Solzhenitsyn proclaimed this when he said, "One word of truth outweighs the whole world." Freedom and truth are inseparable.

You cannot force someone to be free, and if you tried and insisted that you had set them free without their cooperation, you would actually have enslaved them in the name of freedom. Governments are famous for doing this. This is the meaning of the phrase, "We're from the government, and we're here to help you." Therein lies the liberal trap that has been set for those who are less educated and do not have the means of upward mobility. The liberal calling is, "Come all you who are poor and uneducated, and all you who are weary of working for low wages, and we will save you with welfare, food stamps, and a multitude of entitlement programs. We will set you free." What a trap! What looks like freedom and help is nothing more than a trap of enslavement. What the devil calls freedom, God calls slavery.

Freedom is everything. Freedom is so important to Americans; we voluntarily died to achieve its independence, and men and women from every generation in America have voluntarily died around the globe to protect the freedom of Americans and to promote freedom for others less fortunate. There are two words that I love more than any others: ***freedom*** and ***truth***. I believe these two words are the most important words in the history of the world.

Truth is at the foundation of freedom, and if you do not choose freedom, you will never fully live in the truth. You cannot separate the two. If you compromise the truth, you lose freedom.

CHAPTER 3
WHY THERE IS NO TURNING BACK
DON'T BELIEVE POLITICIANS WHO SAY OUR FUTURE IS BRIGHTER THAN OUR PAST

If you see the President, tell him from me that whatever happens, there will be no turning back. Ulysses S. Grant

Politicians love to play to their constituents to get elected and re-elected. This is why politicians make promises they can't keep. It's why they create entitlement programs in perpetuity, and it's why they won't stop the flow of illegal immigration. It's also why they say, "I believe America's best days are ahead of us, not behind." They know that is what people long to hear. They know this kind of positive pie-in-the-sky statement tickles peoples' ears. Even many good and well-meaning politicians have said it. Politicians know that people want to have their ears tickled more than they want the truth. As with many things politicians say, the statement doesn't ever have to prove to be true, and voters do not hold politicians accountable for what they say.

Sometimes the truth is not pretty, and too often, weak-hearted Americans do not want the truth. In fact, many Americans reject the truth in order to accept a lie. We are living in troubling times when politicians who tell the truth can lose to politicians who lie as a strategy to get elected. Politicians know this, and many do not hesitate to play the voters for fools.

If you are a politician or a news anchor, and you have made the statement that you think America's best days are ahead, don't get defensive and raise the walls of self-justification, or you might unwittingly find yourself indirectly supporting those who are compromising our freedoms. Remember, the road to hell is paved with good intentions. Do not become an enabler of liberalism out of misapplied notions of positive thinking.

There is plenty of evidence to demonstrate that the positive statement, "I believe America's best days are ahead of us, not behind us" is one of the most naive statements you will ever hear, at least prior to the election of Donald Trump as our 47th President. As you'll read in the next chapter, we are experiencing nothing less than four simultaneous miracles that are have hit the reset button for the American political system.

Hope for the future can be based on facts or faith, or both. Hope and faith are always appropriate. But denial of overwhelming facts is never wise. If America does have a way out of this deep morass, then we are justified pontificating Tony Robbins' personal motivation principles with national fervor, provided it is mathematically and politically possible and provided we actually know how to do it. So let's take an honest look at what hinders America's progress and threatens our survival.

> *After we've reviewed the iron grip that the deep state has on America and how pervasive the swamp really is, we'll look at the extraordinary plans at DOGE, the new Department of Government Efficiency, and the ideas driving Elon Musk and Vivek Ramaswamy to reverse course and attempt to implement a strategy to make America great again, if it's possible.*

The Key To Understanding The American Political System

Before we get into the current state of the American system as it has morphed over the decades, remember that we have a U.S. Constitution, a Bill of Rights, a form of government called a Republic, not a democracy, which is a representative form of government that allows for all people to be adequately represented through the popular vote and the electoral system, and we have three branches of government that are each tasked with exclusive areas of responsibilities. It should never be forgotten that the Constitution and Bill of Rights were written specifically to limit the power of a Federal Government, not facilitate its expansion and power over the citizens. Bills are proposed and become laws if passed cooperatively in the House and Senate and signed by the President. This description of how laws are passed becomes important in order to understand how we are now operating in unconstitutional territory and how powerful government agencies have been weaponized against American citizens illegally.

Millions of Laws Cannot Be Undone

A massive volume of bad laws are on the books. There are millions of laws at the Federal level. Add millions of state statutes, millions of county and borough codes, and millions of municipal ordinances, and you have a massive legal spiderweb that cannot possibly be unweaved, no matter how good the intentions. First, you would never get a consensus to revoke all the bad laws. Second, who is going to define "bad?" Third, you cannot suddenly eliminate a complex system of laws that was developed over two centuries without creating instant chaos. The majority of laws were well-intentioned and had specific problems they were designed to overcome. Many laws are misguided, and the result of special interests, and many laws have been passed only because they are attached to the approval of another law. Some laws are actually illegal because they violate the Constitution.

If we could revoke bad laws, we would be moving in the right direction to save America, but this is a practical impossibility on a large scale. There is a serious dilemma with rescinding or reversing even a single law on the books. Like throwing a stone in a calm pond, the widening consequences of changing or reversing a law will necessitate re-examining many other laws that are affected. Laws are often built on other laws and on case precedent. Imagine starting to randomly pull bricks out of a wall in a tall building in Manhattan. It cannot be done in a practical way without grave risk.

A single law can result in the creation of a Federal agency, which then creates volumes of regulations overseen by hundreds or thousands of Federal employees, and these regulations and procedures are interpreted over the years by administrative law judges, which are often examined by Federal judges for inconsistency with other Federal laws or mandates. Federal cases interpreting a law and its progeny of sub-laws and regulations become law itself, which then must be considered by the Federal agency overseeing the implementation of the single law that started all this. The interdependent nature of laws, regulations, and judicial interpretations makes even a single law a labyrinthian maze that cannot simply be undone.

A college political science student might suggest that the executive and the legislative branches of government, who have the power to create laws, also have the power to uncreate laws. In the real world, and especially in these times when we may actually have reached the tipping point of entitlement voting, there is virtually no possibility that the executive branch and the legislative branch will miraculously cooperate to undo millions of entitlement laws and millions of bad laws that are destroying our freedoms. But there is another reason politicians would find themselves in an impossible quagmire if they tried to revoke thousands or millions of laws.

Millions of Court Cases Set Precedents

The judicial branch would never let the politicians revoke millions of laws in order to start with a clean slate. There would be lawsuits like we have never seen before. There would be enough challenges to overwhelm the courts. In a very large percentage of the cases, the courts would rule such acts unconstitutional, thereby re-enacting many of the laws immediately. Judges would not need laws to do this. They could use their own case precedents to neuter the politicians. Judges would undoubtedly issue injunctions, literally stopping the executive and legislative branches in their tracks. How could judges do this?

Liberal activist judges are on a mission, just like their political counterparts. This means they are not bound by traditional notions of judicial restraint. Judges might rule that a law cannot be revoked because it implements another law that was required to satisfy a Federal mandate, which was the result of a Federal court case enforcing a judicial ruling that peeled away at the U.S. Constitution. But let's not be naive here. Liberals cooperate with each other, so liberal politicians and liberal judges will not fight each other. They will fight the American people who want their freedom back.

Assume you have good judges for a moment at every level-- municipal courts, state district courts, state superior courts, state appellate courts, state supreme courts, Federal district courts,

Federal circuit courts, and the Federal supreme court. All of these judges have sworn an allegiance to obey court precedent. There are millions of case precedents created over the past two centuries. The truth is that there are thousands of bad cases, and those cases created precedents for more bad cases, which created precedents for more bad cases, and so on. Many bad cases became the basis for bad legislative law, which spawned bad regulations ad infinitum. This massive judicial spiderweb holds us hostage, and it cannot be undone through the same orderly process that created the entire nightmare.

Millions of Regulations Enslave The People

When the legislative branch creates a law, and the executive branch signs it, administrative agencies are tasked with the responsibility of implementing the broad mandate of the law into practical rules for enforcement. A single law, which may only consist of a paragraph, will often need volumes of three-ring binders created by administrators to implement the intent of the law.

But wait, because it gets much more exciting for the bureaucrats. It's not as though one person in one agency can create the three-ring binders to enact a law and be done with it. The creation of a single law and the necessary regulations for implementation often reverberate from the Federal to the State to the Municipal levels of government. Each level of government that is tasked with enforcement must have its own administrators.

And once regulations are created, they must be constantly updated. That requires entire legal staffs to interpret the intent of laws, the intent of amendments to the laws, and how to amend, re-write, or add to existing regulations. Should an administrative agency fail in any of these duties, they can become the brunt of administrative punishment from on high or suffer the humiliation of judicial sanctions. Administrators can get fired for not creating and updating regulations. They even create regulations on how to create and update regulations. And within agencies, especially at the Federal level, there are departments tasked with overseeing the regulatory agencies. In other words, there are regulators of the regulators. And there is massive duplication among Federal agencies.

The point is we could not, even if everyone agreed, eliminate millions and millions of regulations that currently were written for the orderly enforcement of laws on the books. Not only would it create chaos, the judicial branch would not allow it.

It was a law that authorized the Federal government to tax American citizens. The federal tax code today in raw text covers 2,600 pages, but when you include annotations, explanations, and cross-references, it extends to about 70,000 pages and requires over 700 different tax forms. The IRS estimates Americans spend 5.1 billion hours annually merely preparing their tax returns. The Tax Foundation estimates that those wasted hours drain some $194 billion annually from the U.S. economy.

The Federal Registry, which records all of the regulations the federal government imposes on businesses (all of which carry the force of law), now exceeds 75,000 pages. The Office of Management and Budget estimates that merely complying with these regulations, paying lawyers to keep educated on them, interpret them, and implement them, costs U.S. businesses another $500 to $600 billion per year.

The Obama Healthcare law has created the single biggest regulatory nightmare in our nation's history. So massive are the regulations already, no one person or agency seems capable of explaining how they will work. The original bill started with 700 pages, and the regulations to implement the law now exceed 20,000 pages and growing. As massive as the regulations are already, the law has necessitated an endless process of writing and re-writing regulations implementing the law at the Federal and state levels. In addition, companies in the U.S. are being forced to create their own rules for managing Obamacare.

All of this should be taken in context. It was President Obama who said, "This legislation is fully paid for and will not add one single dime to our Federal deficit." Since then, the Government Accountability Office estimates this legislation will add 58 trillion dimes to our Federal deficit. Liberals like President Obama are not just bad liars; they are bold-faced liars.

An Impossibility

Bad laws, case precedents, and regulations are choking economic freedom, the engine that drives the American model. It would seem to be an impossibility to eliminate all laws, court cases, and regulations that have stolen our freedoms and hinder our path to better days.

The great American invention of a political system of checks and balances consisting of the executive, legislative, and judicial branches was unquestionably a stroke of genius. But it would seem that the same executive, legislative, and judicial branches now are part of a system that is enslaving us, thanks to liberalism's chokehold.

It is practically impossible to turn the clock back 50 or 60 or 70 years and recapture freedoms long lost by a massive spiderweb that holds the American people hostage. This is why it has been naive to suggest that, "America's best days are ahead of us, not behind us."

Until The Overturning of The Chevron Doctrine, President Trump's 47th Term and DOGE

Extraordinary new developments in the past year have

presented us with the possibility of doing more to reverse the decline of America than at any time in the last three generations, and it is nothing less than miraculous and consisting of multiple events in all three branches of government. In the next chapter, we'll detail four miracles.

CHAPTER 4
FOUR TRUMP MIRACLES TO SAVE AMERICA
THE GREATEST DISRUPTOR IN U.S. HISTORY

MIRACLE NUMBER 1

The biggest and most amazing change that is a miracle of miracles is the U.S. Supreme Court overturning the Chevron doctrine.

The Chevron doctrine originated from the 1984 Supreme Court case <u>Chevron U.S.A., Inc. v. Natural Resources Defense Council</u>, Inc. In this case, the Court established a framework for judicial deference to administrative agencies' interpretation of ambiguous laws that they are tasked with implementing. The decision created a two-step process: first, determining whether Congress has spoken clearly on the issue, and if not, deferring to the agency's reasonable interpretation. This doctrine has since shaped U.S. administrative law significantly.

In other words, bureaucrats at Federal agencies were given unbridled discretion to write how laws would be enforced, and they were told they could even clarify and explain ambiguous sections of laws and how those sections would be interpreted and enforced on Americans. This remained the law from 1984 to June

28, 2024. During that time, Federal agencies created millions upon millions of illegal regulations they enforced on Americans.

Alas, miracle of miracles: the Chevron doctrine was overturned by the U.S. Supreme Court on June 28, 2024, in the case Loper Bright Enterprises v. Raimondo, which marked a major shift in administrative law. The Court ruled that the Chevron framework—requiring judicial deference to federal agency interpretations of ambiguous statutes—was inconsistent with constitutional principles, specifically those related to the separation of powers and the Administrative Procedure Act (APA).

The Reasons for Overturning The Chevron Doctrine

1. **Violation of Separation of Powers**: The Court argued that Chevron improperly shifted lawmaking authority from Congress to unelected bureaucrats in federal agencies. By allowing agencies to both interpret and enforce laws, the doctrine was seen as granting executive agencies legislative powers, which undermines Congress's role as the primary lawmaking body.

2. **Judicial Independence**: Chief Justice Roberts, writing for the majority, emphasized that Chevron compromised the judiciary's responsibility to independently interpret the law. Courts, under Chevron, were required to defer to agency interpretations of ambiguous statutes if those interpretations were deemed reasonable, effectively limiting judges' ability to exercise their own judgment.

3. **Administrative Procedure Act (APA)**: The APA requires courts to ensure that agencies act within the bounds of their statutory authority. The majority held that Chevron's deference allowed agencies to exceed these limits by filling gaps in legislation with their own policy judgments, which courts were then obligated to accept.

Constitutional Basis for Illegality

The decision to overturn Chevron was grounded in the principle that statutory interpretation is a core judicial function under the Constitution. By requiring courts to defer to agencies, Chevron was perceived to have blurred the constitutional boundaries between the legislative, executive, and judicial branches. The ruling restored the judiciary's role as the arbiter of legal ambiguities, ensuring that agencies cannot unilaterally define the scope of their own authority.

The Court viewed Chevron as unconstitutional because it delegated too much interpretive authority to agencies, undermining both the judiciary's independence and Congress's legislative power. This shift reflects a broader movement to reassert checks and balances in administrative governance.

How Many Federal Agencies Are There?

There are about 430 U.S. Federal agencies, and they have had far greater control over your life than you have ever imagined.

I was in the USAF as a JAG, and I can tell you we had volumes of regulations written by military and civilian employees on everything from blowing your nose to launching a missile. In the claims department alone at Nellis AFB, I had volumes of 3-ring binders with regulations on dealing with claims military members make during a move from one base to another. Unless you've worked for the Federal government, you probably have no idea how much unconstitutional authority has been delegated to unelected bureaucrats.

Here are just 36 of the largest U.S. federal agencies by name who have been unconstitutionally interpreting laws and drafting regulations governing your life.

1. Department of Defense (DoD)

2. Department of Health and Human Services (HHS)
3. Department of Veterans Affairs (VA)
4. Department of Homeland Security (DHS)
5. Social Security Administration (SSA)
6. Department of the Treasury
7. Department of Justice (DOJ)
8. Department of Agriculture (USDA)
9. Department of Transportation (DOT)
10. Department of Energy (DOE)
11. Department of Education
12. Department of State
13. Department of the Interior
14. Department of Commerce
15. Department of Labor
16. Department of Housing and Urban Development (HUD)
17. Environmental Protection Agency (EPA)
18. National Aeronautics and Space Administration (NASA)
19. Office of Personnel Management (OPM)
20. General Services Administration (GSA)
21. Small Business Administration (SBA)
22. Federal Communications Commission (FCC)
23. Securities and Exchange Commission (SEC)
24. Federal Reserve System (Federal Reserve)
25. National Science Foundation (NSF)
26. U.S. Agency for International Development (USAID)
27. Central Intelligence Agency (CIA)
28. Federal Bureau of Investigation (FBI)
29. Drug Enforcement Administration (DEA)
30. Transportation Security Administration (TSA)
31. Federal Emergency Management Agency (FEMA)
32. Internal Revenue Service (IRS)
33. Food and Drug Administration (FDA)
34. Centers for Disease Control and Prevention (CDC)

35. National Institutes of Health (NIH)
36. U.S. Customs and Border Protection (CBP)

I don't have to remind you that overturning the Chevron doctrine would not have happened had Donald Trump not been our 45th President and appointed conservative judges to the Supreme Court. He also made it possible for the Supreme Court to overturn that evil, unconstitutional case called "Roe v. Wade".

MIRACLE NUMBER 2

The election of President Trump as the 47th President is another miracle, and the reversal of the Chevron doctrine would not have a fraction of the potential impact if a liberal Democrat had been elected President. It is the combination and the cumulative effect of the overturning of the Chevron doctrine and President Trump's administration that will be revolutionary.

Trump promised to address excessive government, including Federal agencies as part of draining the swamp. Many of these agencies were weaponized by the democrat party in an attempt to defeat Trump and destroy his most loyal allies. They went after his wealth, his children and their businesses, they engaged in multiple massive propaganda campaigns against him using our own national security agencies to create false accusations, and they actually paid people to perjure themselves with your tax dollars in their attempts to stop Trump from getting into the White House.

Trump was falsely accused in criminal and civil lawsuits, and he was impeached as President also with false charges. He has been called every horrendous name the Democrats could think of, and he has been legally slandered more than any other politician in history. No President has ever been so viciously attacked as this man.

They also covered up massive fraud by the Obama and Biden

administrations to facilitate their efforts. One obvious sin on the part of the Democrats is how they continually project their own evil behavior onto Trump. What do I mean by this? Here are two quick examples, and of course, there are literally dozens that could be listed:

1. Democrats accused Trump of censorship. Censorship is one of their primary policies, and they have done everything to censor freedom of speech, freedom of religion, a free press, and to work closely with big tech to censor search engine results and to strike opinions that are contrary to their democrat narrative. On the contrary, Trump has fought to ensure freedom at every level and against censorship everywhere.
2. Democrats accused Trump of being a threat to democracy, but again they are projecting their own goals to destroy what we have—a democratic republic. Their policies open the borders to let illegal aliens in 24/7, and they fight against policies that would require voters to obtain legal IDs. They stand against laws that would stop them from voting for dead people and voting multiple times for voters who are still breathing. They want illegal votes so they can stay in control. They have a long history of voter fraud and dishonesty. Trump has stood adamantly against policies that would destroy our democratic republic.

They weaponized the Department of Justice against Trump, and they weaponized the FBI and the CIA against Trump. All of this is grotesquely illegal and a blatant violation of our laws and constitution. But this is what the Democrat party has come to in these dark times.

The list of how they illegally and unethically attacked Trump is beyond the scope of this chapter, but it is a long list. Of course, there were also two assassination attempts, so it's hard to think of something that these evil people have not tried to stop him. His personal strength, stamina, and perseverance are nothing less than extraordinary among men.

Before the overturning of the Chevron doctrine and the election of Donald Trump as the 47th President, it would have been absolutely impossible to turn America back from its dramatic decline.

Had the only miracle been the overturning of the Chevron doctrine, there would be some small element of hope over the next decade that would have to deal with thousands of lawsuits and administrative battles that would rage on as the massive regulations on the books were dealt with appropriately. While that would truly have been an amazing miracle in itself, especially with the U.S. Supreme Court overturning its own ruling from 1984, the practical impact of that miracle would have been tragically muted if a Democrat president was elected as our 47th President. They would maintain the status quo with every weapon in their arsenal, and that means turning the entire executive and legislative branches against us as they have for so long. They also turn the judicial branch against the people by appointing life-long terms to radical ideologues instead of rational judges who care about justice and the Constitution.

Let's take the next step. With the overturning of the Chevon doctrine, had a rhino republican president been elected, we also would see about the same status quo with little hope for change as we would have with a democrat president. Most U.S. voters who are not "low information voters" have realized by now that we don't really have a two-party system that counterbalances itself. It is really a single-party system with two apparent parties that work together to maintain their power and wealth and keep the citizens enslaved and powerless.

Regardless of your political beliefs in the past, you must acknowledge that Donald Trump is not a rhino Republican or a party animal or part of the deep state wanting to maintain the status quo and work toward global governance. Donald Trump is a political disruptor, and unless our 47th President were to be a Donald Trump, the dramatic and miraculous overturning of the Chevron doctrine and what his administration is already planning to do would amount to very little to make America Great Again. It could not and would not ever happen under any other President.

MIRACLE NUMBER 3

Behold, miracle number 3 is DOGE, Trump's new department titled the Department of Government Efficiency. There has never been a Federal department like this, and no President, Democrat or Republican, would dare to create such a department except Donald Trump.

Trump appointed two extremely smart men to head up DOGE, and they are both not only geniuses, they are both proven successes in business and the management of organizations. They also are true believers in the limitations imposed on government by the U.S. Constitution. In other words, they are about as far as you can get from career politicians in Washington, D.C.

These two men are Elon Musk and Vivek Ramaswamy, who will work together to head the department. You know they understand the problem from this statement Vivek recently made:

> *Most laws today are not "laws enacted by Congress but rules and regulations promulgated by unelected bureaucrats--tens of thousands of them each year. Most government enforcement decisions and discretionary expenditures aren't made by the democratically elected president or even his political appointees*

but by millions of unelected, unappointed civil servants within government agencies who view themselves as immune from firing thanks to civil service protections"

Without all these miracles, we would not and could not have such hope that we will see better times again in America. Prior to these three miracles, I stated unequivocally that "American will never be great again." But now there is hope, and it is truly amazing that these events line up at this point in time to make the slogan MAGA a real possibility.

This does not mean that America will be great again forever, or that we will become the world force for good for the next century. I hope and pray we do, but you'll want to read books 2 and 3 of this series, because there is such a thing as good and evil, and God and Satan are real, and Bible prophesy details how it all ends.

For now, we have more hope and encouragement than we thought possible, and for that, we must thank Donald Trump. Who else would have been able to give us such hope for the American political system and for freedom?

MIRACLE NUMBER 4

This miracle came slowly over time, but it also started with Trump. It was Donald Trump who, during his first campaign for President, coined the phrase "fake news." Most Americans didn't attribute much to the phrase or Trump's use of it.

Donald Trump, it seems, alone foresaw the seismic impact of those two words—"fake news"—unleashing them to forever alter the American political landscape and deliver a staggering blow to the once-unchecked power of the deep state.

Who knew that benign reference to fake news would be the beginning of a new focus and awareness of how legacy media had abandoned journalism and justice and truth to become an arm of the radical liberal democrat party, and more than that, how legacy media, especially the TV networks, had become massive propagandists and bold-faced liars promoting all kinds of evil and gaslighting Americans 24/7.

As often happens throughout history, singular events occur that become catalysts to related events, and a chain reaction ensues that can revolutionize a culture and even change the world. Such is the case with Trump's repeated use of the phrase "fake news."

While Trump was being viciously attacked by legacy media and by lying politicians, another development unleashed a whole new force for good. This new force has been called the "network society," or you could say the Internet unleashed for individual newscasters.

In other words, the Internet facilitated advances in technology and software, in particular in the areas of affordable video production at home, video publishing and distribution, and podcasting in such a way that individuals and teams of individuals suddenly had the option of producing their own daily news and opinion shows on Youtube, Spotify, Rumble, X (formerly Twitter), Facebook, Apple, TikTok, Instagram, Vimeo, LinkedIn, and other platforms. Donald Trump even started his own direct-to-voters platform called Truth Social.

Lo and behold, millions of Americans were getting weary of the blatant lies and propaganda coming from the legacy TV news, and they began to flock to these individual podcast sites. Those who could be articulate and are knowledeable and know how to produce an entertaining and honest show that informs people and exposes fake news have found their shows growing rapidly with large numbers of loyal subscribers.

The concept of "fake news" grew across the country as Donald Trump launched his second campaign for the presidency, and Americans by the millions, sat up and noticed. At the same time, the legacy TV stations grew more desperate in their forced narratives and became their own enemies by projecting their lies and evil intent on Trump and on Trump followers. Hillary Clinton tried that, and it didn't work out so well for her.

The free flow of information on the Internet through non-legacy media one day surpassed the viewership of the legacy TV stations, and the tipping point was reached. The fake news has been defeated, and their power to use propaganda against us has been crushed.

Who broke the legacy media and crushed its power over you and me? Clearly, Donald Trump. No one else did so much to expose them and destroy them than Donald Trump. No one.

Miraculous Conclusion

All four of these miracles had to happen simultaneously in America at this time to stop America's downward spiral and give us the kind of hope to enthusiastically wear a hat that says "Make America Great Again." The millions of Americans who have been wearing the MAGA hats are not stupid people as the Democrats have claimed. Instead, they are far smarter than the Democrats, and they are far bolder than the rest of the Republicans, who were unwilling to wear a MAGA hat even though they supported Donald Trump and his full agenda.

Timing is everything, so do <u>not</u> miss the point that if a "Donald Trump" had not been elected and did not serve as America's 47th President, America would have gone the way of many nations throughout history—turning to communism or tyranny that would once and for all permanently enslave the people and empower evil rulers to maintain power and control until the next big violent revolution.

> *Do not miss the breathtaking view from 30,000 feet because these four monumental miracles—alongside a cascade of extraordinary events, including the perfect alignment of allies surrounding Donald Trump in his new administration—are converging with a powerful synergistic effect that has driven a stake through the very heart of the Deep State. The Deep State is not yet dead and never will be fully dead until the White Throne Judgment, but no U.S. President has ever achieved such monumental victories against the most seditious enemies the U.S. has ever known, unless perhaps you go back to George Washington or Abraham Lincoln.*

You can say anything you want about Donald Trump, but if you're a Christian, you understand that Romans 13:1 makes it clear that God appoints all Kings and Prime Ministers and Presidents, whether they are Christians or not. You can disagree with Trump's personal lifestyle or unfiltered speeches, but you cannot deny this:

> *Donald Trump is singularly responsible for the miraculous events that are now saving our country from the brink of total collapse. Love him or hate him personally, you owe him a deep sense of gratitude for saving America and giving all of us hope for the future. Whether you are a Republican, a Democrat, or an Independent, Trump's policies and his agenda will do more to improve the quality of your life than any Democrat policies would have by an order of magnitude. Be grateful for Donald Trump. Thank him, and thank God for appointing him our 47th President.*

CHAPTER 5
PUPPETS OF LIBERALISM
MAIN STREET MEDIA EXPOSED AS THE ULTIMATE FAKE NEWS

Never has the political class or the mainstream media that covers them been more out of touch with the American people than they are today. Marco Rubio

"The realization that neither the city's high taxes nor its endless bureaucratic red tape seem to have dampened this explosion of capitalism at all has already begun to shape up the local political scene." This is the philosophy of the liberal press in Seattle, and they cannot help themselves. It is spewed from every issue of the newspaper all year long. This quote is the genius of The Seattle Times' staff columnist Danny Westneat. The title of his article published on March 24, 2013 is *Seattle's An Inconvenient Truth to GOP*.

This was such a dramatic example of the insanity of the left, I have not forgotten it, although it is a dated example. Leftists today hold the same dysfunctional belief system.

What Westneat was saying to the applause of the liberal readership of The Seattle Times is that liberal politicians in Seattle are just getting started. He might as well have written, "You think liberals have done enough with high taxes and burdensome business regulations! Baby, you haven't seen anything yet!" His article exudes that kind of excitement for the liberal cause. With employment improving in the Seattle job market and with massive labyrinthian bureaucratic processes, and with such high city taxes (according to Westneat in his article), this is all the proof Seattle politicians need to go on a new taxing and spending spree, not to mention more regulations.

It is astonishing to the logical mind that liberals would claim that Seattle's improving economy is proof that their brand of socialism works, and that the survival of the American free enterprise system in the midst of socialism is somehow proof that the people love high taxes and want higher taxes. It is amazing that they would boldly claim that the economy not only can bear higher taxes, but the implication is that higher taxes will help grow the economy even more. Finally, according to liberals we are approaching a utopia where higher taxes and more regulations will keep us on this ever-higher spiral of improvement, and it is all an *inconvenient truth* for the GOP. If only Republicans and conservatives would get out of the way once and for all, America could thrive and reach utopian status.

In the same issue of The Seattle Times there is a fascinating article entitled, *Budget-Starved Parks Mark Grim Centennial*, written by staff writer Lynda Maples. The article chronicles how state parks are falling into disrepair and some facilities are going to be closed for lack of money. Almost every paragraph of the article continues the liberal harangue, lambasting common citizens for not paying enough in taxes to support and maintain our park resources. How dare you as citizens of America not pay enough to maintain our massive bureaucratic park systems! You should be ashamed of yourselves!

It has long been known that the Seattle Times is a puppet of the left wing of the Democratic party, but is the mainstream media in America just a puppet of liberalism? It's a legitimate question, but for those who have a heartbeat and a normal EEG pattern, it's a rhetorical question, like "Does the sun rise every day?" We all know the answer.

Mainstream Media as an Arm of Liberalism

There's another way to phrase the issue, which might make more sense today: Is the mainstream media in America an integral part of the liberal establishment? In other words, could it be that the liberal press is not just a puppet on the end of a string for liberal politicians, and that journalists are not just sycophants or good soldiers, but much more? Has the mainstream press become an integral organ of liberalism, functioning independently but giving life and power to the liberal behemoth? If this is closer to reality than the puppet theory, then the mainstream media is far more dangerous than most realize, because their survival would then depend upon the survival of the liberal behemoth itself.

If the mainstream media became an inadvertent puppet for a time, they would surely wake up one day and demand their independence once again. After all, professional journalists for decades have taken great pride in their *independence* from political power and corporate influence. For nearly two centuries, investigative journalists have been an unofficial fourth branch of government, holding politicians accountable when no one else would and saving us from corruption and bias.

Bob Woodward and Carl Bernstein brought down a President unworthy of the office. But where in the mainstream media are the Bob Woodwards today? What happened to investigative and objective media coverage? Even the Bob Woodward of the Nixon era is not the same Bob Woodward today. He has turned to the dark side and fights for the Deep State and liberal causes bent on destroying truth and freedom in America.

Willingly Hoodwinked

The mainstream media has had plenty of time to wake up and realize they've been hoodwinked. They have had all the time they could possibly have needed to wake up from their long sleep and cut the strings of their puppet-hood. Alas, they have chosen not to do so. Why? Because they are no longer simply puppets. They are an integral and vital part of the liberal machinery. That means there is no turning back for the liberal media. Their purpose for being is no longer objective reporting or questioning political power. Their mission today includes the steady daily brainwashing of Americans. But to what end? The liberal media is hellbent on promoting liberalism, which includes an agenda for the destruction of personal freedoms and the advancement of an all-powerful Federal government.

Mainstream journalists are playing a much larger role in liberalism than just playing the part of puppets. Mainstream journalists represent liberalism at its best. Just like the Democratic leaders in America who are stalwarts of liberalism, American mainstream journalists are an integral arm of the liberal movement. They don't just follow and obey the Democratic leadership, they are the liberal leadership. Today the phrases "democratic leadership" and "liberal leadership" include the same small universe of people.

Remember that the leaders of the liberal media, including the news anchors, have shown an extraordinary level of arrogance that masquerades as independence. Name every famous mainstream news and opinion anchor of the past five decades, and then name one who wasn't incredibly arrogant. If you can name anyone (Peter Jennings?), I guarantee the list will be very short. They are and always have been too arrogant to submit to any political leadership. This created a tremendous difficulty for the liberal media, but they came up with an ingenious way out.

False Media Independence

If the mainstream media could redefine its role within the liberal movement, maintaining at least an appearance of independence, it could intellectually satisfy their claim of "objective independence" and at the same time ride the crest of a wave that they believed would take them to the seats of power and money. And they could fool the masses and essentially act as a liberal propaganda machine. That strategy has proved unbelievably successful.

What this means is that the mainstream media has refused to outwardly bow down to the liberal politicians, maintaining their precious independence (at least in appearance), while at the same time joining the liberal movement with daring displays of their own liberal strategies.

Many Americans have been mystified as to why the mainstream media would so fervently promote liberalism with such a blatant lack of objectivity. The answer is right in front of us. The media has become a machine seeking to destroy conservative values and promote liberal values. Independent news reporting is no longer their mission. The singular mission of the mainstream media that underlies everything else they do and report is the promotion of liberalism. How could this possibly be?

Mainstream Media Lost It's Identity

The explanation is simple but astonishing. The key leadership in the media have had a passion that eclipsed their historical role. Their passion has been a liberal passion to change America and to play a major part in a quiet revolution. Their motivation is rooted in a hatred for capitalism and freedom, and includes a lust for personal power and control.

The owners of the media conglomerates have become some of the wealthiest individuals in America. What do people who have everything and more money than they can ever spend want next? They want power, control, and more wealth. They want to fulfill their destiny and their place in history. They want to play God. This is where money and power combined with radical ideology are extremely dangerous. Give these same people an open door to the White House and the Halls of Congress, and they will feel like Gods.

> *Today, we can see that the mainstream media has gone so far overboard that they actually have lost their identity in America. Their liberal agenda is no longer under the radar and invisible to average Americans. Their agenda is in our faces every single day of the week on the front pages of newspapers and on T.V. all day long. Those who would deny this are themselves liberals who passionately promote the liberal cause, the truth and facts be damned.*

As for the puppets (or loyal soldiers), many well-intentioned journalists did not sign up for a full frontal assault on the Constitution and personal freedoms. They did not work hard in college to become good writers and labor late hours for newspapers for years with the goal of destroying America. Nevertheless, far too many journalists now have fallen into the trap of becoming puppets of the liberal media that signs their paychecks. Unfortunately too many of these good people, they undoubtedly feel like there is no turning back. They may recognize now that they accidentally got passage on the Titanic, but they feel they cannot get off. For most of them, to get off would mean the end of their "successful" careers. It would feel like jumping off the Titanic to avoid the iceberg. So long as they can convince themselves that the iceberg isn't too close in the path of the ship, they will stay on the Titanic rearranging the deck chairs with nervous smiles.

Major course corrections for America take time, a lot of time, but we would have to have the cooperation of those who are navigating the ship. We don't have that cooperation between Democrats and Republicans, and we are running out of time. So long as the media continues to recklessly facilitate steering the ship toward the iceberg, America will get closer to being irreparably ripped apart and then . . . slowly sink into darkness.

The Rise of Independent News

Thank God there is some light at the end of the tunnel in news reporting, and that good news comes from totally independent news reporters who have created their own Youtube news channels. There are some crazies out there, and bad players have been embedded in YouTube to spread their propaganda, but we are for the first time in decades, getting some level of filtered truth from a small handful of dedicated, honest, and professional news reporters.

> *We are deeply in debt to our 45th President, Donald Trump, for coining the phrase "fake news" because it alerted all of us to what was actually true—that the legacy media was fake, full of false information and misinformation, and propaganda galore. And thank God he has been elected our 47th President to continue exposing the fake news and opening doors for unfiltered news and information.*

Thank God for Elon Musk and X

The hero of our time on the subject of blowing up the chokehold legacy media had on Americans is surely Elon Musk, whose purchase of Twitter (now X) has put freedom of the press back into the hands of the people. No longer do Editors in Chief decide what Americans should be focused on and what we should be thinking. The citizens get to decide what news is important and how to think for themselves in what is being called a "Network Society" in which citizens have taken control of the news and information on the Internet.

This has spawned a new industry of individual podcasters and small newsgroups broadcasting to the world every day. These new and gifted podcasters are experiencing massive success with viewership numbers that dwarf CNN, MSNBC, ABC, CBS, and the liberal newspapers. Finally, we are seeing the acceleration of the slow and painful death of the legacy media we have been watching for two decades.

> *It is no coincidence that Elon Musk will play a major role in the Trump administration! We are in the midst of a massive tectonic shift as a result of Trump's election as the 47th President, and this is just the beginning.*

CHAPTER 6

LIBERALS OWN THE INTERNET

GOOGLE + FACEBOOK + AMAZON + APPLE + MICROSOFT = LIBERAL POWER

The Internet empowers individuals to play a more active role in the political process, as Obama's campaign has manifested.
Al Gore

Why would I suggest that liberals own the Internet? That's easy. Because the founders of the most powerful Internet technologies are in bed with radical liberals, and the most advanced technologies are being used to promote liberalism. You may have suspected this, but the mainstream media keeps this on the down low, so most people are unaware of how Democrats have courted some of the most powerful people in the world of Internet technology.

In the first and second Obama campaigns, the world's most powerful social media genius and founder of Facebook, Chris Hughes, pushed Obama over the finish line to elect him president. In 2009 Fast Company Magazine's cover article was entitled, "The Kid Who Made Obama President; How Facebook Cofounder Chris Hughes Unleashed Barack's Base, and Changed Politics and Marketing Forever."

The organization that Hughes created using a massive network across the country where young people anywhere could plug in and be part of volunteer groups for Obama, and the billions of dollars that were raised using technology gave liberals the tools they needed to take control of the most powerful campaign machine ever created. Liberals own that. Obama would not have been elected apart from Hughes' ability to plug millions of people into the campaign. This alone would give liberals a gigantic advantage in politics, but it doesn't end there.

Here's a list of Internet powerhouses who give entirely or heavily to Democrats:

- Mark Zuckerberg, Facebook
- Michael Eisner, CEO of Disney, 1984-2005
- Bill Gates, Co-founder of Microsoft
- James Kimsey, AOL's founding CEO
- Thomas J. Meredith, CFO of Dell, 1992-2000
- Craig Newmark, Founder Craigslist
- Dan Rosensweig, COO of Yahoo, 2002-2007
- Howard Schultz, founder of Starbucks
- Terry Semel, CEO of Yahoo, 2001-2007
- Yahoo's new CEO Marissa Mayer, an Obama bundler.
- SalesForce.com founder Marc Benioff
- Google's Sergey Brin
- Adobe co-founder Charles Geschke
- John Warnock, the other half of the Adobe co-founders
- Reid Hoffman, founder of LinkedIn
- Netflix founder Reed Hastings
- Sean Parker, co-founder-Napster, 1st chairman-Facebook
- Mark Pincus, the founder of Zynga
- Comcast CEO Brian Roberts
- Al Gore sits on the Board of Directors of Apple.

You may know that many of these titans of the Internet have also given to Republicans, although disproportionately in favor of Democrats. Some would argue that if they give to both parties, they are neutral. Nonsense. Supporting Democrats is helping to promote liberalism, which means the shredding of the U.S. Constitution, the loss of our precious freedoms, and the continued destruction of America. You have to marvel at how some of our most successful capitalists in America support the very politicians who are trying to destroy capitalism. Unwittingly, many of these billionaires are helping destroy the great economic system that made them so wealthy.

Microsoft has done what many companies do. They ride the fence trying not to make any enemies. The company and employees donate to both parties. Trying to be friends with both liberals and conservatives is actually an incredibly dumb strategy, although most American corporations have taken that approach. I would say to corporate America:

Go ahead and play neutral and sit on the sidelines while the free enterprise system and constitutional protections under which your company was built and has thrived is slowly destroyed. Go ahead and wait until the government taxes and regulates you to death. When you are put out of business, will you then stand up to fight for the values that built your company? What will you do after America's free enterprise system is no longer?

Liberals have played America's CEOs for fools, and they have done it using the very inventions that these great companies created. Liberals have understood that whoever controls the most powerful means of communication today wins. Consider that the Democrats control (or are strongly supported by) mainstream media, Hollywood (movies, T.V. series, games), and the single most powerful form of communication today--the Internet. I can only imagine how used America's tech giants and billionaires feel after they realize this. If they don't feel humiliated, they are fools helping to destroy America. Geniuses but fools.

Many would object to this argument that liberals own the Internet, but a big reason this is true is because many liberals in technology are passionate about helping liberalism. Unfortunately, almost no conservatives in technology have the courage to take liberalism on. They are afraid their businesses will come under scrutiny by Federal agencies, and they are afraid they will get on a blacklist and see no more government contracts. Their fears are not unfounded. Remember, liberals do not play fair. If you were a tech billionaire would you risk your fortune and the wrath of shareholders if you thought the Feds might target you, and if you thought that liberal hackers might coordinate a worldwide attack on your servers? Conservatives have to worry about that.

Internet Companies in Bed With the Feds

All of the major Internet companies have been cooperating with the Feds to share confidential personal information on millions of Americans. This includes Microsoft, Google, Yahoo, Facebook, Linkedin, and many more. They are intimidated by the Feds to participate in gross violations of constitutional protections. The Feds use threats of administrative sanctions, threats of Federal lawsuits that could cost a company billions of dollars, threats of the loss of Federal contracts, and threats against subsidiaries and affiliate companies. Corporate America has been turned by the Feds against the people, and in some ways it could be argued that corporate America has become a weapon of the Federal government.

Americans Should Protect Businesses

A conservative Internet billionaire (or millionaire) cannot stop the Federal government's intrusions into our personal lives by himself, even with powerful technology. What he needs is the American people to stand up for the Constitution and be a shield between an abusive power-hungry government and his private company. Americans have been fooled by Democrats into thinking that corporate America is evil. In fact, liberals have been so successful with their decades-long attack on American businesses that they have a huge percentage of Americans joining them in the attack against corporations whenever the opportunity presents itself. Unfortunately, these Americans don't realize they are attacking their own freedoms and their own constitutional rights.

When corporations can be attacked and manipulated, taxed and regulated to death, and threatened with potential government scrutiny and investigations, guess who really loses? Retirees who have their retirement funds invested in those companies' stocks will lose (perhaps billions of dollars). The corporate employees who are raising their families and paying taxes are hurt. Americans who stand by while their right to build their own small business is denigrated are set back every time the Feds unfairly attack an American business of any size.

While most people realize the Internet is big, most don't realize how it has been used by Democrats to promote liberalism and take control of the White House. Democrats have tapped into the most powerful communication technologies of the day.

Passion Drives Liberals

This should be no surprise. Liberals are extremely passionate about their cause. Most extreme liberals will die for the cause. It is their life, it is their destiny. It is their religion. They are working night and day, 365 days a year.

Republicans, however, are not so passionate and have no heart to die for some cause, no matter how great the cause. Republicans are working and raising their families, going to Church, and working in their communities. They are not staying awake at night plotting and scheming like liberals. What an advantage this is for liberals and what a disadvantage for Republicans!

Liberalism and The Contradiction of Wealth

For extreme liberals, the sacrifices are not necessarily great sacrifices. Liberalism has rallied vast financial resources from around the world, and many extreme liberals have become very wealthy. Al Gore is said to be worth over $100 million, money earned from his network with liberals. Liberalism has gained the support of billionaires who passionately support the cause. One has to marvel that Apple would have Al Gore as a member of their board of directors. This is another example of a powerful corporation sucking up to liberal power. Al Gore talks about the Internet and about technology as if he is some kind of leader, and as if he is a strong proponent of the inventive genius and entrepreneurship of Steve Jobs, but he is not. Al Gore's most passionate beliefs and his entire life represent a hatred for all that an incredible company like Apple stands for. Al Gore hates capitalism unless liberals control it. Don't think the other board members don't know this. They certainly do, but they must do what they must do to survive, or so they think.

The Great Liberal Advantage

One of the points that I hope becomes apparent in this book is that liberals have an advantage in many venues that help to promote liberalism. They have an advantage in the natural processes that flow out of bureaucracy. They have an advantage with the natural tendency of people to be lazy and slide into an entitlement mentality. Liberals have an advantage over everyone who hates God, and there are millions of people who hate God in America today. They have an advantage with labor Unions, and they have a strong following among the women's liberation movement and gay rights activists. Notice that all of these groups are some of the most impassioned and rabid liberals in the country. They work harder and longer than Republicans every day. Liberals have such a huge advantage in so many ways, it is no wonder America's best Republicans are losing battle after battle. The evidence is overwhelming: America is losing the war against liberalism.

> **<u>Until now</u>**. *The election of Donald J. Trump as the 47th President is already dramatically shaking the heavenlies. With this election, already tech titans are beginning to yield and change their loyalties, including Zuckerburg and Gates.*

CHAPTER 7
THE DEATH OF TRUTH
AND THE RISE OF MASSIVE LIES, MISREPRESENTATIONS, AND DECEPTION

A lie gets halfway around the world before the truth has a chance to get its pants on. Winston Churchill

Ten years into twenty years of practicing law, I came to a terribly disappointing realization. The truth no longer rules in our justice system. Discovering the truth is no longer the prime objective in the American military justice system, nor in the civilian justice system. I practiced in both systems. As a JAG in the USAF, I saw the careers of innocent enlisted members destroyed. As a civilian attorney, I watched judges unjustly rule against good, honest men. The great misconception is that truth will win the day. It does not always win, and it is a tragedy that the American justice system is full of people who care nothing for truth and justice.

I sat through a military trial in which the defendant was a decorated 12-year veteran with an impeccable record. He was proud to wear the uniform, and he was a man of honor and integrity. He was also an African-American. He was accused of rape by a Las Vegas prostitute who admitted on the witness stand that she had accused eight other men of rape, and she admitted that she was a regular drug user. Her testimony was full of holes and inconsistencies. An 8th grader would have acquitted the sergeant.

The military jury consisted of other commanders on base. In the military, a commander has the responsibility to bring charges against any member of his unit who may have done something wrong. In other words, they play the role of an attorney general at a state level or the county prosecutor at a county level. They sign charges against the soldier or airman. They are also expected to serve on the equivalent of juries. In addition to this bias, the judge in a military court has almost always been a prosecuting attorney in the military for most of his career. His mission for almost his entire military career has been to seek and destroy. Prosecutors are taught to convict, not to question guilt.

But here's the real kicker. Generals and Colonials often make it clear that the defendant must go down regardless. They need a fall guy, and they have one, and the truth is often irrelevant. I have been both a military prosecuting attorney and a military defense attorney, and I could go on and on about the injustices of the military justice system. So could many whose military careers have been unjustly ended.

During a recess of the trial of this sergeant who was falsely charged with rape, I stood with his mother and father in the hallway. I grew fond of these parents who stood by their son and who knew he was not capable of the allegation of rape. I asked his mother how she was holding up, and just as though it was yesterday, I could see her with tears on her cheeks. Looking up slowly into my eyes she said, "I see what they are doing to my son, and there's not a damn thing I can do about it."

The court reached a verdict of guilty very quickly, despite all the evidence to the contrary. This man who had served so honorably in our military was sent to Leavenworth Penitentiary as a felon for a five-year term. I am haunted to this day by that case. What kind of job could an African-American convicted of rape with five years in a federal prison ever hope to get? I doubt he could even get a job as a janitor. Can you imagine the laughter if he should ever say to anyone, "I was innocent." Yet he clearly was innocent. I sat through the trial and observed the evidence.

After the conviction, I went into the office of the Major who was the chief prosecuting attorney. I said, "Sir, you know he is innocent, and yet he is going to prison for five years, and his life might as well be over." The major leaned back in his chair and put his feet up on his desk, and his words still echo in my mind. With a cavalier response, he said, "Well, yeah, that's the way it goes. Hey, we did our job. The jury did theirs." Then he actually chuckled slightly. I remember being repulsed by his attitude. Some months later I left the USAF and a military justice system that cared little for truth or justice.

The civilian justice system is no better, and I would venture to say it is worse. But my point in this chapter is that the truth no longer is all-important in our justice system. Few judges care about the truth enough to make sure the attorneys don't play games and lie in the courtroom. Even for the judges who do care, the rules of evidence and procedural rules govern their behavior so that the end result is the same.

Attorneys Lie Every Day in Courtrooms

On many occasions, I stood in a courtroom while the opposing attorney told lie after lie about the facts and twisted the application of the law. On one particularly bad session of bold-faced distortions by the opposing attorney, I decided to speak up. "Your honor, with all due respect to counsel, he has intentionally stood in front of you and completely disregarded the truth and misrepresented the facts." I thought that was a diplomatic way to call the other attorney a liar in the courtroom, but it wasn't diplomatic enough for the judge. Judges don't like to hear anyone in the courtroom challenged for telling bold-faced lies. Judges think that everyone gets their day to lie in the courtroom, but that's simply not a constitutional right. A judge has the right to tell attorneys practicing in his courtroom that he does not condone lying, but they won't do it. The vast majority of judges once stood on the other side of the bench telling lies all day long. They simply don't care about the truth when they become judges.

To be fair, there are judges who do care about the truth. I've known some, but they tend to fall into line and operate like all the other judges. They are terrified of getting caught violating a judicial rule of conduct. But here's the real clincher. In county and state courts the judges are voted into office by the local bar association members. Judges need the votes of the attorneys in their courtrooms, or they won't get re-elected. This means judges don't want to offend these attorneys who exaggerate and lie in their courtrooms. They let them lie with no accountability. Truth and justice in our courtrooms is a fantasy in this modern era of American culture.

As a footnote to this discussion, have you ever wondered why an attorney would become a judge? If you think it's because they have a passion for truth and justice, think again. I've talked to many judges off the record, and they all told me they took a big pay cut when they became judges, so it's not the money. They told me it's the power and respect they feel as judges. That's why they become judges. Judges are treated like Gods in the courtroom, and they are treated with great respect in their communities, and judges tell me that feels good. That's why attorneys become judges.

Attorneys Get a Free Pass to Lie

Americans don't like it when witnesses or defendants lie on the witness stand, but Americans give lawyers a license to lie in the courtroom, and they think nothing of it. This is true from the opening argument to the closing argument of thousands of cases around the country every day. Let me show you exactly how this happens.

Consider the opening arguments of a prosecuting attorney in a criminal case. If it is a murder trial in which the jury ultimately acquits the defendant, thereby establishing as a matter of fact that the defendant did not commit the murder, then we must conclude that when the prosecuting attorney stated in his opening argument that the defendant "planned to murder the victim, broke into her apartment and ruthlessly bludgeoned the victim to death with no mercy and without giving any thought at all to the value of human life," the prosecuting attorney was lying. We know after the fact that he boldly lied because the jury found, as a matter of fact, that the defendant was completely innocent of all charges. Isn't it interesting that for some strange reason, Americans give that prosecuting attorney a license to lie and make up facts out of thin air, but no one later goes back and holds that lying attorney accountable even though the jury clearly found that he lied to them?

Throughout a trial, attorneys lie about the facts. They lie about the application of the law, and twist facts and testimonies to win their cases. And regardless of the outcome of the case, Americans don't even give the lying attorneys a second thought. Distorting the truth and twisting justice are terrible sins, but lawyers do it every day in courtrooms around the country. I know this to be true, because I practiced as an attorney for over 20 years in two states and in the Federal courts, and in both the civilian and military systems.

Many Americans understand that the code of ethics states that it is an attorney's job to "zealously represent his client."

Unfortunately, Americans are under a terrible misconception that means it's okay for attorneys to lie in the courtroom. It is not. Attorneys are supposed to be *ambassadors of justice*, not liars who twist justice for their own purposes.

The American misconception about the practice of law has given lawyers a license to lie about anything anytime. Where in the U.S. Constitution does it say lawyers can lie in a court of justice? It does not. Where in the Bill of Rights does it say lawyers can lie to protect their clients? It does not. Where in the Bible does it say lawyers are free to lie when they represent their clients? It does not. Lawyers have no legal, ethical, or moral right to lie in our courtrooms, yet they do it every day of the week and Americans excuse it!

Some would jump on this issue and argue that the 5th Amendment protects you from testifying against yourself. That is true, but not testifying at all, and lying are two different things. The prosecution has the burden of proof, and the 5th Amendment does not obligate a defendant to help the prosecution. But bold-faced lying and making up facts and distorting law are in a whole different category of evil.

A Thousand Deaths

Truth has died a thousand deaths in America, and our justice system is just one place where truth has been rendered irrelevant. It is no coincidence that the widespread practice of lying for attorneys has spread to politicians, since most politicians are lawyers. Politicians now stand up and, without any hesitation, tell blatant lies. I've seen a President increase taxes, and give a speech in which he said, "I have reduced taxes for all Americans." Instead of booing the President, the audience responded with enthusiastic applause. Americans seem incapable of discerning what is true and what is not true.

Here's an assignment for you that will require nothing except that you increase your powers of observation. When you watch any liberal being interviewed, notice that they almost never answer a direct question. This is especially true when a liberal is asked a direct question that challenges his liberal beliefs or his facts. He cannot answer the question truthfully and directly, because it would expose him for misrepresenting or distorting the truth. Of course, many liberals are totally sincere, but that does not prevent them from being sincerely misguided.

One way liberals play with facts or conceal the truth about a matter is by redefining words. The meaning of words has been distorted and twisted so that many of our words no longer mean what they have for centuries. This is a major victory for liberals. When they can obliterate the plain meaning of words and introduce other meanings masquerading as truth, they can support any argument and defend any position to the masses.

Liberals Promote Lies and Hate the Truth

Destroying the truth is a never-ending strategy for liberalism. Liberals have been hard at work destroying America's true history, and they have been hard at work on many levels in government, in Federally promoted educational programs, in Hollywood, in newspapers and on T.V. They have been busy rewriting American history books to suit the liberal cause. All of this plays into a well-planned long-term strategy to brainwash weak minds.

Two thousand years ago, a man who embodied "Truth" faced an accuser who sarcastically said, "What is truth anyway?" I can imagine when Pilate said that, he almost certainly sighed with disdain and waived one hand in a dismissive manner. Pilate was one of the great liberal leaders of his day, and if he were alive in America today, he would fit into the Democratic party perfectly.

But imagine the significance of that moment in history. Pilate stood in the presence of Jesus Christ, who was and is the Truth, not just for Pilate's time but for all of time. Jesus' appearance on the Earth is the central point in time, the single most important event that we can comprehend on the Earth. Jesus called Himself the Truth. And it was to the Truth that Pilate actually said sarcastically, "What is truth anyway?" What an extraordinary display of arrogance and stupidity on Pilate's part. No one in all of history was ever more wrong than when Pilate spoke these words to the Son of God.

Pastor John Piper spoke about the loss of truth in America on December 20, 1987:

That is the tragic and cynical cry of our age: What is truth! Not because there's a passion for truth, but because there is so much skepticism that any such thing exists. And the effect of this skepticism and relativism is moral and intellectual and personal and family bankruptcy. Why do many families come apart? Because they have no anchor of truth. The husband and father has no clear vision of why he or his children exist. And so all he can do is pass on a few tips for how to make more money or stay healthy. And the emptiness gets deeper and deeper with each unbelieving generation.

Over 2,000 years ago the Truth was crucified. Today the truth is being crucified again and again in our courtrooms, in our newspapers, in movies, in books, in Washington D.C, and all across America, and the emptiness gets deeper and deeper. America's future is gravely threatened by this callous disregard for what is true and right, and we stand at the threshold of self-destruction.

CHAPTER 8
WHEN FACTS DON'T MATTER
LIBERALS HATE FACTS THAT CONTRADICT THEIR WORLD VIEW AND THEIR SECRET AGENDAS

Political language... is designed to make lies sound truthful and murder respectable, and to give an appearance of solidity to pure wind. George Orwell

We live in an America where emotions trump facts. Greed trumps facts. Selfish motives trump facts. Ideology and bad theology trump facts. There is one thing that does not trump facts--truth. Truth and facts live in harmony.

The degree to which facts do not matter to liberals is sometimes astonishing when you are faced with an example of extraordinary boldness. In a speech given in Cape Town, South Africa, President Obama while talking about George Washington, said, "He understood that Democracy can only endure when it's bigger than just one person. So his willingness to leave power was as profound as his ability to claim power." George Washington would turn over in his grave to hear his political opposite now purport to use him to promote the kind of government George Washington stood so vehemently against.

First, George Washington did not "claim power." He was

drafted by the American people to be their humble leader. He never sought power and fame, but he acquiesced to the call and became a great President. President Obama is the one who claimed power, and he thrives on power and fame. Look at his Presidency, and it seems orchestrated with famous Hollywood actors and musicians to broadcast his fame and prestige. Obama is blatantly arrogant, and there is little humility in him. Barak Obama is the moral and political opposite of George Washington.

Second, George Washington left power to keep government under control, to make sure that every President after him understood that the President is not a King and that the President of the United States yields power to the people. President Obama stands for the opposite. In his first term alone, he expanded the Federal budget more than ALL previous presidents combined! The Federal government under Obama has exploded bigger than ever, and with the Healthcare Act and a thousand other Federal initiatives, Obama is nothing like President Washington. Washington sought to safeguard citizens' constitutional rights. Obama usurps them at will.

The large audience listening to Obama's theft of George Washington's humility and heart for limited government did not even pick up on the incredible irony. The audience actually applauded enthusiastically. They were clueless.

The Great Manipulator

Many have called President Obama a great orator. They are wrong. Obama has learned how to use the English language to misrepresent and manipulate, and he can do so with a smile while exuding confidence. But that does not make him a great orator: It makes him a great manipulator.

What has happened in America is a reflection of what has happened around the world, even in South Africa. People seem incapable of clear thinking. I cannot help but think that President Obama could say anything, and people would applaud and say, "Isn't he wonderful!" I would like to see what would happen if Obama gave a speech to Americans like this:

First, I want to thank all my sycophants for supporting me in this great adventure of remaking America into an example of democracy and opportunity for the rest of the world. It is an exciting adventure, and we are in it together. [Pause, smug smile, look across the audience with confidence. Look stately for the cameras.]

Second, I want to be straight with you as I always am. I am very thankful that Americans, Americans like all of you listening, are so gullible and so incredibly naive. It has been so easy to manipulate you, to promise you one thing and then do the opposite, and none of you seem to even notice. I love the way I can tell you bold-faced lies, lies that are completely the opposite of what I just did, and you all applaud me enthusiastically. Before I came into office, I heard that all I had to do as President was make the promises people wanted to hear. "Just keep tickling their ears," I was told, and Americans are too stupid to pay any attention to reality or the facts. If I just said what people wanted to hear, and if I just did so with an air of confidence, I would become a great President. And you have all proven that to be true. I am a great President. By your own standards my fellow Americans, but only because you are all so naive and frankly far dumber than I ever imagined. God bless America. [No doubt followed by great applause and a standing ovation.]

Apparently nothing Obama says has to connect with reality. A sign of the times?

Facts Are Irrelevant to Liberals

Liberalism is bound by neither facts nor truth. Liberalism cannot be bound by facts or truth, or it would implode. This is why liberals make so many arguments that distort historical facts.

This is why liberals refuse to answer direct questions that challenge their notion of reality. For liberalism to succeed, facts must not be allowed to get in the way.

Liberals often find themselves in a serious dilemma when they cannot refute a fact, so they go to great lengths to persuade weak minds that either the facts don't matter, or that the facts are the opposite of the conservative position. Or they will make a lengthy argument that takes a labyrinthian route to completely disarm listeners. There's an old saying among lawyers, and paraphrased, it goes like this, "If you don't have the facts on your side, argue the law. If you don't have the law on your side, argue the facts. If you have neither, confuse the hell out of everyone."

Liberalism excels at denying objective reality, denying black-and-white facts. Liberalism makes up its own facts, often with no nexus to any known fact on Earth. Liberalism has reached extraordinary levels of intellectual dishonesty. The liberals who have risen to power today in politics have spent a lifetime learning how to talk and say nothing. Said another way, they have the ability to talk for any length of time without substance, but with the use of intellectual concepts and words that tickle the ears of their sycophants.

Ask a Democrat any question, and he is off running with the perfect answer to promote his cause. It doesn't matter how many facts you throw at a Democrat that prove his position wrong, he marches forward with intellectual superiority. The more you prove him wrong, the more adamant he gets, the bolder he gets, and the more he mockingly presents his case. Today a Democrat can look right in the camera and tell a bold-faced lie with an extraordinary air of confidence and cockiness. The average person is persuaded by the confidence. So much for discernment.

How can Democrats lose if facts no longer matter? How can Democrats lose if the truth is irrelevant? As long as the majority of voters don't care about facts or truth, Democrats will continue to gain votes. It's a vicious cycle of "Dumb and Dumber" where dumb politicians get dumber voters to elect them, and then the two incestuously support each other right off the cliff. Note that dumb in this context does not mean they don't have a public education. Many of the politicians are lawyers and doctors, and some have Ph. Ds and master's degrees. But don't mistake an American education for wisdom. Many well-educated Democrats are some of the dumbest people you will meet in your life.

Republicans' Great Disadvantage

Republicans have been at such a disadvantage in this war for America's soul. First, honest conservatives (which includes many but not all Republicans), do not have the advantage of being able to lie at a moment's notice on any issue on any day. Don't think that isn't an advantage for liberals. It's a huge advantage for liberals precisely because the majority of Americans are no longer able to discern the difference.

Watch a conservative and the best liberal intellectual argue opposite sides of an issue. At the end of five minutes, can you tell who won the argument? The vast majority of Americans cannot. The reason is that the intellectual arguments are so twisted and confusing that even smart Americans don't know who won the argument most of the time. In addition, liberals make up facts and lie at will to support their arguments. An honest opponent in a debate with a liberal is at a huge disadvantage.

Second, conservatives simply do not have the intellectual prowess to promote the conservative cause. Of course, there are a few who do, thank God, but today conservatives are still looking around for another Ronald Reagan. Reagan was such an extraordinary man, he made the most powerful conservative arguments sound simple. He was a master of both facts and truth. He was a persuasive man and a great intellectual.

You'll remember how liberals worked very hard for years to try and redefine Reagan as a bumbling old man. This is just another example of how liberals try to convince Americans of something by turning the truth around 180 degrees. Liberals knew Reagan was not a bumbling old man but the greatest and most powerful enemy they had faced in a long, long time. They were devastated by Reagan's sharp tongue which spoke the truth with persuasive clarity.

Where Are The Great Conservatives Today?

There are conservatives with the intellectual prowess to put liberals in their place in debates, but these conservatives are not politicians (with a couple of exceptions). The great conservative intellectuals are behind the scenes, and since William F. Buckley's passing, Ayn Rand's passing, Ronald Reagan's passing and others less known, there are few powerful conservative minds well grounded in liberalism who know how to defend our freedoms. America desperately needs a conservative leader who can think and debate like Reagan. Better yet, we need thousands of conservatives who can think and debate like Reagan.

> *Thank God we are now seeing such people rising from the ashes of the collapse of the legacy media with podcasts that are now legitimately called the mainstreet media by virtue of their massive numbers of viewers. As a result, more people are taking the red pill and suddenly seeing clearly as if waking from a long slumber.*

There is another group of people who have risen to one of the most important roles in America today in the fight against liberalism. There is a small segment of the media that is not part of the mainstream media. This small segment of dedicated journalists, investigative reporters, opinion and news anchors have hung onto the traditional independent calling to pursue the facts and to be honest in their reporting. These people are our greatest hope for educating Americans with the real facts and with an honest perspective of what is happening in America. News without bias and manipulation is refreshing. In the news world dominated by the mainstream media, Fox stands almost alone against media gone wild. But even objective reporting and conservative intellectuals cannot persuade Americans if the majority of Americans care nothing for the truth.

If liberals cannot win on the facts alone, if they cannot win based on the law, and if their best efforts to redefine the issues and confuse the electorate are not working, they go into high gear with their last and most powerful end strategy: They set about with a concerted and well-coordinated strategy to personally destroy the reputation and credibility of their enemy. This is why they went after Ronald Reagan with slander and misrepresentations. It's why they ramped up such attacks and went after Donald Trump with a level of viciousness we have never witnessed before.

You Are The Enemy

Liberals think of conservatives as their enemies. Republicans think in polite terms, like "political opponent," but liberals have no such weakness. Liberals may not publicly use the term "enemy" very often, but for liberals all conservatives are enemies. For liberals this is war. They intend to take the country, and if you stand against them, you are their enemy.

Liberals seek to not just disable conservatives in office, they seek to destroy them forever. The level of vindictiveness among hard-core liberals is almost beyond the imagination of good, honest conservatives.

Since facts do not matter to liberals, you cannot win an argument with a liberal based on facts. Try this next time you are in a debate with a liberal. After arguing the facts logically and patiently and getting nothing in return but vitriol and denial, ask this question, "If I could prove to you that the facts are contrary to what you believe, would you then be persuaded that my conclusion may be valid?" The answer will be one word spoken adamantly and loudly, "**No!**" Facts truly do not matter to liberals.

CHAPTER 9
THE TURNING POINT IN AMERICA
GOD GIVES AMERICANS A REPRIEVE

The accelerated destruction of America started with Lynden Johnson (who coordinated the false flag, the Gulf of Tonkin, that launched the Viet Nam war, killed 50,000 Americans and hundreds of thousands of Viet Cong) and America's decline continued with Richard Nixon, and even under Ford, Carter, and Reagan. But the decline accelerated dramatically when the liberals got Presidents in office who fully embraced their agendas.

From George H.W. Bush to Bill Clinton to George W. Bush to Barak Obama to Joe Biden this nation has fallen from grace and into such evil, the vast majority of Americans cannot begin to comprehend the full depth and breadth of this evil. An entire book could be written specifically about how President Obama accelerated the decline of America's greatness and its collapse. There are many factual and prophetic reasons America is compared to Babylon by theologians. More than any other president, Obama was the puppet of the deep state who brought their evil agenda to fruition.

Joe Biden was merely a placeholder, a facilitator, and a puppet on strings who would continue the liberal agenda during his term. He never had an original thought, but the deep state didn't want a President with original thoughts who they could not control and manipulate. The fall of America continued according to their plans for a one-world global government, and that global plan necessitated the end of American power and influence.

By the time we got to the 2016 presidential election, let's not forget how the deep state represented by the Democrats had spent well over half a century to accomplish the extraordinary by:

- filling all Federal agencies with a majority of employees of democrat supporters,
- managed to pack the Senate and House with rabid democrats fully on board with the liberal agenda,
- packed the Senate and House with rhino Republicans more than willing to sell their souls for power and money,
- took control of America's education system from kindergarten through the Ivy League Universities,
- built a massive military-industrial complex that cost Americans trillions of tax dollars, guaranteed constant wars around the world, and created a source of funding for democrats in the billions of dollars while also assuring the continuation of the "revolving door" that would make so many of the players filthy rich,
- creating many organizations below the public radar that promoted liberal causes, including multi-billion dollar non-profit organizations, many of which receive federal grants to facilitate the deep state agenda,
- took complete control of the legacy media and turned it into an arm of the Democrat Party, and developed what was long called the "main street media" into the most powerful propaganda weapon in world history

(far bigger and more effective than the propaganda of Adolph Hitler, Joseph Stalin and Xi Jinping),
- in a stealthy way, they also managed to infiltrate all of America's national security agencies (all 14 of them), and turn them into unbelievably powerful weapons against the American people in order to fulfill the liberal agenda,
- including the CIA, FBI, and DHS,
- created a secret back channel of cooperation and contracts between these national security agencies and the biggest tech companies in the world, including Google, Facebook, Microsoft, Twitter, YouTube, and many others,
- facilitated the most aggressive propaganda and brainwashing agenda in world history, focused not just on Americans, but extending to the control of other nations, which even included regime change and the funding of America's enemies,
- weaponized government against conservatives and Christians and political opponents,
- essentially took over the three branches of government, including the judiciary from the lowest levels of superior courts to the highest court in the land,
- and much more that would extend this list for many pages, but you get the picture.

And so it was in 2016 when Hillary Clinton was "on deck" to finalize the deep state plan to bring America to its knees, complete the shredding of the U.S. Constitution, and once and for all to enslave all Americans with only the 2nd Amendment standing in their way, the Democrats and their deep state masters (aka puppeteers), were absolutely certain their plan that had taken almost three generations of democrat politicians was finally about to be completed with Hillary Clinton's installation as President.

How was it that these deep-state Democrats were so cocky about keeping control and installing Hillary in 2016? Even their media reported that Hillary's odds of winning were close to 99% over Donald Trump. The Democrats had no doubt whatsoever that it was a done deal. Hillary walked around like the most confident and arrogant presidential candidate in history. Every anchor on every legacy media channel laughed and mocked Donald Trump for even thinking he could beat Hillary and become President of the United States. The rich and famous in Hollywood laughed incessantly at Trump's chances. Political pundits and University think tanks all mocked Trump.

Hillary and the Democrats and their deep state funders were so confident because they had every reason to be confident. Review the long list of accomplishments above again, and it tells us that no one would stand a chance to go up against the deep state candidate. But add to this the fact that the entire Federal government, including all three branches, the military-industrial complex, all of the biggest tech companies in America, had a deep and loyal network that joined all their forces, all their resources, all their money to support and install Hillary Clinton as President so life could go on as usual for all of them.

And do not forget the other insurmountable problem Donald Trump had. Actually, he had at least three insurmountable challenges. First, he had never been a politician and was like a fish out of water. Second, he is not a professional speaker who has spent a lifetime crafting words and phrases to persuade people to vote for him, and the man has no filter. This was Hillary's forte. She is one of the most effective liars in political history. Third, Hillary's campaign had spent a record $1.2 billion to defeat Trump, while Trump's total campaign spent about half that.

All of that money spent on Hillary's campaign gave her a massive propaganda advantage, but she actually got many times that in free legacy media advertising and help with big tech censoring. It is my opinion that the free advertising and censorship that Hillary got from these sources had a value of approximately three times her total campaign budget. It could have been as much as 10 times, but let's be conservative with this estimate.

So shocked was Hillary Clinton on the night of the election when Donald Trump beat her, she was literally unable to face her supporters on election night. She could not speak, and she left without any statement. Since Hillary had spent her life crafting words as a politician, and she loved to hear herself talk, it was quite remarkable that she was speechless.

Why was she speechless? Because she knew beyond a shadow of a doubt, and the deep state Democrats knew, that she had this election in the bag. There wasn't any doubt. They had all the cards, all the money, all the networks, all the legacy media, and they had effectively censored opposition on the Internet and on social media, and they thought they owned the American voters. They had spent decades feeding voters propaganda, and the voters had been quite gullible to believe almost all of the propaganda.

And don't forget, they also thought they controlled the voting machine hardware and software to manipulate the vote totals. It wasn't until the 2020 election that they actually perfected voter fraud that they were able to generate almost 20 million fraudulent votes that still have not been accounted for. But we also have whistleblowers, personal testimonies under oath, and video recordings of blatant voter fraud in 2020. The issue of voter fraud in 2020 is no longer an argument. It is a fact.

So what happened in 2016? Why didn't Hillary Clinton win?

The Democrats are good at cheating, lying, manipulating, committing voter fraud, and paying off many people and companies to get their support, but there is one thing the Democrat Party and their deep state operatives do not control and do not account for.

God. They always leave God out of their formula. In 2016 God intervened. And in 2024, once again God intervened and Donald J. Trump has been elected our 47th President.

I don't want to get side-tracked from our primary focus in this book, but these five presidents have taken us down a very dark path. Our politicians and the main street media have covered up the truth and protected the evildoers so that Americans have been unaware of most of the most heinous crimes in presidential history.

Most Americans still think George W. Bush was a nice man and a Christian who did his best to lead our nation in difficult times, and they have no idea how he was involved in the biggest false flag in our history. We don't have the time or space here to go over the thousands of hours of evidence that expose 9-11 as a false flag event, but it was.

Briefly, we now have proof no plane crashed into the Pentagon, no plane crashed in Pennsylvania, and the two towers and building seven were taken down by planned demolitions, not by fires and not by commercial airplanes. This false flag event then caused the U.S. to enter its longest war, spend trillions of dollars we cannot afford to spend, and cost thousands of precious American lives. Then there are the hundreds of thousands we have killed in the Middle East justified by 9-11, a false flag event coordinated by the deep state and some very evil people.

Yet, to this day, the lies have been covered up, and the truth is not widely known among Americans about 9-11. While George W. Bush is often seen as the least of the evil presidents in recent years, he may, in fact, be the worst. 9-11 was certainly a turning point for America.

The Real Turning Point

But one could argue that the definitive turning point for America was reached when Barak Obama had been in office for a few years, and Hillary Clinton was Secretary of State. It was then that America entered its darkest history with massive fraud, International crimes, national security breaches, human trafficking coordinated by HRC's people, the selling of our uranium to our enemies, treasonous agreements with our enemies, and payment of U.S. tax dollars in the billions to our worst enemies, and treason this nation had never seen on such a scale.

It is a matter of undisputed fact that Hillary Clinton compromised national security with a private server that was hacked by more than one foreign spy (China and Russia most likely), and then she violated Federal law and her own oath by destroying the servers and physically destroying hard drives as well as hiding over 33,000 emails from a legally issued subpoena.

During the Obama/Clinton reign, DNC secrets have been guarded at all costs, including the assassination of Seth Rich and others. Voting by illegal aliens reached an all-time high, and Democrats insisted on allowing illegal voting because illegal aliens know who feeds them, and so they vote for Democrats. This is why Democrats fight so vociferously against any kind of voter ID card. Notice how they twist the truth with lies and hidden agendas by accusing Republicans who want an honest voting system in the U.S. of being racists.

Hillary Clinton was recorded as saying that she wanted "no borders" at all between the U.S. and Mexico. She wants to welcome criminals of all kinds, murderers, drug dealers, gangs, and so on. Why? Think about it.

The Clinton Foundation has been exposed for massive fraud in the billions of dollars. The Clinton Foundation has also been identified as being involved in the Haiti human trafficking business. The Haiti government official who was to testify about the fraudulent transfer of funds was killed the day before he was to testify. They called it suicide, but his family and friends who knew him said there was no possibility it was suicide.

Many have died this way over the years when they were about to testify against the Clintons going way back to the Arkansas drug operations and money laundering business when Clinton was the Governor of Arkansas. It was out of that operation that the CIA built the largest drug distribution network in the world. Our own CIA! This knowledge puts a new spin on Nancy Reagan's theme to stop drug use with her famous phrase "Just say no." While our own CIA had a massive International drug distribution network, we were saying out of the other side of our mouth, "Just say no" to the end users.

During the Obama/Clinton reign, the CIA and FBI were exposed for treason in trying to overthrow a sitting President of the United States by framing him for a crime he never committed. Hillary Clinton and the DNS (and possibly Jeb Bush) paid for the fake Russian dossier. The whole world knows about this, and we still haven't seen any of these traitors go to prison.

Never in this nation's history has there been this kind of attempt to take out a President with a coup involving so many Federal employees in so many high positions in so many departments. The deep state is real.

The list of fraud and crimes of the Obama/Clinton era goes on and on, but I want to stop there. You could actually call this era the Clinton/Obama/Clinton era, because Obama was sandwiched between Bill and Hillary, but for simplicity I'll just call it the Obama/Clinton era.

What the Obama/Clinton era represents is a crescendo of the

fight against all that is true and good. It represents a time in America's history when the compounding effect of massive lies, fraud, manipulation, and deception have reached a point of ultimate crisis, leading to the ultimate fall of America as we know it, or the destruction of the deep state by an America that rises against the evil and stands for the truth.

The Turning Point is Upon Us Now

The significance of Trump's 47th presidency is not lost on the deep state. They understand that he will be their doom, unless they stop him. They understand that it is during this administration that all they have worked to accomplish their entire lives may be destroyed.

They live for their deep religious ideologies, although they deny the true God. They are driven not just by political ideologies, they are driven by much deeper and more powerful forces, including their worldview and religious beliefs. Let there be no mistake about their religious beliefs. They do not believe in the true God, but many of them are deeply involved in private fraternities or associations that are shrouded in secrecy.

For example, many of the people involved in the attempted coup against President Trump in his first term (and the destruction of truth in America) have been or are still members of Skull & Bones, The Free Masons, the Illuminati, The Bohemian Club, The Trilateral Commission, and many others. [See a partial list at Wikipedia Fraternities.]

The deep beliefs and goals they have through their associations with other like-minded and sick people are the powerful driving forces behind everything they do, although those goals and associations must remain absolutely below the radar and kept from the public.

You see, unlike hard-working conservatives who are raising

families and pouring their energy into productive and good things, liberal fanatics are driven by their evil religious and philosophical beliefs. Many liberals today will die for their cause.

You see that in how they have manipulated their liberal constituents to commit crimes of violence against Christians or conservative people. They willingly and with great enthusiasm participate in riots where they attack innocent people and break windows and trash businesses, and encourage thieves to do likewise.

They express their hate for America, for the U.S. Constitution, for the freedoms this nation has, and against the symbol of our freedom—the American Flag. These are the liberal Democrats who are doing all this to destroy America, not conservative Republicans.

If you think that President Trump's second term will solve all our problems and make America Great Again forever and ever, think again. Granted, he won a mandate with a landslide victory, and Republicans have the majority in the Senate and House, and the U.S. Supreme Court has a conservative majority. All of this is wonderful news for conservatives, true American patriots, and Christians, but evil never rests, and the War of the Ages is far from over.

In a YouTube video (Nov 7, 2024) titled "The Enemies of Liberty Will Not Go Quietly into the Night" Peter Boghossian said it plainly when speaking about the Democrat response to Trump's victory:

> *"I predict that we will see a ferociousness and a tenacity and a pathological vengeance by the people and the cronies that we have thrown out of office, the people who have basically terrorized the United States and the rest of the world at the very minimum for 12 years."*

What Is Coming Very Soon

What many do not understand on both sides of the aisle, and what President Trump may not understand either, is that Bible prophecy will unfold exactly as God has planned. What does this mean for us as Americans?

This means that many on both sides are wrong about what will happen. Many good people who are in the fight against the deep state but who are not themselves believers and students of the Bible are predicting that the deep state will be destroyed and that America will rise to greatness and we will all live happily ever after.

The evil people trying to destroy America are still hoping that they will overthrow Trump and take over America, most likely through false flags and violent events (possibly war, planned terrorist attacks, a massive man-caused plague—Bill Gates predicts 33 million will die from a coming plague). And let us not be naive. They tried to assassinate Trump twice during the campaign, and they are so unspeakably evil, does anyone doubt they will try to assassinate him again?

God determines what will happen to America and when it will happen. He has always known. The Bible has never been wrong about any prophecy, and it won't be wrong about the unfolding prophesies now.

<u>Will America Be Great Again?</u>

Where does all of this leave MAGA, the great theme of Trump's campaign—Make America Great Again?

We are already seeing gigantic positive changes even prior to him taking the oath of office. His agenda has a mandate from American voters, and it's an excellent agenda that turns our nation from hundreds of wicked agenda items to a much more righteous list of good for all Americans.

Your worldview about the future will hinge on whether you are a Bible-believing Christian who understands biblical prophesy or an unbeliever who believes in a secular view of America, human behavior, and the future. It is my conviction that an accurate view of current events and prospects for the future must consider both a secular understanding of worldly events and spiritual insight gained from a deep knowledge of the scriptures and prophesy.

In the third book of this trilogy, you'll see a careful analysis of the spiritual realm and how America plays its part. That certainly influences how we view the statement "Make America Great Again."

CHAPTER 10

THE KAVANAUGH HEARINGS

WHERE ADMISSIBILITY OF EVIDENCE,
WEIGHT OF EVIDENCE, AND CREDIBILITY
ARE ALL LOST

The Senate confirmation hearings of Judge Brett Kavanaugh as a Trump appointee to the U.S. Supreme Court exemplified what is wrong with America. It's like seeing the tip of the iceberg, and now we have a better view of what is below the surface, and it's not pretty. It's not just the behavior of the democrat Senators on the committee that reveals what is wrong with America—it's how Americans have divided into two groups of people, and one group has completely fallen for all the lies, all the manipulation, and all the deception of the Democrat leadership.

We're not talking about a mere difference of opinion on political issues or economic issues. We're talking about something much deeper and much more sinister. The Kavanaugh hearings help us identify the real issues that are below most people's radar.

Before we look at the evidence against Kavanaugh, it is important to have at least a fundamental knowledge of the rules of evidence and important legal concepts, like the admissibility of evidence, the weight of the evidence, and the credibility of witnesses. In addition, the evidence must be weighed based on whether it was contemporaneous with the alleged event or distant in time, and the corroboration of witnesses' testimony (or lack thereof) plays a critical role.

These vitally important legal issues have been developed and refined over centuries, so we have a very strong legal foundation upon which to interpret the Kavanaugh documentary evidence and testimonies. Fortunately, I was an attorney for 20 years, so I can help with that.

Mainstream Media Not Reporting Facts Objectively

Before we get into the facts, we must acknowledge that the mainstream media did not report all the facts objectively. This is a tragedy because millions of sincere Americans rely on the media for their facts and even their opinions. The media has joined the Democrats to distort the facts, misrepresent the issues, and they have aggressively and passionately expressed opinions intended to sway public opinion against Kavanaugh.

That so many Americans don't see this for what it is . . . is nothing less than tragic. But who really bears the responsibility for what they watch, read, and listen to? American citizens are responsible for the information they believe. If they choose to be deceived, it is most likely because they are deceived.

Remember what Jesus said:

> *For this people's heart has grown dull, and with their ears they can barely hear, and their eyes they have closed, lest they should see with their eyes and hear with their ears and understand with their heart and turn, and I would heal them.'* [Matthew 13:15]

> *Let them alone; they are blind guides. And if the blind lead the blind, both will fall into a pit."* [Matthew 15:14]

It is truly disappointing that Americans can be so easily misled by the mainstream media, because this is history's best known form of brainwashing used by dictators throughout history. The mainstream press were all important components for every dictator, including these:

Adolf Hitler's Nazi Germany, Hideki Tojo's Japan, Benito Mussolini's Italy, Francisco Franco's Spain, Joseph Stalin's Soviet Union, Mao Zedong's People's Republic of China, and North Korea.

Christine Ford Testimony and Evidence

Christine Ford's personal testimony is that 36 years ago, someone she alleges was Brett Kavanaugh, grabbed her, pushed her down on a bed, and touched her over the top of her clothing in a private area, and allegedly put his hand over her mouth, and then stopped. That was the end of it. She did not make any claim that anything happened with regard to any kind of sexual assault or rape. Her clothing remained intact, and she immediately left the room and the house. That is the entire event.

Did Christine Ford have witnesses? She named four witnesses, but all four not only would not corroborate her testimony, it was worse than that. All four refuted her testimony under penalty of federal perjury.

Christine Ford's best friend at the time of the alleged incident testified that Ford had not told her about the event at the time. Not a word. That friend also testified she never met Brett Kavanaugh.

Christine Ford cannot remember when this event took place, nor can she remember the house. And she cannot remember how she got to the house or how she got home. But oddly enough, she remembers for sure that she only had one beer. Why are Democrats so willing to believe Ford? If your own middle school or high school child was telling you this story, would you believe it? Democrats are more than willing to believe it, because the Kavanaugh hearings are not actually about the facts or his qualifications.

Ford's ex-boyfriend came out to explain that her personally witnessed Ford coaching someone on how to pass a polygraph test, and Ford denied involvement in polygraph testing when she was under oath. Her ex-boyfriend also said Ford loved to fly, and Ford admitted that she flew all over the world. This is relevant because her excuse for not wanting to fly to Washington, D.C., to the hearing was that she was afraid to fly. So that turns out to be another lie. But it's a double lie, because she was on the East Coast when she represented that she did want to fly from her home in California.

In addition, Ford did not report the event to the local police, her parents, her friends, or anyone. This raises the issue of whether the event ever occurred. Any woman who was sexually assaulted tells people and some report it to the police, but at a minimum, such a woman would tell her best or closest friend. Ford told no one.

There is not a single corroborating witness, and there is not a single piece of documentary evidence contemporaneous with the alleged event that supports her allegation. This is a 36-year old allegation with no corroboration whatsoever.

These are all incontrovertible facts based on Ford's own testimony and her own witnesses' testimonies. You do not have to be a lawyer to understand that all of this boils down to an uncorroborated allegation by one woman with a foggy memory of events of something she says happened 36 years ago.

Lastly, we had a 7th FBI investigation and report, and the FBI found that there was no corroborating evidence of any kind to support Ford's single allegation. In other words, there is no case.

Dr. Ford's allegation against Brett Kavanaugh has collapsed completely, and she has no credibility herself.

Notice I have not even included a personal opinion here. This is all judicial language and interpretations of actual evidence based on our constitutional rights and rules of evidence, which includes due process and the core American principle that one is innocent until proven guilty.

Brett Kavanaugh's Massive Documentary Evidence

The Senate already had more information, more documents, more FBI reports (6 prior FBI reports), and more judicial opinions on Brett Kavanaugh than any other judge in the history of judicial nomination hearings. USA Today reported:

> *Senators have begun the deepest dive ever into the writings of a Supreme Court nominee, digging into a record 1 million-plus pages of legal opinions and emails from Brett Kavanaugh's career as a federal judge, White House attorney and assistant to the prosecutor who investigated President Bill Clinton. The volume of Kavanaugh's records dwarfs those of the past two Supreme Court justices to be confirmed: Neil Gorsuch and Elena Kagan. Senators reviewed about 182,000 pages of documents on Gorsuch and about 170,000 pages on Kagan.*

What did the Senate do with this massive documentary evidence? Absolutely nothing! The questions and the hearings focused entirely on attacking Kavanaugh personally based on one uncorroborated 36-year-old allegation of a very disturbed woman.

Brett Kavanaugh's Testimony and Evidence

Brett Kavanaugh's personal testimony is that he was not at the house and he never assaulted Ford or any other female in his entire life.

Kavanaugh did have documentary evidence that was contemporaneous with the alleged event, and that was a handwritten calendar he kept of his activities and where he was. His calendar showed he was in other places and busy with other activities on the weekends that were most likely the time of the alleged event. A contemporaneous documentary piece of evidence like this is given great weight in a courtroom.

Kavanaugh also had a lifetime record with not a single blemish on it. He has been married to one woman all these years, had an extraordinary career as a judge, was first in his high school and law school classes, and to this day is loved by hundreds of people who know him intimately and have worked with him for decades. 65 women signed a letter giving him the highest praise as a man and as a judge.

These are all incontrovertible facts based on Kavanaugh's own testimony, his calendar, and the character testimonies. This would all be admissible evidence in a courtroom.

The Missing Evidence

Notice what is missing in the evidence locker against Kavanaugh. This is important, because in any case there is affirmative evidence and there is evidence that is conspicuous by its absence. Here is what is missing, and this shouts loudly from the mountain tops:

- Kavanaugh did not lie even once (those who say he did are lying)
- There are no inconsistencies in his personal testimony under oath

- There are no inconsistencies in all of his documentary evidence
- There are no witnesses who contradict his testimony
- There are no witnesses who refused to corroborate his testimony
- There was not a single witness (other than Ford) who refuted his testimony
- No Senator had an issue with any of his 300 plus judicial opinions
- No Senator had an issue with his last 12 years on the bench
- There was no evidence that disputed Kavanaughs integrity

All of this is of huge importance. The man Kavanaugh withstood the toughest test of independent FBI investigations and Senatorial investigations, and he came out with not a single blemish or single piece of evidence or a single witness, other than Ford, who could attack his record or the man.

When you balance Kavanaugh's record and testimony and documents with Ford's, there is no comparison. Kavanaugh is perhaps 100 times more credible than Ford.

I would submit that not a single Senator, and not a single American that I know, myself included, could stand up to the lifetime of integrity, loyalty, faithful service, and honesty that Kavanaugh has. The man's record and service are nothing less than incredible. And this is the man the democrats sought to destroy forever!

Not So Subtle Facts (Unreported by Main Street Media)

After Dr. Ford's testimony, it was instantly popular for nearly everyone to announce that her testimony was "very credible" or "compelling," but the truth is not so pretty. Her testimony was neither credible nor compelling.

With time to reflect on Ford's testimony and her own alleged witnesses and alleged corroborating evidence, it turns out she has zero corroborating witnesses and zero corroborating evidence of any kind. Her own alleged witnesses have not corroborated her testimony, and worse than that, they refuted it.

But there's more. Ford's claims that she is afraid to fly on airplanes turns out to be a lie on her part. Evidence came out in her own testimony that she flies all the time all over the world for fun. If you were a lawyer who has tried cases based on witness testimonies, you would know how critical even small pieces of information like this are, and how they demonstrate the lack of credibility of a witness.

It also turns out that Ford has been a CIA employee, and she has taught others how to take lie detector tests. And it turns out Ford lied under oath about her lie-detector experience. This is just more evidence that hurts Ford's credibility.

It really does not take a psychologist or an experienced attorney like me to understand from Ford's testimony that she is a deeply disturbed individual with serious personal unresolved issues. This is not a personal attack on her, but a purely evidentiary analysis that comes from years of experience in both military and civilian trials.

I've heard hundreds of witnesses testify in hearings and trials, and there are patterns of behavior that indicate sincerity and honesty, and there are patterns of behavior that indicate insincerity and dishonesty. Ford's body language was not supportive of honesty, and her childlike voice, as though she was an eighth grader, was very bothersome. 36 years after the alleged event, which did not involve any sexual activity whatsoever, this woman was an emotional wreck. Ford was not a woman who came to the hearings with emotional and intellectual maturity and credibility. Far from it. She lacked credibility by all standards.

So why did so many people on both the Democrat and republican sides, as well as President Trump, all say immediately after Ford's testimony that her testimony was very credible? Because in this politically charged environment that is considered the correct thing to say, but more than that, to suggest anything other than that in this politically correct time would subject that person to a vicious and relentless attack by democrats, and they all knew that.

Now we have a break-in and theft of senate offices before a vote has been taken on Kavanaugh's nomination, and the theft was of several GOP senator's home addresses and personal information, including Senator Lindsay Graham's. There has been an arrest already, and it is a Democrat intern.

A number of other grotesque allegations have been made against Kavanaugh, bizarre claims with absolutely no corroboration made by people with no credibility. I won't give them any credit here by describing those allegations. Even the Democrats have let these other allegations go without further examination. Who is behind such false allegations? I would only state that it is not in the interests of Republicans to promote such lies, but it is in the Democrats' best interests and consistent with how they have conducted themselves from the moment Kavanaugh was nominated. Many of the extreme protestors on the street have cited these unsubstantiated allegations in their angry comments. The democrat leadership is playing their constituents like a musician plays a violin.

Deceptive Legal Games Democrats Are Playing

For those of us who have legal experience and understand

how to evaluate evidence and witness testimony, the games and lies and manipulation are so obvious, but for the average Americans who don't have this kind of experience, the democrats are involved in some of the most deceptive and evil manipulation of average American I have ever seen. Many of the democrats involved with these hearings are lawyers, and they know they are lying and involved in one of the biggest con games we have ever seen.

I recommend listening to Joe diGenova's analysis of Ford's lack of credibility.

Democrats have repeatedly claimed that they need more time and more investigations, but remember that it was Diane Feinstein who secretly sat on the letter from Dr. Ford for 45 days before bringing it out at the 11th hour to torpedo the nomination hearings. It is more than disingenuous for Democrats to then claim they need more time to investigate Ford's claims. There has always been a procedure for handling a claim like this within the Senate, but Feinstein violated standard procedure to lay in wait as she did to sabotage the nomination.

Then democrats kept asking Kavanaugh why he wouldn't demand or ask for another FBI investigation. Everyone who has experience with the law, these kinds of hearings, and the FBI protocol for investigations know that Democrats were again being disingenuous because they knew they were only asking the question to manipulate their constituents back home. Kavanaugh had no legal authority to demand or ask the FBI to do anything. He is a nominee at a Senate hearing, and his only job is to answer questions under oath.

It is the Senate that conducts these hearings and collects information for their decision. The Senate asks for FBI reports and reviews them, and Feinstein could have asked for an FBI investigation 45 days earlier, but she chose not to. For Feinstein to shirk her Senate duty and then to try to put that duty on Kavanaugh was a kindergarten tactic that everyone at the hearing could see through. But the average American was fooled by democrat tactics and manipulated to oppose Kavanaugh.

Then, after Trump asked the FBI to do another investigation (the 7th FBI investigation into Kavanaugh's life and career) to satisfy Democrats, they refused to accept the result of the independent FBI report, now accusing the FBI of being manipulated. Anyone who doesn't see what the Democrats are doing is simply blind. There's no other way to describe it.

On October 4, 2018 prior to the Senate vote, the Wall Street Journal published a letter written by Brett Kavanaugh in which he wrote:

> **Going forward, you can count on me to be the same kind of judge and person I have been for my entire 28-year legal career: hardworking, even-keeled, open-minded, independent and dedicated to the Constitution and the public good. As a judge, I have always treated colleagues and litigants with the utmost respect. I have been known for my courtesy on and off the bench. I have not changed.**

These are the qualities that should be considered for any nominee for the Supreme Court, but the Democrats don't care at all. Kavanaugh's statement will make absolutely no difference to Democrats. The democrats have not examined his judicial opinions or his qualifications to sit on the court. They don't care about his qualifications.

There are a number of problems with the testimony on the Ford side of the ledger. For example, her own witnesses have refuted her testimony. That's huge, and should cause everyone to question her credibility. She has no supporting witnesses. That puts her credibility on the line. She can't remember where the event occurred, nor can she remember when it occurred. That should raise questions about Ford. Her demeanor during her testimony should raise questions about her credibility. And then there is this issue as explained by Senator Grassley:

> *Grassley writes: "The full details of Dr. Ford's polygraph are particularly important because the Senate Judiciary Committee has received a sworn statement from a longtime boyfriend of Dr. Ford's, stating that he personally witnessed Dr. Ford coaching a friend on polygraph examinations. When asked under oath in the hearing whether she'd ever given any tips or advice to someone who was planning on taking a polygraph, Dr. Ford replied, "Never." This statement raises specific concerns about the reliability of her polygraph examination results."*

This is damning evidence that raises a legitimate question, "Is Dr. Ford credible at all? Is anything she said true?" This is not a biased statement—it is a legitimate question that any jurist would ask if they were truly objective and seeking to flush out the truth in the midst of contradictions, lack of corroboration, and credibility issues. But the cumulative problem with Ford's evidence and testimony is gigantic, while Kavanaugh doesn't have any problem with lies, contradictions, or witnesses that refute his testimony. The talking heads on the Main Street media are claiming Kavanaugh lied, but they cannot produce one example of any lie told by Kavanaugh, either under oath or in his entire life.

Democrat Response to Final FBI Report

In response to the final FBI report, which President Trump ordered at the request of the Senate, Senator Chuck Schumer demonstrated their classic obfuscation with this quote, "Given how limited the scope of this investigation was, we are reiterating our call that the documents be made public." There is absolutely nothing about this whole investigation that could be defined as "limited."

Remember the USA Today report above that said no judicial hearing has produced so much documentation, and Kavanaugh has already been investigated by the FBI six times, more than any other judicial appointment in history. The Senate had all the time they wanted to ask questions of the witnesses, and they asked questions ad infinitum. After all that, they demanded a 7th FBI investigation. The FBI completed the 7th investigation, and the Democrats want another delay because they are claiming the investigation is too limited.

This 7th FBI report included more damning information for the Democrats. It reported that Senator Chuck Schummer is responsible for leaking Dr. Ford's letter. It also came out that Ford's best friend, Leland Keyser, who had testified that she would not corroborate Ford's story, was approached by some of Ford's people and asked to change her story to help Ford. Lying, manipulation, and deception are clearly the approach the Democrats have taken. This whole affair from the democrat side stinks to high Heaven.

The Vote

On the afternoon of October 6th, 2018 a vote was taken in the full Senate on Brett Kavanaugh's nomination to the Supreme Court, and he received 50 votes to 48 nays. He was sworn in quickly so he could go to work and fill the 9th seat on the Supreme Court.

Now do you think the democrats will apologize to Brett Kavanaugh and his wife for how they tried night and day to completely destroy Kavanaugh's good reputation without credible evidence? Absolutely not. The Democrats are unrepentant. They will never apologize or admit they were wrong. They will never admit that Ford's testimony was not credible, and they won't even admit that Ford's own witnesses refuted her testimony or that Ford lied about the polygraph tests. Instead, the democrats will bear down on their radical views, and they will continue to insist that Kavanaugh is guilty of all crimes as alleged by one witness who has no credibility, regardless of evidence to the contrary.

It doesn't matter whether you are a Republican or a Democrat; this behavior and how the Democrats have conducted these hearings ought to be repulsive to any fair-minded person who cares about truth and justice. And here's a bigger point. If you are a Democrat who identifies as a Christian, you owe it to yourself to re-examine the gross unbiblical behavior of the Democrats and ask yourself if you identify more with Democrats than you do with God. It may be a time for many "Christian democrats" to re-examine their party and their own relationship with God.

How Can Democrats Behave This Way?

The rational person who is normal, mentally and psychologically, has a great deal of trouble trying to understand how extreme liberal democrats can behave as they have during these Kavanaugh hearings. To the normal person, their behavior makes no sense. It appears that these extreme liberals often defy blatant facts, lie boldly with no apparent remorse when they are exposed, and never apologize. Many of these democrats seem to care nothing for people, even their constituents, and will use anyone with no consideration for their welfare. If this sounds just like how Democrats have handled the Kavanaugh hearings, that's because it is precisely how they have behaved.

They used their own secret weapon, Dr. Ford, against her

urgent request to remain private and confidential, and they threw her to the lions without any hesitation and with no remorse whatsoever. Then they went after a good man, Brett Kavanaugh, who has an impeccable reputation over an entire lifetime, and they sought to destroy him personally and professionally (and humiliate his wife and children) forever based on one uncorroborated allegation. These democrats have no shame, and they are as ruthless as anyone we have ever seen in politics in all of history.

The Democrat Party Has Been Taken Over By Sick People

Apart from the Biblical warnings about such people and how they are spiritually blind, I want to share this amazing explanation in this video that will do more to explain Chuck Schummer, Diane Feinstein, Dick Durbin, Patti Murray, Mazie Hirono, Elizabeth Warren, Nancy Pelosi, Maxine Waters, Harry Reid (ret.), Bill Clinton (ret.), Hillary Clinton (ret.), James Comey, Richard Blumenthal, Cory Booker, and Jerry Brown, than anything else we can say.

If you are reading the paperback, go to https://bit.ly/3VjDPaF

Rational human beings have been saying for quite a while that the Democrat leadership in America has gone completely off the rails, that they have gone insane, that the "Trump Syndrome" is a real sickness, that the Democrat leadership is poisoned with irrational arguments, viscous personalities, hatred, a "no-rules" mentality, a total disregard for their American constituents, a total disregard for the U.S. Constitution, bitter hatred for all things Christian, and the apparent inability to recognize their own sins compounded by an inability or unwillingness to ever apologize to anyone for terrible wrongs committed.

The Tipping Point for America

The Kavanaugh hearings are part of a major tipping point in America. These hearings are not just about the appointment of a Supreme Court Justice—it is about the future of America, our constitutional rights, the power and control of the Democrats and the deep state. When you understand that these hearings are part of a much bigger power move on the part of the Democrats, you begin to realize how much is at stake.

The Democrats know that if they lose the Supreme Court, they are in serious trouble. Why? Because they know the American people are waking up to their dishonesty to get illegal votes (they oppose voter ID cards and promote illegal alien voting), their lies to their constituents (blacks are waking up to how they've been used for decades), and voter fraud of the software in voting machines in Florida has been tracked to democrat programmers. There are many other serious problems of fraud and various crimes among democrats that Americans are slowly waking up to.

The Democrats and the so-called deep state are gripped by fear, dreading the possibility that their most sacred cause and the core of their identity could be dismantled if conservatives seize control of the Supreme Court. The driving force behind their every move, the issue that fuels their very existence, is nothing less than what they deem untouchable—the darkest, most heinous act imaginable: the taking of innocent lives, cloaked under the term "abortion." **Lo and behold, since this first edition was written, <u>Roe v. Wade</u> has been overturned, and it has devastated the Democrats and fanned their hatred for Donald Trump. Hallelujah!**

The democrats have turned to un-American ways to stay in control, and that includes getting judges on courts throughout the country who do not play their judicial role as the third branch of our government system. Instead, these are judges who are fiercely loyal to the democrat causes, and before their appointments it is known that they will legislate from the bench on behalf of the democrat party. That is a violation of our constitution.

This is why Democrats are rabid about stopping Kavanaugh. If they do not stop him, they lose their ability to control the Supreme Court for liberal anti-American purposes.

This is important for another bigger reason. Since it is apparent that democrats are losing their decades-long control of the executive and legislative branches, and therefore all our Federal agencies, including our DOD, DOJ, and so on, their last hope of stopping Republicans is with judicial reversals at the Supreme Court where liberal judges have been more than willing to legislate for democrats.

Now, do you see why Democrats are uncontrollably rabid and have gone to extremes to stop Kavanaugh? For Democrats, not stopping Kavanaugh in these hearings is equivalent to being on the Titanic the moment you find out why the deckchairs are beginning to slide. For democrats, this single battle represents a life-and-death battle for them.

What Happens Next?

The question has been asked of some Republican leaders, "Is this kind of contentious battle between republicans and democrats the new order of business, or can everyone get past this and back to business as usual?"

The question is a good question, but the answer of republican leaders demonstrates their incredible naiveté. Several have given answers that start with the phrase, "I hope so . . ."

Oh come on! Does anyone really think these democrat psychopaths are suddenly going to become nice people and humbly work with Republicans to do the people's business? Does a sheep herder say, "I hope the wolves will be willing to work with the sheep amicably so we can all get along."

The operative phrase for our republican party leaders and for all Americans is "Wake up!" Democrats are dragging this country straight to hell while everyone sits around and says stupid things like, "Can't we all just get along?"

What happens next is not good. On a short-term basis, it will appear that Republicans are making great strides to drain the swamp and kill the poison of the DNC that is destroying America. There definitely will be short-term progress, and some of this progress will represent huge victories.

Draining the swamp is not just a campaign slogan. It's not just President Trump that is passionate about draining the swamp. There is a large contingent of the conservative leadership in this nation that is pouring tremendous resources, time and money into a master strategy to drain the swamp of evil and traitorous people.

As the swamp creatures are cornered, many liberals will be devastated, because this will involve many big names of people they have worshipped, and some of these big names will have horrendous crimes on their indictment sheet. Too many Americans have placed some alleged crimes in the conspiracy theory category. Unfortunately, many of the conspiracies are turning out to be real and not conspiracies at all.

All of this is short-term progress in an attempt to regain America's heritage, but it really is too late. In the long-term what will happen?

The damage that was done to America over the past sixty years by democrats, extreme liberals, self-acclaimed communists and socialists, dysfunctional sycophants of radical leaders, those who hate God, heretical church leaders, a powerful military-industrial complex, and the deep state (an amalgam of all of the above plus more), cannot simply be undone by a magic political wand.

As I wrote in my book, ***The War for America's Soul: Will America Fall Into Darkness*** in a Chapter entitled **Why There is No Turning Back**:

> There are millions of bad laws are on the books. There are millions of laws at the Federal level. Add millions of state statutes, millions of county and borough codes, and millions of municipal ordinances, and you have a massive legal spiderweb that cannot possibly be unweaved no matter how good the intentions. First, you would never get a consensus to revoke all the bad laws. Second, who is going to define "bad?" Third, you cannot suddenly eliminate a complex system of laws that was developed over two centuries without creating instant chaos.
>
> There are millions of precedent setting cases on the books. The judicial branch would never let the politicians revoke millions of laws in order to start with a clean slate. There would be lawsuits like we have never seen before. There would be enough challenges to overwhelm the courts. In a very large percentage of the cases, the courts would rule such acts unconstitutional, thereby

re-enacting many of the laws immediately. Judges would not need laws to do this. They could use their own case precedents to neuter the politicians. Judges would undoubtedly issue injunctions, literally stopping the executive and legislative branches in their tracks.

<u>There are millions of regulations on the books</u>. When the legislative branch creates a law and the executive branch signs it, administrative agencies are tasked with the responsibility of implementing the broad mandate of the law into practical rules for enforcement. A single law, which may only consist of a paragraph, will often need volumes of three-ring binders created by administrators to implement the intent of the law. But wait, because it gets much more exciting for the bureaucrats. It's not as though one person in one agency can create the three-ring binders to enact a law and be done with it. The creation of a single law and the necessary regulations for implementation often reverberate from the Federal to the State to the Municipal levels of government. Each level of government that is tasked with enforcement must have its own administrators.

It is virtually impossible to turn the clock back 50 or 60 or 70 years and recapture freedoms long lost by a massive spiderweb that holds the American people hostage.

The Kavanaugh hearings became a tipping point in America for sure, but in the long run America is not tipping toward utopia —it is tipping toward rapid decline and total destruction. This isn't what most dreamers want to hear, but you only have to look at Bible prophecy to realize that man is on a downward spiral of sin and decadence, and the end result is not a sudden, "Oh, we're sorry, God. We've been wrong all this time, and now we will behave."

Not even close. You don't have to be an agnostic rocket scientist or a devout theologian to see the signs from Bible prophesy. Even without spiritual wisdom, any person who examines political world history and is paying attention to the depravity in the world today and especially in the United States, can see we are not going to experience a miraculous reversal, except on a short-term basis with the miracle of Trump's election as our 47th President.

Democrats will not cooperate with a reversal to all that is good and righteous and civil in a republic form of government, and mankind is not suddenly going to turn to God en masse and save this Titanic at the 11th hour. Folks, any other thinking is just fantasy.

This book is primarily a political analysis, but you cannot escape the fact that this country and this world will someday face God's wrath. You can deny it if you are an unbeliever, and I respect your freedom of choice, but the Bible has laid out a very clear scenario for the end days, and faithful believers around the world are absolutely convinced we are in the last days now.

President Donald Trump is doing more to drain the swamp and slow the self-destruction of the greatest nation in world history than any other President ever has, but make no mistake about this President's role. While we love his theme to "Make America Great Again," America is in decline, and the best he can do is slow the decline. It may even appear he has reversed the decline, and he can in many ways, at least in the short-term. A long term view tells us America eventually continues its decline until God's wrath comes to settle all accounts.

Many would justifiably argue that President Trump keeps wining, and anyone who goes up against him loses. That would appear to be the case, but it is not actually Trump who is so powerful and so smart. The Bible tells us that all leaders, kings, presidents, and prime ministers are appointed by God. God chose Donald Trump for such a time as this. What President Trump accomplishes has been ordained by God, and what President Trump cannot accomplish is also ordained by God.

> *Be grateful. Had Donald Trump not been our 45th President, we would be in a world of hurt right now, and if he had not been elected the 47th President, America as we know it would be gone in the near future.*

CHAPTER 11
LIBERALS DO NOT BARGAIN
LIBERALS HAVE NO INTENTION OF COMPROMISING WITH THEIR ENEMIES

Liberalism is totalitarianism with a human face. Thomas Sowell

Rule No. 1

Republicans bargain. Republicans play nice. Republicans forgive and forget.

Rule No. 2

Democrats do not bargain. Democrats do not play nice. Democrats never forgive, and they never forget.

Today radical liberals are driving the Democratic party train. Some moderate Democrats claim they are not in agreement with the radicals of their party, but that would be a nonsequitor. So long as they vote Democrat and stand with liberalism, they are part of the problem.

Imagine two card players. One is honest and plays by all the rules and is so naive; he assumes his card-playing opponent is also honest and plays by the same rules. As a result, the honest player is not suspicious, and he does not watch his opponent's hands carefully or how he plays the game.

The other card player is a master deceiver, cheats when it appears he may lose, and considers his opponent weak because he is honest and does play by the rules. If the two play for two hours, two nights a week, who wins the majority of the games by the end of one year? At the end of 10 years?

Let's play a more subtle game of truth or perjury. Suppose you are a trial lawyer, and your client is absolutely honest and will always tell the truth on the witness stand no matter what he is asked. Let's assume the opposing party will not hesitate to perjure himself to win his case. He is willing to say anything to avoid losing. In fact, he is more passionate about avoiding a loss than he is about winning.

The truth-teller is careful to answer accurately, so he tends to pause and think before he answers. If he is not sure, he says so. On cross-exam, his credibility is questioned, and under oath, he does not appear to know all the facts that well, but only because he hesitates to speak the precise truth. He actually does know the facts very well. Unfortunately, juries and judges assume this witness is less credible. This gentle and humble and honest witness comes off as a weak witness in the courtroom.

The liar is slick. He has an immediate answer to every question, and the answer always supports his case perfectly. He can make things up in an instant and never misses a beat. His answers are directly on point, and there is no hesitation or uncertainty in his voice or mannerisms. He speaks clearly, sits up straight, and looks his questioner right in the eye, and his eyes casually connect with the judge and jury. They have no idea his every word and every gesture are well coordinated. He has a lifetime of practice. He has been manipulating and fabricating since he was in elementary school. He is a great actor, and what he says seems so believable, judges and juries think it must be the truth. After watching a master liar on the witness stand, a truth teller seems almost boring.

After over 100 trials (both military and civilian), I can testify that in the courtroom, the liar has the advantage over the truth-teller in almost every case.

And so it is in the liberal movement. Liberal Democrats don't play by the rules. They make their own rules. They don't care about truth. They abhor losing, and they are determined to win no matter what it takes. It doesn't matter that most Democrats are sincere, that they believe their own lies. The results are the same. America is being ripped apart by liberalism.

Liberals are more passionate about <u>not</u> losing than they are about winning. This means that before Democrats will allow Republicans to win big, they will sink the whole ship out of perverted ideological fanaticism. Liberal Democrats would rather America implode economically and sink into darkness than allow conservative Republicans to prove them wrong and save the country with conservative policies. For liberal Democrats being wrong is a fate worse than death.

Liberals Hate American Success

If conservatives did win America back and the country thrived as a direct result of conservative policies, liberal Democrats would be rabid with anger. When Ronald Reagan took the White House, turned the entire economy around with conservative strategies, and almost single-handedly brought down the Soviet Empire, liberals were livid and redoubled their efforts to come back with a vengeance. The Reagan revolution, which spurred national and economic vitality, and which brought the power of American righteous freedom to the rest of the world, should have been something all Americans praised. While Republicans did praise Reagan's incredibly successful policies, Democrats hated what they saw, despite that it meant prosperity and freedom for Americans and others around the world.

How could Democrats and radical liberals hate such successful conservative policies during the Reagan Revolution? Remember that it is not America that liberals love. What liberals love is the idea of an America that they would remake. They don't hate capitalism because it doesn't work. They know it works, although they cannot admit that in public. Our history is replete with obvious examples of how well America flourishes when free enterprise and personal freedom rule the day. Liberals hate capitalism and personal freedom, because these powerful forces hinder the implementation of the liberal agenda, which is the creation of an entirely different America.

Imagine a man saying to a woman, "It's not you I love, it's the idea of loving you that I'm in love with." How do you think that would go over? Not very well. If Democrats were being absolutely honest with the American people, they would say, "It's not America that we love. What we love is the idea of an America that we would completely remake."

For liberals, this whole battle is not about saving America or thriving economically or giving the people freedom to be happy. It's about something very sinister. It's about power and control and ideology, the people and the country be damned.

Liberal Deception is The Key

When you realize this is true, and when you realize how deep it goes into the heart and soul of liberalism, you also realize how horribly deceptive liberals are when they tell the poor and less fortunate that their policies will help them. Liberal policies are not about helping anyone get a step up. Liberal policies are about keeping the voters down and facilitating the power and control that liberals so enjoy over Americans.

Consider how wealthy many liberal leaders become while claiming to live and breathe for the poor. They are always talking about how the rest of us need to redistribute our wealth, but they use their Democratic offices to become rich, and they do not share their wealth with the less fortunate.

John Edwards, who ran for the Democratic presidential nomination in 2004 was said to be worth 21 million dollars, wealth earned while being a personal injury attorney. He once said that his whole law practice was about helping the less fortunate, but if that was true, and if he really believed in the Democratic policies of redistribution and "fair share," why didn't he give his wealth or most of it to the poor? Even his fees were taken out of his client's recoveries. Personal injury attorneys take 30% to 40% of their clients' judgments. If Edwards practiced what he preached, why didn't he just keep 5% or 10%, instead of taking so much from the poor?

Al Gore is said to be worth $100 million, but he hasn't given it away. President and Mrs. Clinton are worth a fortune, but they haven't given it away. Ted Kennedy didn't give his wealth away. Where's the redistribution among these hypocrites? Go down the list. Harry Reid is rich, but he doesn't share his wealth. Nancy Pelosi is wealthy but she likes to keep it all. Liberals are some of the most selfish people in America!

The danger for all of us is this: If liberals realize they cannot win, they will choose not to yield but destroy the country. Remember, liberals will not bargain, even if it means the country will be devastated.

Had the Republican Party leadership understood all of this, they would not have lost so many games at the card table. Republicans have been compromising for decades, and each time they compromise, they yield to liberals. Each time they compromise truth, they move the country further toward liberalism. After decades, Republicans look like the Democrats of 20 years ago. Now our country stands at the crossroads of self-destruction.

For liberals there is no turning back. While Republicans think that the battles they fight with liberals are all just politics in a great Democratic society, liberals have a completely different mindset. Democrats believe they are at war. Liberals consider mainstream Republicans amateurs who are so naive they have no idea what is coming. I hope Republicans awake from their long slumber. More than that, I pray American voters will wake up and actively join **The War for America's Soul** before it is too late, if it isn't already.

CHAPTER 12

THE TRUTH ABOUT CAPITALISM

AND HOW LIBERALS HAVE BEEN LYING TO AN ENTIRE GENERATION

Capitalism should not be condemned, since we haven't had capitalism. Ron Paul

Liberalism teaches that capitalism is an evil economic system that enslaves people and creates great division by making the rich richer and the poor poorer. For those of us who have had a modicum of education in the subject (I have a B.A. in Economics), we know that the truth is quite the opposite--that capitalism sets people free to be successful if they work hard.

Socialism and communism inevitably spawn a self-destructive system that crushes ambition, strips individuals of their drive, and paves the way for a ruling class of wealthy, power-hungry elites. Meanwhile, the masses are left to languish in deeper poverty, their hopes and opportunities drained by the very ideology that claims to liberate them.

Liberalism's single greatest crime is persuading people that the truth is a lie so that the lie may become accepted as true. You will never see any organization or any people work so hard and so passionately for a cause as the liberals do to destroy truth. There's almost a Biblical sense to liberalism's violent assault on truth, like Satan's hatred for the Truth and his non-stop, all-encompassing war against all that is true and good. Liberalism does hate God, and more specifically, Liberalism hates the one true God of the Bible while accepting and promoting all other religions.

What is the truth about capitalism? To play off Winston Churchill's quote about democracy, I'll say that "Capitalism is the worst economic system on the planet, except all others." This is one intriguing way to say that capitalism is not perfect, but it is better than socialism or communism or any other economic system ever created by man.

The reality is that any system that man operates will fall short, especially in a fallen world. There's nothing perfect about our world or our economic system. As long as human beings are less than perfect living in an imperfect world, there will be no such thing as a perfect economic system. However, that does not disqualify capitalism from being the best system in this world.

The strategy of liberalism, and of all world despots and communist leaders, has been to point out weaknesses in a capitalist society and then claim that such weaknesses are proof that capitalism is evil and does not work. A rational mind will readily recognize that is a leap of illogic.

The Liberal Distortion of Society

Let's take an imaginary society of 100 people. If 70 of these people work very hard to feed and house their families by working seven days a week, and the other 30 choose not to work at all, how would liberals interpret this society?

First, liberals would define the problem this way. It is unfair that the 70 get to live in their own homes on their own property while dressed in their own nice clothing and eating healthy. This plays, of course, to the 30 who are not working, and who do not own their own homes, cannot afford nice clothes, and are not eating healthy meals. Liberals define the 30 as those who have been cheated out of their birthright, who are being robbed by the wealthy, and who deserve their **fair share** of the spoils that the wealthy earn.

Second, liberals then provide the solution. The solution is to take from the 70 and redistribute to the 30. The majority must pay their fair share, but the 30 don't have to pay their fair share. The 30 don't have to work. The 30 don't have any responsibility in society. The 70 must figure out how to make a living for themselves, and they have to make more than that, because they must also take care of the 30.

This destroys the motivation and financial incentive of the 70 to do better and to build a brighter economic system for everyone. In addition, by replacing the rewards of success with punishment, those who are poor will have no incentive emotionally or financially to achieve success through hard work. Those who have been successful will not be motivated to build more or bigger businesses that could employ more people.

The Hidden Agenda

This is the great hidden agenda of liberalism. Claim to be fair and to help the poor while actually destroying their future. Here's the irony of liberalism. You can almost hear it from the liberal bastion of wealth and power:

Let's destroy the poor's opportunity to rise up and become economically powerful, while at the same time getting them to vote for us and to permanently keep us in power.

It's almost too ironic even to believe. Imagine boasting that you have a plan to destroy an entire segment of society while at the same time winning the undying loyalty of those same people so that they vote for you and keep you in power. This is the greatest victory of liberalism, yet the poor are so naive they do not know what is happening to them. Many do not want to know. Many are in their second or third generation of entitlements. For these victims, Liberalism has sucked the life out of them, and they don't want to live free anymore. They have chosen slavery over freedom.

There is an uprising that seems to be gaining momentum among blacks and Hispanics consisting of some very intelligent leaders who have seen the light and expressed their views that they have been used and abused by Democrats all these years. There's also a new movement called "Walk Away Campaign" for anyone who sees how Democrats have used them and is encouraging Democrats to walk away.

The truth about capitalism is the opposite of liberalism's claim that capitalism is evil. Liberalism is evil. Capitalism is far from perfect, but it is not evil. Capitalism can be harsh, but it is never as harsh as liberalism. Capitalism sets people free to succeed. Liberalism destroys the psychological, emotional, and financial motivation upon which the greatest nation in the world was built. Capitalism gives the poor the opportunity to work hard and lift their station in life without limitations. Liberalism enslaves the poor and seeks to keep them in poverty forever.

The truth about capitalism is exactly the opposite of what Democrats claim.

CHAPTER 13
THE DEATH OF PRIVACY
HOW AMERICANS JUST LET IT HAPPEN

> *The Constitution is not neutral. It was designed to take the government off the backs of people.* William O. Douglass

Politics has a way of reframing important issues, changing people's focus, and often distracting everyone from the real issues. Hidden agendas pollute the environment, and power and money infect the entire process. The complicated issue of privacy is constantly being reframed, distorted, and pushed with hidden agendas by people in powerful positions and by organizations with trillions of dollars at stake. No wonder Americans have trouble keeping their eyes on the ball in the magician's hands.

Privacy is undoubtedly one of the most important constitutional issues for all Americans, yet the debate over the right to privacy has been derailed by specious arguments. In addition to intentional efforts to change the perspective so Americans are unaware they are losing vital freedoms, there are also a host of complex issues that cloud people's ability to stay on point.

The debate about our privacy has been sidetracked from the constitutional right of privacy to a discussion about the need for unfettered access to Americans' private data for national security purposes. In other words, to protect us from terrorists, the government claims it has the right to our personal conversations and activities with virtually no limits. Have Americans forgotten that the cure can be worse than the disease? At what point does our own government's infringement of our constitutional rights exceed the terrorist threat? When does our own government become a terrorist?

A Terrible Mistake

Many good Americans are making a terrible mistake, including prominent "conservative" Republicans, by supporting the government's need for this data based on national security. If our Federal government was perfect and could keep all the data they collected absolutely confidential, if they had software that automatically searched for key terrorist phrases between two destinations, and if we knew they would expunge all data from the government database permanently, then we might give up certain privacy rights for the sake of our security. Those who believe the government will faithfully do all that while protecting our privacy rights are making a dangerous assumption.

There's a disaster lurking in the dark when government no longer believes in protecting the constitutional right of privacy of its citizenry. That nightmare is something that has snuck up on us because no one saw it coming until it was too late.

First, we didn't know our own government had dropped the "hammer" to capture all our personal data, and second, we did not anticipate the power of technology in the private sector to facilitate this theft so quickly and so thoroughly.

Google, Facebook, and Amazon have stolen more private information from individuals around the world than anyone else in the history. And guess who their primary partner has been in the greatest theft the world has ever known? It is the United States government, through its primary agency of deception, the CIA, and all 14 national security agencies of the federal government. Some of these agencies appear to share databases with each other, but most do not. This means your entire life is on multiple databases on the government side and in the private sector.

The truth is we don't know the extent to which our personal private information has been shared across a massive network of corporations and government agencies. We do have substantial evidence to indicate that there is almost nothing about you they don't already know.

If this were just a simple theft of private information, it would be no big deal, but this is about much more. This is about expunging the 4th Amendment of the United States Constitution without a single vote. It's about knowing everything you've ever done and predicting everything you ever will do in the future. It's about knowing your political and religious beliefs and proclivities, so that you can be controlled. It's about preventing you from doing something before you even plan to do it.

We've learned that the Federal government regularly serves subpoenas on telephone companies and Internet companies like Google, Yahoo, and Microsoft demanding the personal communications of Americans. Many of these companies willingly release the data requested rather than be subject to a full frontal assault by Federal agencies that can cost a corporation millions of dollars in investigations, not to mention a lot of bullying and potentially lost Federal contracts.

The greatest threat to our freedom and privacy today in America is the dark labyrinthian maze involving a web of Federal agencies in partnership with private sector corporations.

This dark affiliation of the government and private sector has unlimited power, including the police power of the state, the executive power, the judicial power, and unlimited funding under the taxing authority of the Federal government through the IRS as well as funding through undisclosed sources called "black projects," which are not even revealed to the President or congress.

That's just on the government side of the ledger. Now add the power and money in the private sector. Facebook, Google, Amazon, Apple, and Microsoft have almost as much power as God.

This unholy alliance between government and the private sector eliminates the normal protective mechanisms in a constitutional republic, because the government is no longer motivated to protect the citizens from abusive technology or theft or violations of privacy rights. On the contrary, government now becomes a partner with the technology companies to steal and violate our rights.

The alliance is virtually unbreakable and probably permanent, and here is why. There are two steps to understanding the power of this alliance. The first step is understanding the government's role and their motivation. The second step is understanding the private sector's role and motivation.

The government finds its power, and what it now thinks is its mandate, in collecting all information on all people, organizing that data, and creating applications that will allow them to use that data to recall it and interpret it in a matter of seconds for billions of Americans. This is why there is such a strong push to implement facial recognition in every public place in America. (The private sector has already accomplished audio and video recordings in your home without your knowledge.) Facial recognition is what makes it possible to bring all the other personal data they've already stolen about you and me to a computer monitor instantaneously. AI can even issue commands at that point, which could include administratively issued orders for surveillance, search and seizure, and arrest.

The private sector in this arena primarily includes the evil triumvirate of Google, Facebook, and Amazon, although there are many other companies that also are stealing our private information. The private sector's mandate is to make a profit, and they make billions and billions of dollars selling our private information. They do this primarily through their business models, which are advertising models. If you track the income of these businesses, they are selling advertising. Do not be fooled, these are not social media or search engine companies — they are advertising companies.

There is another ugly entanglement in this web, which guides policies and relationships. The U.S. Government grants multibillion dollar contracts to these technology companies in what can only be described as a dark web of mutual benefits, and which motivates them to cooperate secretly. Contracts and activities are even outside the scope of disclosure to congress if they are classified by a government executive as "national security interests." This means there is no oversight by the judiciary or any other person or agency, nor is there any disclosure to the people. This is the fertile soil of illegal operations that are regularly conducted by the U.S. Government, often with third-party independent contractors who remain anonymous and untraceable.

It gets more complicated, because these private sector companies were not just created to sell your private information through their advertising model. They were also created to collect every bit of personal information on every single human being in America and eventually the entire planet. Why? Because they knew that whoever knows everything about everyone has all the control and power and money. And they were absolutely right.

If they know everything about you, they control you. If they control you, they own you. If they own you, you are not free: You are a slave.

Do not expect this powerful dark alliance to be broken by any do-gooder politician. Even President Trump doesn't have that kind of power and influence. The web of power throughout multiple Federal agencies and the multi-billion dollar technology companies is so vast and so well funded (Internationally) that it is unlikely the alliance can ever be broken.

President Ronald Reagan was a patriot. He was also absolutely right when he said "Big government is the problem, not the answer." Apparently, not even President Reagan anticipated the great dark alliance between the government and the private sector, which is now upon us. It would seem no one did, except one — President Dwight Eisenhower, who famously warned us on January 17, 1961:

In the councils of government, we must guard against the acquisition of unwarranted influence, whether sought or unsought, by the military-industrial complex. The potential for the disastrous rise of misplaced power exists, and will persist.

How prophetic were his words! Notice he said it "will persist."

> *Every single Federal agency has been taken over by liberal extremists. It's taken them decades, but they've done it. I give you the IRS (caught trying to destroy conservative organizations), the CIA and FBI, the State Department, DOJ, FEMA, ATF, DOC, DOD, DHS, DOT, VA, DEA, Fannie Mae, GSA, USGS, HHS, HUD, DOI, SEC, SBA, TSA, and we could go on and on. All of these agencies have become part of the dark alliance.*

In a recent Twitter conversation conducted by Fox on the right to privacy, the question was raised, "Regardless of who is in the White House, do you trust the government to properly balance privacy versus law enforcement?" The answers demonstrate the extraordinary level of naiveté on the part of average Americans. Here are two responses. "The government can only be trusted when a non-overtly political person goes to the White House," and "Yes, if a President commits to the oath taken to 'support and defend' the Constitution. It's about character and honesty."

With such incredibly naive voters, no wonder liberalism is having such success infringing on our right to privacy and on our constitutionally protected freedoms. Once all your private and confidential information for your entire life is in a government database, you cannot undo that. Americans have already allowed that to happen, but we don't have to continue to let the government collect more information.

It was out of 9–11 that the Patriot Act was born.

In the post-9/11 bureaucratic frenzy to never let a similar attack happen again, the Congress rushed to pass the Patriot Act, a domestic-surveillance wish list full of investigatory powers long sought by the FBI. And the government created the Department of Homeland Security, an unwieldy amalgamation of agencies united under a moniker straight out of a bad science-fiction novel. [Wired Magazine on Privacy]

This summary from the American Bar Association of how our privacy has been stolen ought to scare everyone:

Americans' right to privacy is under unprecedented siege as a result of a perfect storm: a technological revolution; the government's creation of a post-9/11 surveillance society in which the long-standing "wall" between surveillance for law enforcement purposes and for intelligence gathering has been dismantled; and the failure of U.S. laws, oversight mechanisms, and judicial doctrines to keep pace with these developments. As a result, the most sweeping and technologically advanced surveillance programs ever instituted in this country have operated not within the rule of law, subject to judicial review and political accountability, but outside of it, subject only to voluntary limitations and political expedience. [See Privacy Lost from the American Bar Association]

The 4th Amendment guarantees our right to privacy:

The right of the people to be secure in their persons, houses,

papers, and effects, against unreasonable searches and seizures, shall not be violated, and no Warrants shall issue, but upon probable cause, supported by Oath or affirmation, and particularly describing the place to be searched, and the persons or things to be seized.

The persistent shredding of our constitutional rights over a period of decades means that the Constitution will someday be nothing more than a footnote in history. We will have no defense against government bureaucrats for anything they choose to do. Without absolute limits on the Federal government, we become "subjects" or "slaves" with only lip service to constitutional rights.

Americans should have drawn the line in the sand long ago, but they did not. Today Americans need to know exactly where that line should be, where their right to privacy stands absolute. And then Americans need to back the Federal government up to that line. And Facebook, Google, and Amazon need to be held to account.

CHAPTER 14
THE BOLDEST LIBERAL MISREPRESENTATIONS
LIBERAL POLITICIANS DO THE OPPOSITE OF WHAT THEY PROMISE THEIR CONSTITUENTS

I know that the vote of 9 out of 10 black Americans for the Democratic Party or for leftist kinds of policies just is not reflective of their opinions. Clarence Thomas

If all Democrats could see through the boldest liberal misrepresentations of the Democratic party, many of them would leave the party in disgust. The majority of Democrats never intended to get caught up in a party involved in a web of policies that destroy our freedoms and the American economy. After all, who would get on a ship if they intended to help sink it?

Most Democrats have been raised with a liberal worldview and have been brainwashed so long they don't want to believe anything but the liberal talking points. Still, if they knew the bold misrepresentations made to them all these years by their party leaders, who have been playing their own constituents for fools, I believe they would leave the party in disgust.

What are these bold misrepresentations? This has been the Democratic Party platform for a long time. It has become a boilerplate sales pitch of bold lies. Here is an outline of some of the boldest misrepresentations you will ever see in a party platform. Their goals and their results are some of the most blatant contradictions in modern history.

<u>Rebuilding Middle Class Security:</u>
Putting Americans Back to Work
The Middle Class Bargain
Cutting Waste, Reducing the Deficit, Paying Their Fair Share

<u>Economy Built to Last:</u>
America Works Everyone Plays by The Same Rules
Wall Street Reform
21st Century Government: Transparent and Accountable
Lobbying Reform and Campaign Finance Reform

<u>Greater Together:</u>
Strengthening the American Community
Protecting Rights and Freedoms
Ensuring Safety and Quality of Life

<u>Stronger in The World, Safer and More Secure at Home:</u>
Responsibly Ending the War in Iraq
Disrupting, Dismantling, and Defeating Al-Qaeda
Responsibly Ending the War in Afghanistan
Preventing the Spread and Use of Nuclear Weapons
Countering Emerging Threats

<u>Strengthening Alliances, Expanding Partnerships, and Reinvigorating International Institutions:</u>
Promoting Global Prosperity and Development
Maintaining the Strongest Military in the World
Advancing Universal Values

I will highlight the inconsistencies of a few of these party misrepresentations, perhaps the most glaring ones, but it would be a great exercise to go through the entire platform and examine it with the actual consequences of liberal policies and their hidden agenda.

Putting Americans Back to Work

The platform claims Democrats will **put Americans back to work**. This would be humorous if it wasn't such a tragic misrepresentation. Let's examine reality. Democratic policies are anti-small business, anti-big business, anti-entrepreneur, in favor of higher taxes for all businesses, in favor of higher taxes on all Americans, and in favor of more regulations on anything that moves or doesn't move. All of these strong Democratic policies kill jobs and cause unemployment.

But it doesn't stop there. Democratic policies are anti-self initiative. Their policies discourage Americans from creating businesses and inventing things and building financial independence. Throughout all Democratic policies is a theme that pushes people onto welfare and unemployment and entitlement programs. Of course, what Democrats say and what they do are two different things. That describes the Party Platform, too.

Democratic policies to increase the minimum wage were proven by Milton Friedman to actually cause unemployment, not promote jobs. Small business owners have testified all over the country that they cannot pay someone more than they are worth, and they will lay them off instead, or they simply will not hire new employees.

Democratic policies promoting unions have a history of harming businesses, which means people get laid off. A fundamental economic principal that is lost on many Democratic leaders is that you cannot legislate employee value to a business. An employee has value based on his individual contribution to the production of a product or service, and unions usurp that free enterprise concept by forcing economic decisions on employers. This is another example of how Democratic policies do not create jobs, they destroy jobs.

The other side of the coin for the Democratic party is that they want and need more people in poverty, on unemployment, fewer educated, more on welfare, and more in entitlement programs, because that is where they get so many votes. That is the ugly side of liberalism. Democrats don't want to promote jobs. They want votes so they can stay in power. Democrats win by keeping the people down.

Do you want an example of what happens when Democrats have their way? I give you Detroit. Liberal unions, massive government programs, entitlement spending, bureaucracy and regulations, liberal housing programs, high taxes, government budgets out of control, and unkept promises. This is the Democratic way. This is what happens when Democrats are in control and implement their grand policies for the people. The result? A city devastated with poverty, broken down houses, hundreds of commercial buildings waiting to be torn down, thousands of homes and buildings boarded up, a dwindling population, a city in administrative shambles, 50% of the property owners unable to pay their property taxes, unemployment that is through the roof, increased crime, and tragic environmental implications. At a White House Jobs Summit Detroit Mayor Dave Bing said the true unemployment rate in Detroit was "probably close to 50 percent." For the past 40 years since Detroit has been rapidly declining, guess which party controlled the city? A Democrat has been mayor since 1962.

Some would argue that Detroit's demise was the result of the failure of manufacturing in Detroit, particularly the automotive industry. While that is part of the story, it is not the whole story, because you have to ask why manufacturing collapsed in Detroit. The answer is the implementation of liberal policies as outlined in detail in the previous paragraph. But Chuck McDougald of *The Daily Journal* told the rest of the story this way:

In Detroit, state and city employees also negotiated generous pensions and lifetime health care benefits. As a result, it has accumulated long-term debts of at least $18 billion, including $3.5 billion in unfunded pensions and $5.7 billion in underfunded health benefits for about 21,000 retired workers. The rest is owed to bondholders and other unsecured creditors.

Does any of this remind you of our Federal government?

For the past four decades, Detroit has been a liberal experiment in a science lab for all the world to observe. The liberal Democratic policies that destroyed the city have been laid out before us to observe all these years, and now we have the final result--total collapse and economic devastation. Even when this obvious experiment and the consequences are staring us in the face, Democrats refuse to admit their policies failed the people of Detroit. I hope the rest of America can see the obvious.

By the way, the people Democrats claimed they would help the most in Detroit, have been hurt the most. Blacks are hurt the most in Detroit. I give you liberalism. Would someone please tell blacks in Detroit they have Democrats to thank for what looks like a nuclear disaster?

Cutting Waste and Reducing the Deficit

This item on the Democrat Party platform is another glaring contradiction for any American who pauses to think clearly for 30 seconds. I'm almost embarrassed even to have to address this misrepresentation. The current Democratic administration has done everything but cut waste. Regular stories of fraud and abuse keep coming out of this administration to the tune of billions of dollars.

President Obama has increased the federal budget more than all previous U.S. Presidents combined, yet the same party says they are the party of "Reducing the Deficit." What a bold-faced misrepresentation.

The language "fair share" sounds like something right out of Lenin's writings, and it is. This is not the language of an American free enterprise system. This is the language of a socialist or communist regime. We live in America. Our free enterprise system promotes hard work, independent initiative, reward, and the pursuit of happiness. Democrats hate such talk, because their agenda depends on a redistribution of wealth where personal initiative has been destroyed, where free enterprise has given way to an all-powerful Federal government, and where personal liberty and happiness are controlled by the government.

Government Transparency

Another bold-face kick in the teeth to all Americans is the Democratic Party platform item, **"21st Century Government: Transparent and Accountable."** Democratic politicians are rarely transparent and accountable, but the current administration has been one of the most non-transparent administrations in this generation. Consider these major Obama scandals: Benghazi, the IRS targeting conservative organizations, the administration going through reporters' personal phone records and the Attorney General's perjury regarding the charges, the Fast and Furious scandal, the extraordinary waste of Federal funds by the GSA and the VA, the massive government losses with Solyndra and other green energy projects favoring Obama friends, and the list goes on and on.

Now we have what may be the biggest debacle in public policy and administration in the history of the United States, and this one involved outright fraudulent misrepresentations over a period of many years. I give you Obamacare, also known ironically as the Affordable Healthcare Act. This is a blatant and tragic example of how liberals hate transparency when it exposes their lies, misrepresentations, and fraud. Obamacare is nothing less than "fraud in the inducement," and liberals knew it was fraud, and now they have never been transparent and open about the law and the devastating consequences for Americans and American businesses.

And here's a point that deserves its own paragraph. Every single one of these scandals has involved and continues to involve cover-ups, lies, misrepresentations, dodging questions, and government employees claiming their 5th Amendment right not to answer questions, lest they incriminate themselves. It's painful to watch people in the current administration dodge questions in interviews about every single one of these scandals. If fifth graders dodged questions so blatantly and repeatedly, their teachers would hold them accountable, but there seems to be no accountability to the American people at all from Democrats on these scandals. The extraordinary boldness of the lies and the refusal to cooperate with congressional investigations is setting new records for American government corruption. If all these disgusting scandals, coverups, and lies are not shocking enough, President Obama actually referred to these scandals as "phony scandals." Does this Democratic President have no shame?

This is all standard operating procedure for liberals today. Have you ever wondered how in the world liberals sleep at night? I know the answer to that question. They sleep like babies. They have no moral compass. They have no conscience connected to what is right and true. They sleep just fine.

Protecting Rights and Freedoms

The Democratic Platform claims it is "**Protecting Rights and Freedoms.**" Who doesn't know that the Democratic party stands for the polar opposite? Clearly, their policies are about taking away freedoms and rights, not protecting them.

Democrats want to take away people's right to own guns. They have been chipping away at religious rights. Not all religions--only the Christian religion. Liberal policies are anti-free speech, anti-equality, racist (conveniently disguised as the exact opposite), and anti-personal privacy. Liberal policies promote heavy control and regulations into people's personal and business lives, which is certainly not protecting rights and freedoms.

Democrats have taken away the rights of Americans to seek out and obtain their own health coverage of their own choice. Their greatest victory, the Obama Healthcare Plan, will put Doctors out of business (thousands have said they will leave or retire from medical practice). This will have the effect of reducing healthcare choices for individuals and raise costs. Businesses will be charged penalties for not providing healthcare in a system where insurance premiums are suddenly skyrocketing. For people without company insurance, their own premiums are going up dramatically, not down like Obama promised. Our healthcare choices are less, not more with Obamacare. This is what the Democratic Platform calls "protecting rights and freedoms?"

If liberals could draft the perfect law, one that would promote the liberal agenda most effectively, what would that law look like? It would transfer control of a major area of people's lives to the government. It would give the government greater power and control over the people. It would increase the size of the government, justifying many more government employees, and ideally it would require entirely new departments, which would also justify increasing taxes on the people. It would give the government more power to capture private information about Americans, and it would give all government agencies the ability to share personal information that could be used against Americans. It would give government agencies broad powers with grand administrative discretion without any accountability. The perfect liberal law would create a web of legal obligations on states and on businesses in private industry. It would give the Federal government control over a major sector of our economy or several sectors. It would place major life decisions of the people in the hands of government bureaucrats. Ideally, this law would grant the most threatening Federal agency with enforcement powers, specifically it would give the IRS enforcement powers. The perfect liberal law would control life and death decisions of Americans.

I give you the Obama Healthcare law, the perfect liberal law. In one fell swoop, Democrats have accomplished more for the liberal agenda with this one law than anything they have accomplished in decades. What a masterful addition to the Democratic Platform philosophy. It's perfect, because not only does it advance the liberal agenda in many ways all at once, but it does it with extraordinary levels of deceit and manipulation, a core competency of radical liberals.

National Security

The entire section in the Democratic Platform on **national security** is a cruel hoax. Their plan weakens our national security, has humiliated and weakened our military and reputation abroad, and erodes our ability to defend our own borders with an open border policy. Democrats have made sure we have open borders so they can keep increasing their voting constituency.

Democrats are vociferously against voter ID of any kind, because they need all the votes they can get, and they truly do not care if they get illegal votes as long as they get them. They want to get elected, and how they get elected doesn't matter to them. Their argument that voter ID disenfranchises voters is incredible nonsense and nothing but a smoke screen. All Americans must have IDs of all kinds, and what is more important than making sure that only Americans entitled to vote actually vote. But again, Democrats don't care about voter fraud, because it is voter fraud that will help them stay in office. That's not what shocks me. What shocks me is that the majority of Americans don't care.

Foreign Policy

The section on **Strengthening Alliances, Expanding Partnerships, and Reinvigorating International Institutions** is an example of doing exactly the opposite of what they claim in their platform. It's really astonishing. Our current President, who is the perfect Democrat for our time, began his presidency with an International apology tour, and proceeded to lose the respect of world leaders around the globe. President Putin openly disdains President Obama in public.

One of our Ambassadors was attacked and murdered overseas during this administration, and our elite strike force teams were ordered to stand down. Since our ambassador's murder, this administration has shown weakness like no other U.S. President in history. Don't think this has gone unnoticed among foreign dictators and terrorists. It is seen as a great victory against the U.S.

Speaking of terrorists, this liberal administration excuses terrorists, defends them, and refuses to call them out. Wanted posters of known terrorists were placed on the sides of Seattle buses recently, but this administration bowed under pressure and removed the posters. As one Democrat said, "this gives the impression that all brown skinned people are terrorists," or words to that effect. Have liberal Democrats lost their minds? The answer may be yes. It was Billy Graham who said, "sin is a kind of insanity."

Glaring Misrepresentations

The Democratic Party platform is full of blatant misrepresentations. It does not take a rocket scientist to recognize the glaring misrepresentations in the platform if you can think clearly. Of course, that is the great dilemma of our day. So many Americans seem incapable of thinking clearly. This has worked out beautifully for Democrats, because the less clearly Americans think, the more likely they are to keep voting Democrats into office.

This is a crisis of major proportions. The fate of our nation hangs by a hair, not on common sense, not on historical fact, not on the simple mathematics of federal spending, nor on the strength of reason, but on the broken psychological associations of dysfunctional people. Greed, selfishness, laziness, and an entitlement mentality have all paid off for Democrats in spades . . .

Until the election of Donald Trump as the 47th President. Everything is about to change.

CHAPTER 15
THE 20 RULES OF THE LIBERAL TEMPLATE
AKA: THE SECRETS OF STALIN, ZEDONG, HITLER, AND OBAMA

Liberalism in general, is based on not trusting the American people - a belief that big government is better for people. Bobby Jindal

Liberals have a template that they have been using for many years, and while they continue to tweak the template based on new developments, this template has proven to be extremely powerful and effective. Many have recognized parts of the template and have warned us, but most Americans have ignored the warnings. What follows is the tip of the iceberg of what I call the Liberal Template, which consists of many adaptable rules.

Liberal Rule No. 1

This rule may be old hat to conservatives who have been around a while, but this remains one of the most powerful tools in the liberal arsenal. In the liberal way of thinking, no crisis should be wasted, because it is during a crisis that people are most easily manipulated and so willing to give up their freedoms. This is true when there is a natural disaster or human violence. The recent Zimmerman trial is a glaring example of how the use of a crisis can be exploded into promoting the liberal agenda in a dozen ways. For liberals it has become a racial issue, a white supremacy issue, a Wall Street issue, a big banks issue, a capitalism issue, a civil rights issue, and on and on. Liberals love crises. Liberals know that they need crises, and the worse the crisis (the more people hurt), the more liberals thrive.

Liberal Rule No. 2

It is the most elementary of rules for liberals to ignore incidents that would disprove the liberal talking points on any issue. Hide contrary facts, disguise them, or bury them, lest people find out the truth. Whatever it takes. Ignore the truth if at all possible. The media has been an important arm of liberalism in this regard. I'll share only two simple examples here, but there are hundreds. Stories of how good Americans have successfully defended themselves and their families with guns from violent attacks by criminals rarely appear in the media. Such facts would be an inconvenient truth for liberals.

Secondly, the media jumps on any crime involving a white and a black where the black is either hurt seriously or killed. Immediately they want to play the race card, and the white is to blame even when an American jury acquits the white. The media ignores black-on-white crimes. The same media ignore the substantially larger number of black-on-black violent crimes. These inconvenient truths would not promote the liberal agenda.

Liberal Rule No. 3

Manipulation and distortion have always been mainstays of liberal movements throughout history. The **truth** is the single most dangerous weapon opposing liberalism. Hidden agendas cannot long remain hidden if the truth shines light into the darkness. Those who thirst for power, money, and control over the people hate the truth, because it can lead to their total destruction.

Most of the national liberal leaders in America have become

very powerful and wealthy promoting liberal causes. That's another part of their manipulation. They use people while claiming to help them. Worst than that, the very policies liberal leaders claim will set people free actually enslave the people. They have to manipulate and distort or they would be out of business.

Liberal Rule No. 4

Liberals are very adept at enlisting a broad liberal network to go to work night and day to send a coordinated dishonest storyline to Americans on any issue. The network includes some of the most powerful organizations and wealthiest Americans who are deeply passionate about promoting liberal causes. It includes loyal party members, non-profits, media, famous people, street level attack dogs, and millions of passionate uninformed Americans who go into the streets like puppets to conduct violent protests. *Note that it isn't coordinating or rallying forces for a cause that is evil. It's that they are coordinating lies. That's why this is evil.*

Republicans claim to be able to rally their forces on important issues, but they are novices compared to Democrats in rallying support. Of course, it doesn't help the conservative cause that the vast majority of Republicans are not passionate enough to fight as hard as liberals. The one issue on which Republicans have fought the hardest is gun control. Even then, the vast majority of conservatives around the country have simply sat on the sidelines.

Here's something to keep in mind. While love is more powerful than hate from a theological perspective, hate-driven by deep passion is far more powerful than love when it comes to political action. Democrats are far more passionate about their liberal agenda than Republicans are about protecting their constitutional rights. Ergo, when it comes to rallying the forces, guess who has far more volunteers who are very passionate?

Liberal Rule No. 5

Liberalism taps into long established principles of human behavior. For liberalism, manipulating human behavior is far more central to their strategy than worrying about the facts or what is true. One of the important strategies liberals have mastered is repetition. It's not the use of repetition that is wrong; it's the use of repetition to persuade Americans of lies. Americans generally seem oblivious to the brainwashing effect of the liberal repetition machine. Oblivious.

Liberal Rule No. 6

Liberals have learned to use the most powerful marketing and advertising venues to promote their agendas. This means using newspapers, television stations, and media conglomerates. Using the media gives them large audiences and the power of repetition along with the appearance of credibility. Liberals courted the mainstream media, and won them over a long time ago. Republicans have few friends in the mainstream media. What a one-sided battle this has been for the last three decades. The importance of the liberal media's role cannot be over-emphasized. I don't think liberals would have such a dominant influence today had it not been for the media over the past few decades. America would be a different country today had the media not joined the liberal movement.

Liberal Rule No. 7

Liberals use some of the most influential Americans to persuade weak minds. This is how totally unqualified Hollywood actors end up testifying before Congress on issues of national importance. Famous musicians, actors and actresses are recruited by liberals 10 to 1 over conservatives. Liberals do not hesitate to use unqualified people to promote agendas, because it isn't about the facts or the effectiveness of policies (or lack thereof): it is all about manipulating people.

Liberal Rule No. 8

Liberals love to use third-party entities organized specifically to promote liberalism, but quite regularly, they do so secretly. When an accusation is made by an organization other than a lead

Democrat, there is the appearance of credibility. Attacks from supposedly independent organizations can be ruthless, and they regularly conduct terribly destructive personal attacks against good conservatives with no accountability to anyone. Since most Americans seem to pay little attention to the credibility or source, these attacks are quite effective for Democrats.

Liberal Rule No. 9

Liberals personally attack individuals who stand on the front line to protect constitutional rights. There is no limit to the methods used to personally discredit conservative Republicans, and especially conservative Christians. Anything goes, and this includes personal attacks on spouses and children and friends.

Liberal Rule No. 10

Liberals enlist the help of key government employees for the cause. A recent study of the Connecticut office of the IRS during investigations of IRS targeting of conservative organizations, showed that 100% of the IRS employees in that office had given personal donations to President Obama or another Democratic candidate in their voting district. Of course, now we know that the order to target conservatives came from much higher than the Connecticut office, and there has been a massive coverup effort.

The IRS and its leadership and employees have been caught red-handed targeting conservative organizations. I marvel at Americans who are shocked at such government abuse for the liberal cause. What did they think has been happening all these years? And don't believe for a second that liberals will stop either. Even long after the IRS scandal was exposed and long since the congressional investigations started and continue, it is now being reported that another IRS agent and whistleblower from the inside has come out with news that the IRS is still targeting conservative organizations. My God! Can liberals not stop even after they are caught red-handed and exposed? No, they cannot. They cannot stop.

Liberal Rule No. 11

Liberals use government resources to promote every liberal cause. Liberals have been getting away with this for decades. Use entire departments, use agencies, and use Democrats on the Federal payroll. Use tax dollars to create infomercials and nationwide campaigns promoting liberal causes. Billions of dollars.

Of course, there can be no appearance of impropriety, but it only takes an eighth-grade mentality to avoid getting caught. If everyone employed in a government agency is on the government payroll with a sweet retirement plan, and they are all on board with the liberal agenda, how would anyone ever find out what they are doing? The only way liberals on the inside get caught is when a whistleblower comes out of the woodwork. And in today's caustic big government environment, the difference between a whistleblower and a traitor is no longer so clear.

Liberal Rule No. 12

When liberals get caught in fraudulent activities, government corruption, or some kind of scandal, their first defense is absolute denial. Their denials are bold, confident, and they feign shock. They're good actors. Their second defense is to use incoherent babble to try to derail any talk of an investigation. This is when they give a long answer using the English language and some long nouns and creative adjectives, but later when you reflect on what they said, you realize they said nothing. Their third defense is to accuse Republicans of going on a witch hunt or politicizing the issue, another way to try to discredit someone. Notice in all three defenses, truth is totally irrelevant.

Liberal Rule No. 13

If most or all of the other rules of attack do not apply or are not working, liberals will weave a racial argument into any issue. It doesn't matter if a racial argument doesn't fit, or if it is a stretch of the imagination. It always works for at least 15% of the American voters, and it creates a great diversion for another 40%.

Liberals rely heavily on the divide-and-conquer strategy. By dividing America into racial groups, they can play one race against the other, and more significantly, they can play Republicans against all minorities. Democrats have successfully moved nearly the entire black population to vote Democratic.

This is especially astonishing for those of us who know that Democratic policies actually hurt blacks more than any other voter segment. If Democrats lied to Republican voters to actually do some good and help their black constituency, there would at least be some semblance of loyalty, however perverted. But not only do Democrats lie to Republican voters, they lie to their own constituency and use the very people they promise to help. Liberals have no integrity.

Liberal Rule No. 14

One of the oldest liberal strategies is to promote class warfare based on income and employment. This is old hat because it actually comes right out of Lenin's fundamental writings on class warfare. Combined with the liberal technique of creating racist issues where none exist, engendering class warfare has been one of the greatest liberal tools since the 1960s.

Liberal Rule No. 15

Liberalism seeks to diminish the value of human life and the uniqueness of each human being. This is a common theme throughout liberalism. Liberal euphemisms used to diminish the value of life are so bold, they are shocking to the rational mind. For example, murder is called "freedom of choice." On the subject of abortion, liberals promote the murder of children with an argument that they support life and choice for the mother.

Liberals diminish human life by taking away people's motivation to work and build something for themselves and their families. Democrats should be congratulated for creating entire generations of low self-esteem entitlement voters. Actually, liberalism has created something very unique--low self-esteem entitlement voters who are very angry and who become vociferous protestors and loud promoters of all things liberal. Liberalism has created an army of violent soldiers.

These voters have become permanent Democratic supporters by virtue of their dependence. Like a wild animal born and kept in captivity in a fake environment and fed artificial food in a zoo, people can lose their connection with their origins. They can lose their deepest motivations and hopes and become totally helpless. Democrats love helpless people. Only people who seek to diminish human life would love to keep people helpless. The Democratic Party platform sucks the life out of people who need a helping hand the most. It's sad.

But Democrats also love angry, pissed-off people. Democrats recruit pissed-off people. They make the best Democrats. Many are turned into rabid sycophants who will enthusiastically march in the streets, scream obscenities into a camera, physically attack conservatives (especially Christian conservatives), get arrested, go to jail, lose their jobs, or even die for the cause. Democrats incite unrest and then proclaim themselves saviors of the people.

Slavery diminishes human life, and the Democratic party is the party of slavery. Liberals diminish human life by stealing constitutional and God-given freedoms from people and enslaving them with government mandates, regulations, and bureaucracy that serves government, not the people.

Liberals diminish human life by taking over personal healthcare choices and creating mandates that adversely effect people's ability to get medical care. With promises of lower medical insurance premiums, Democrats blatant misrepresentations are obvious as premiums are skyrocketing. Are Democrats apologizing for this? Of course not. Democrats never admit they are wrong, and Democrats never apologize. This is another example of how liberalism deceives people with promises of dinner with the King while giving them scraps of soured food in a dark alley.

Liberal Rule No. 16

Words have meaning. Daniel Webster created a masterpiece with the Webster's Dictionary, helping us to communicate better for two centuries. Every language known to man uses words with specific meanings. Using words that have meaning is so fundamental to human communications, who could ever doubt that words have meaning? But what if they changed the meanings?

What if you had a cause, and to achieve your cause you could not be honest with Americans, because the truth would stop you dead in your tracks? What if the truth would expose your manipulations? What if your agenda was so full of goals that Americans would oppose, you could not possibly let them know what you were up to?

You would have to create a strategy that would fool the best educated Americans. You would have to redefine key words in the English language. An important element of this strategy would be to define Federal terms in such a way that they hide the truth from Americans. The Federal definition of unemployment is a perfect example of deception. When people who are unemployed cannot find a job long enough, and they quit looking for a job because there are none, they are no longer counted in the Federal definition of "unemployed." Under this deception, you could have 70% of Americans unable to find jobs, and yet the Federal unemployment rate could officially be only 7.8%. This is the kind of evil game liberals are playing. Unfortunately, Republicans are doing nothing to fix this Federal deception.

I give you one of the most powerful strategies of liberalism ever conceived. Granted, it was not conceived in one fell swoop. No one said 50 years ago, "Let's re-define key English words to obfuscate their meaning and to hide what we really intend to do to the American people." Liberals really fell into this strategy over a long period of time and it was only recently that a more concerted effort has taken this strategy to entirely new levels. They have redefined thousands of words.

Liberals have also charged key phrases with powerful emotions. It doesn't matter which side you are on, just saying these phrases raises the blood pressure. In addition, liberals have managed to classify entire groups of words into a new category that has been cursed as "politically incorrect." All of this has been amazingly effective for Democrats. It is wrong, of course, but it is much worse than that. It facilitates evil, therefore it is evil.

Liberal Rule No. 17

Pacifism is a tenet of liberalism. It is at the root of almost everything they promote. The one exception is the use of the military to defend ourselves when attacked. Liberals will use aggression against the U.S. to their advantage to gain power and control over people. It used to be that liberals would also defend Americans who were attacked overseas, but not anymore. American Ambassadors can be murdered now inside an American Consulate on foreign soil and liberals' pacifist theology prohibits them from defending Americans.

Pacifism is everywhere in the Democratic party. Violent criminals are victims now, whether they are in prison or out. Liberal pacifism reaches extreme conclusions when a good law-abiding American defends himself with a gun from an attack by a repeat offending criminal, and the law-abiding citizen gets charged with hurting the criminal.

Terrorists are victims of poverty. Liberalism actually makes excuses for terrorists and for extreme Muslims who publicly announce that their goal is to wipe every American off the face of the earth. In the face of such unmitigated hatred and violence, only liberals could respond with, "Can't we all be friends here?"

A woman who is attacked and raped is told she has no right to use a gun to defend herself. Instead, she is told by liberal pacifists that she should consider spitting on her attacker or even "peeing" on her attacker. No one could make this stuff up!

The liberal answer to raising children would be an entire encyclopedic series on pacifism. Parents cannot physically discipline their children. They could end up in jail. Parents have no legal right under the liberal model to make many life-critical decisions for their minor children, including birth control and, in some states, abortion. This is where pacifism overlaps with the liberal agenda to dehumanize and interject government control into parents' private lives.

Teachers now live in a pacifist world in American schools. Of course, they cannot discipline children in any physical way, but they also cannot discipline in any way that is politically incorrect or could be construed to be psychologically harmful from a liberal perspective. The subject of self-esteem has turned into an entire dogma, and is almost a religion itself to promote pacifism.

Mothers who abort their children are victims and not responsible for their own behavior. You have to marvel at how liberals could persuade so many people that the murderer is a victim. But that just reminds us of how liberals make victims out of criminals, too. Liberalism is insanity with polite language. And sometimes not so polite.

Liberal Rule No. 18

What a web liberals do weave! Liberal leaders preach peace but promote violence.

George Zimmerman was acquitted of the murder charges for the death of Trayvon Martin. Martin was not white, nor is Zimmerman. Zimmerman is Hispanic. A jury of his peers acquitted Zimmerman, and the "justice system" found him not guilty after an extensive examination of all the available evidence and the testimonies of many people, including experts.

Furthermore, neither the prosecution nor the defense introduced any evidence that race or prejudice was involved, nor did anyone in the case argue race. The FBI conducted a 16 month investigation, interviewed about 40 witnesses, and found no basis whatsoever of racial prejudice, racial bias, or racism of any kind. And they certainly looked for it.

In addition, the case was purely a self-defense case, and the jury decided as a matter of fact that Zimmerman had the right of self-defense against the violent attack by Martin. The case did not hinge on the "stand your own ground defense" under Florida law.

It was established beyond question by an expert witness that Martin was on top of Zimmerman when he was shot. Zimmerman's statement that he was attacked, on his back, and being beaten by Martin was supported by substantial and incontrovertible evidence. The jury ruled that Zimmerman was not guilty.

You would think that would be the end of the case. Everyone did their job, and everyone goes home now. That's how the justice system is supposed to work. Despite my criticisms of the justice system, in this case it would be hard to find fault with a jury of six women that listened to all the testimony and examined all the documentary evidence and found that Zimmerman did not murder Martin. The verdict is justified and supported by the evidence. The jury even considered manslaughter, but determined that Zimmerman was not guilty of manslaughter either. He is a free man.

"But not so fast," say the liberals. Liberals have an agenda, and by God, the facts do not matter. The jury doesn't matter. Only the liberal talking points and agenda matter.

Jesse Jackson, who fancies himself a civil rights leader is the master race baiter. During the entire trial there was not a shred of evidence that Zimmerman, who is not white anyway, had any racial motivations against Martin. Yet, **Jackson's agenda is to preach peace while promoting violence**. How did he do that in this case? He kept holding up the race card every opportunity he had, even though there was absolutely no evidence in the case that Zimmerman was a racist. And immediately after Zimmerman's acquittal, Jackson said this:

That race is not a factor, among other factors, with this young black boy going home pursued by Zimmerman is to be blind and deaf to the pain . . . matters of racial justice and gender equality must matter for Americans. We cannot deny it. We cannot avoid it.

Immediately before Jackson said this, he was asked if he would encourage a peaceful response to the verdict, to which he said yes, and then he immediately launched into these race baiting talking points, which do promote violence. Notice the extraordinary contradiction. Jackson claims to promote peace, and then everything else he says and does inflames African Americans against the entire white race. Zimmerman is not even a white poster boy, but Jackson could not miss the opportunity to jump on this liberal bandwagon, which is off and running at full speed.

One cannot help but notice how nonsensical Jackson's words are. Reread that quote again, and ask yourself what did he actually say? It doesn't make sense, and it is horrible grammar and an incredibly uneducated use of the English language. But here's why Jackson has had success inflaming blacks with his language. He is a race-baiter, and he uses emotionally charged phrases. You can see them in the quote. To his audience, it doesn't really matter what the rest of his words are, or whether he said anything at all. The value of his mini-sermons is to inflame blacks against whites and to promote violence. In a nutshell, that has been Jackson's entire career.

The liberal media, liberal Democrats, liberal leaders like Jackson, the Democratic party machinery, liberal organizations, and Hollywood actors are all jumping on board to promote racial tension and indirectly racial violence.

Social media exploded immediately after Zimmerman's acquittal, and Hollywood took a lead role in promoting racial tension and violence. Actress Kirstie Alley tweeted, "White people used to make black people drink from separate drinking fountains. Now we just shoot their children." This is a direct exhortation to blacks to start violent protests. What a bizarre and sick way of thinking not connected to the facts of the Zimmerman case, nor to reality on planet earth. Then again, this is the ideal liberal response that promotes their agenda. It promotes violence, and liberals need violence to succeed.

Toni Braxton tweeted, "Today I'm embarrassed to be an American." Katy Perry re-tweeted this comment "American justice is still color blind as long as you're white." Isn't it fascinating that we have all these rich white people engendering violence in society with harsh statements against a defendant who is not even white. Zimmerman is Hispanic. But truth must not get in the way of progress.

After Zimmerman's acquittal, the United States Attorney General, who is a liberal Democrat, made a speech in which he promised that there would be an investigation to see if the United States could charge Zimmerman with any other crimes related to race. Liberal organizations are already threatening civil lawsuits against Zimmerman for alleged violations of Martin's civil rights. The mainstream media is all over this.

The day after the Zimmerman verdict, there were violent protests conducted by liberals, and Democrats planned 100 protests in 100 cities, all based on racism. Street violence is exactly what happens when liberals like Jesse Jackson, Al Sharpton, and Eric Holder, promote violence with their racist agendas. Notice that it is the very people who claim to be protecting blacks from racism who are actually engendering racism. It wasn't conservative or Republican rhetoric that encouraged violent street protests. It is liberal rhetoric.

The connection between this liberal onslaught on Zimmerman and violence is not so tenuous. There's a news report of a group of blacks beating a Hispanic man shouting epithets about the Zimmerman acquittal. Where's the outrage in the Hispanic community? Why is no one protecting George Zimmerman or his innocent family?

Do not miss out on another very important reason that liberals hate George Zimmerman and what he stands for. He is a Christian. Liberals have a special hatred for Christians. There is one person liberals hate more than any other, and that is a conservative Christian. Zimmerman has been cast into the role of a conservative Christian. Unless strong American leaders stand up to put a shield of protection around Zimmerman, the liberal machinery will not stop until Zimmerman's life is destroyed. How can anyone not see that liberals are violent?

Liberals are using the Zimmerman acquittal to attack American values, capitalism, Wall Street, and everything they hate about America. Only an uninformed person could get so caught up in such outlandish rhetoric. One liberal on a megaphone at a liberal rally the day after the verdict announced, "We don't get democracy. We get capitalism. We get white supremacy." Likewise, in San Francisco a speaker at a liberal protest shouted, "We got to water our seeds and we got to let a new society grow! A people society! Not one where Wells Fargo, the Federal Reserve, all these big banks . . . The whole damn system! Shut it down!" This was followed by the crowd chanting together repeatedly, "Shut it down!" They were shouting about shutting down America. This is the heart of liberalism.

Father Michael Pfleger gave a hate speech at Saint Sabina Church in Chicago in response to the Zimmerman verdict in which he reiterated his belief that America is a racist country. It is more than interesting that when liberals give speeches about how people's civil rights are being violated and how rotten to the core America is, they do so with vicious language, faces contorted as if possessed, and shouting and ranting with visible anger. They are clearly some of the most angry and hateful people in America, and while they are so pissed off, they are preaching to us about peace and love. If anyone doesn't understand that liberals are full of hate and deep bitterness, they just aren't paying attention. Liberals hate America. They hate freedom. They hate truth. They hate the one true God. This kind of hatred is a prerequisite to being a true liberal.

The Zimmerman family had to go into hiding because of threats by liberal Democrats. Notice that conservatives, Christians, and Republicans do not threaten people's lives to promote their agendas. But Democrats do all the time.

The Zimmerman case is one example of many to follow that all have the same narrative and the same evil purpose. The George Floyd case was proven to be another opportunity for the media to twist the facts to fit their narratives, and cause tragic and violent street riots. Racism has become a primary weapon of the liberals, even when it does not exist.

January 6th, the alleged insurrection of Donald Trump and the attempted coup in Washington D.C. was another lie that has been thoroughly established to be a setup and false accusations that Donald Trump was an insurrectionist. It was Trump who told everyone to march in peace, and we know that because we have his audio recording saying that. We also know it was Trump who requested the National Guard be called to keep the peace, but Nancy Pelosi refused to call the National Guard. We also have whistleblowers who have testified that the FBI had many agents assigned to incite a riot.

The Democrats use hate-filled speech and have repeatedly called for violence against Donald Trump. Their rhetoric is likely the cause of the two assassination attempts against Donald Trump. A survey of Democrats revealed that a many as 25% wished that Trump had been killed in the July 6th attempt in

Pennsylvania. This is the violent history and theme of the Democrats, not Republicans.

Liberal Rule No. 19

Liberals came up with a strategy that is nothing less than genius. By making everything an environmental issue, they managed to create government laws that reach deeply into everyone's life and everyone's business. If the progress of capitalism is evil and harms the environment to the extreme, then businesses can be heavily taxed, regulated, and capitalism's driving force--profits--can be reduced or even eliminated.

Conservatives first seek to get definitive answers on whether global warming is a reality, and if so, whether man is really the cause of global warming. Then while conservatives would seek to do a cost-benefit analysis, liberals have no interest in the cost, even if it is unemployment and poverty. But of course, unemployment and poverty play right into the liberal agenda and inevitably gets them more votes.

While the effect of man's presence on earth is questionable in terms of environmental impact, and thousands of credible scientists have plenty of documentation to argue that man is not causing global warming, liberals don't care. Liberals created such a massive year-after-year campaign with constant repetition, many Americans have believed the unproven claims. So ineffective or nonexistent has been the conservative defense on this subject, that many in America assume that man is causing global warming as an established fact. But it is far from established fact. Nevertheless the idea of global warming plays right into the liberal agenda for big government programs, greater regulation and taxation of corporations, and the resulting unemployment that gets Democrats more votes.

As with most liberal agenda items, it's not the facts that matter--it's all about what you can get the American people to believe.

Liberal Rule No 20

Liberals are smart. I know I've said that before in other ways, but they are so far ahead of Republicans when it comes to the psychology of human behavior, it gives them extraordinary advantages in controlling and manipulating the average and uninformed American. Perhaps most Republicans are simply not motivated to manipulate Americans, and I'm not suggesting they should be, but you can certainly raise a stronger defense if you understand the psychological warfare games that Democrats play. Republicans seem oblivious to this entire front on the battlefield. This front involves human behavior and ethics.

One way liberals have achieved an advantage is by setting different standards of behavior for themselves than they set for Republicans. Notice that Republicans are not in charge of setting the standards. Liberals are. You have to marvel at how liberals managed to guard the Keep on ethical standards. You see, presidents like the Bushes who had high ethical standards throughout their presidencies, do not change the ethical standards. They maintain high ethical standards by not lowering the standards with grotesque and embarrassing behavior, but this means they don't change the standards. However presidents like Clinton and Obama lower the standards dramatically with their behavior. So it is unethical presidents who control the ethical standards by lowering them.

When Republicans do anything that could even be ethically suspect, liberals are all over them. Liberal leaders give speeches of condemnation, newspapers print parallel attacks, and the media lights up with another opportunity to destroy a Republican. And they will stay on the stories and rumors for weeks and sometimes months. When a Republican actually does something bad ethically, he is so viscously attacked for so long, he might as well give up his political career. So liberals set standards that might be thought of as Biblical standards with the rhetorical question,

"What would Jesus do?" Then they hold Republicans to that standard.

But the same high standards have no place at all in the Democratic party. Liberals have no standard, or perhaps it would be more accurate to say that their ethical standards are so low, it's really impossible to define how low they are. As soon as you think you know the bottom, some Democrats stoop lower.

When a liberal Democrat does commit a horrible ethical breach, that Democrat is immediately excused by the party. A blind eye is turned to the story by the media. If Republicans try to bring it to the public's attention, they are demonized in a variety of ways, and the entire liberal machine goes into overtime to redefine the issue, to bring race into the issue, to personally attack the Republicans, and to implement the liberal strategies that have been so successful to cover up the truth.

Bill Clinton took this liberal weapon on ethical standards to new record lows. Before Clinton, who could have imagined that the President of the United States would have sex with an intern in the Oval Office? It was, to most Americans, incomprehensible. But that was only the beginning of his treachery to ethical standards. In classic liberal form, Clinton did not genuinely repent and come clean to the American people. He looked right into the camera at the American people and said he did not have sex, and then came his famous words, "It depends on what the meaning of the word 'is' is." He committed perjury, and he survived an impeachment attempt.

As low as Democrats' ethical standards were before Clinton, they fell off a cliff with his presidency. It wasn't just that Clinton committed horrendous acts that violated the decency and office of the President, it was that he lowered ethical standards for liberalism by nearly eliminating the bottom rung. The Monica Lewinsky affair was only one of many Clinton ethical breaches.

Today Clinton is a God among Democrats. Democrats have no shame.

Presidential affairs were at one time considered so horrendous that they were kept absolutely secret, and that only goes back to J.F.K.'s time. Then Senator Ted Kennedy showed us that ethics and questionable character could be taken to lower levels by driving drunk and walking away from an accident that killed a woman under questionable circumstances. He didn't even report the accident for over nine hours. That was Chappaquiddick. Good Americans with a moral compass would have fired Ted Kennedy and would have wanted an intense criminal investigation. The man was unfit to be a United States Senator. Instead, Democrats put this unethical man on a pedestal. He became one of America's greatest liberal Democrats.

Anthony Wiener, a New York congressman, was exposed for taking pictures of his penis and texting them to girls. He got caught and after a very ugly public disgrace, he resigned and said he would never text his penis again. Now Anthony Wiener is running for Mayor of New York, and he's back at texting his nakedness to girls. The man is very sick, and yet, somehow, he is at home in the Democratic party. Does that not bother anyone in the Democratic party? People like to say character matters, but apparently it doesn't for Democrats.

Does anyone else think it's surreal that this man's last name is actually Weiner? Truth really is stranger than fiction.

Conclusion

True liberals have made all 20 of these liberal rules a part of their DNA. They live by these rules. They breathe them 24/7. Each of them and all of them together make up the fabric of all that they do and think.

This is why conservatives have such a hard time comprehending why and how liberals can think like they do, defying common sense sometimes, lying other times, distorting facts so often, and disregarding ethics and good character. You would have to really incorporate all of these liberal rules into your mind, emotions, and spiritual life in order to think like a liberal. Neither a true conservative nor a true Christian can think like a liberal. It's too evil.

Another reason Trump's election is so significant is because:

It is no coincidence that Donald Trump stands opposed to every single one of these practices that make up the liberal template.

CHAPTER 16
LIBERALISM AND CHRISTIANITY
DEMOCRATS PLEASE STOP SAYING YOU ARE CHRISTIANS! YOUR BEHAVIOR IS ANTI-GOD!

No other political Party has ever assaulted religious freedom as Democrats are doing today. Dr. Kevin "Coach" Collins

The subject of religion is important because it goes to the core of why the United States was founded. Our founding fathers sought to escape from a state-mandated religion and religious persecution. Therefore, how liberalism affects our constitutional right to be free to practice our own religion without government control or prejudice is one of the most important subjects of the day.

Liberalism stands in stark contrast to Christianity and is opposed to fundamental Biblical doctrine. Many devoted Believers find themselves shocked and repulsed by much of the liberal agenda. However, a very large number of Christians in America cannot articulate where liberalism defies Biblical doctrine. When confronted by an extreme liberal who challenges their Christian beliefs, many Christians have no defense. They cannot explain where liberalism goes off the reservation.

Why is there so much confusion about liberalism among

Christians? I believe most American Christians do not have a deep understanding of the Bible. This means liberal Democrats can claim to be Christians with extreme anti-Biblical positions, and the vast majority of true Christians have no idea how to address the contradictions. As part of the liberal movement, Democrats have become good at using the English language to go all over the map, to touch the stars with adjectives, to plummet the depths of human needs with examples, and to wax eloquent while talking about spiritual matters.

Christians today who hope to put up a good defense for their faith and to put evil in its proper context must not only know doctrine and the Word, they must be experienced debaters who are articulate and understand the methods of liberals. This is no small challenge, but the very first challenge for American Christians is knowing the Bible intimately.

If you don't know where the line in the sand really is, it is easy to get hoodwinked. If you don't know the truth well, how can you recognize the counterfeit? When FBI agents study to recognize counterfeit money, they don't spend all their time examining the hundreds of variations of counterfeit bills. Instead, they spend almost all of their time studying the real thing. By knowing all the details of a true $20 or $100 bill printed by the U.S. Treasury, they recognize a counterfeit in a heartbeat. Knowing the truth intimately is the key to recognizing anything that is not true. Knowing the truth well is the best way to instantly recognize when a belief or practice contradicts fundamental Christian beliefs.

The value of knowing the truth is that when issues or questions come up, most of the time, you will instantly know which way to go. The truth becomes part of your mind, emotions, psyche, spirit, and every fiber of your being. The truth becomes embedded in your identity and in your thought processes. When a complex issue is raised, a mature Christian has an immediate intuitive sense as to what is true and what is not.

Christians Do Not Understand Liberalism

It is my contention that American Christians don't understand liberalism and are not deeply grounded in the Word. No wonder Christians don't know what positions to take on union disputes, tax proposals, foreign policy, military defense, national security, personal freedom, the entire Bill of Rights, the behavior of our politicians, social issues, entitlements, fiscal and monetary policies, and even abortion and homosexuality. Does the Bible answer all of these questions definitively? Of course not, but what is true and right does answer most of them. Does anyone think Jesus would not know which side to take on all these issues? Of course, he would. And on almost every issue, liberalism takes a position that is in direct contrast to a Biblical view.

Have you ever tried to convince a liberal that their facts are wrong or that their understanding of economics or human motivation is upside down? They seem incapable of being persuaded regardless of the facts. In a very real sense, they are incapable of understanding because of the worldview they have grown up with, which has become such a huge part of their personal identity.

This is a serious problem for many Christians whose entire belief system was built when they were very impressionable in a home environment that was a disaster of dysfunctional, irrational, and unbiblical beliefs. None of us grew up in a perfect environment with perfect parents, but there is such a thing as a domestic disaster, and far too many adults today grew up in exactly such a chaotic environment.

Anyone can grow up and personally mature in a healthy way, even with a less-than-ideal childhood, if they are willing to be teachable and humble and if they have the opportunity to learn from someone who can mentor them. Anyone can, but few hard-core liberals are teachable and humble. Therefore, they become more determined, more bitter, and more violent in an effort to prove themselves right. Liberals who are teachable and open to learning that their belief system may be upside down are the good people who eventually leave the Democrat party.

The Liberal Filter Denies Objective Realty

Many Democrats are sincere, but their worldview is a filter through which they see everything with a liberal interpretation. That filter can hinder their ability to see clearly. You may say one thing very articulately, but their filter may actually have translated what you said into something entirely different. Their worldview brings in neurological associations from their youth, which can trigger emotional switches and suddenly result in irrational or angry behavior.

At the least, it can connect a series of thoughts to draw a wrong conclusion. False beliefs can certainly cloud a person's thinking and affect their ability to even see themselves clearly. The worst thing about deception is that the one deceived has no idea that he or she is deceived.

But let's not be naive. There are also Democrats who are not sincere, but are driven by their own evil desires. This is part of what makes it so hard for Christians to understand Democrats. Christians are repulsed by the evil behavior of radical Democrats, but then they meet a Democrat who is a nice person but still holds radical liberal beliefs. For true Believers, it is an extraordinary contradiction for a Christian to hold radical liberal beliefs that are anti-God, disregard the truth, and are destroying our constitution and our freedoms, not to mention murdering babies in the womb.

Even good people with sincere intentions can be sincerely

wrong. If a person has always seen a corporate CEO as greedy and part of a conspiracy that separates classes of people and deprives the less fortunate, such a person may be incapable of seeing a CEO as a generous, kind humanitarian who volunteers to teach prison seminars on weekends. You could show this liberal the prison list of attendees for the weekend with the CEO's name on it, and he still wouldn't believe it. He would probably ask if you forged the signature. If he finally agreed that the CEO did attend, he would immediately argue that it was all a ruse, that conservatives don't care for the less fortunate, never mind that it was a Republican, not a Democrat, who devoted the rest of his life to founding and faithfully serving Prison Fellowship Ministries. Facts don't matter. A person's worldview, like a computer program, controls how the data is interpreted. The data will be filtered and interpreted consistent with their life long belief system.

For nearly all radical liberals, facts won't even make a dent in their radical perspective. Conversations with a radical liberal can be very frustrating, because it is like talking to a brick wall. Actually, it is much worse than talking to a brick wall. A brick wall won't yield, but it doesn't defy what is true, it doesn't say ridiculous things, and it doesn't attack you personally. A conversation with a vicious liberal can be very unsettling for the rest of the day.

We all have a worldview, but a worldview can help you grow in truth, or it can hinder your ability to recognize what is true and good. The liberal worldview hinders one's ability to see right and wrong, good and evil, and truth and lies. And what is so sad is that most liberals think they are thinking clearly, that they have the truth, and that Christians and conservatives are really out in left field. For the best explanation of how this can happen, I strongly recommend you read the **Appendix: How Can People Be Blind to The Truth?**

While not all conservatives, and certainly not all Republicans, are devoted Believers in Jesus Christ, those who are set aside their personal greed and motivations for something bigger than themselves. They are willing to make sacrifices for the sake of truth and to serve others with genuine humility. God's grace and mercy are constantly at work in their hearts. These people are much more likely to see outside their own mental and psychological constraints. Conservative Christians tend to be teachable. They seek to grow and to become better. They are never perfect, but they admit that, and they acknowledge humbly that they are a work in progress.

Liberals Are Not Teachable

This is in stark contrast to radical liberals, who rarely are teachable. They behave as if they know it all. Their worldview is in sharp contrast to the Christian worldview. Their own pride hinders their personal growth. Does any of this sound like the humble spirit of Jesus Christ? Of course not, because it isn't.

Liberals Hate Everything Christian

This explains how liberals take so many positions that are anti-God. Liberals hate nearly everything Christian. Many of us would equate such attitudes with being anti-American precisely because liberal positions are the opposite of the values upon which this country was founded. This country was clearly founded upon Christian principles. There's no doubt about that at all. The evidence on that is overwhelming, although liberal educators and Democrats have done everything in their power to try to erase any sign of Christian faith in our history. That's another gigantic indication Democrats are un-Christian.

It's not front-page news anymore that liberalism seeks to destroy all Christian influence in America and replace it with anti-

Christian theology. If you want to know which side of a political issue liberals are on, all you have to do is ask which position is anti-God, and that will answer the question almost every time. While liberals try to keep their radical anti-God theology out of the press and below the radar, sometimes their rabid hatred for God and Biblical values gets the best of them.

The Washington Post reported such an incident on July 3, 2013. In Texas when Governor Rick Perry called for a second special session to pass an abortion law that would prohibit the procedure past the 20th week of pregnancy, those supporting the Governor and wanting to protect human life assembled peacefully on the steps of the Capital and sang "Amazing Grace." And what did Democrat protestors chant? Protestors supporting abortion tried to drown out their enemies by loudly chanting **"Hail Satan!"**

No more blatant example could demonstrate that liberalism is anti-God. The video is on Youtube as of this writing, and you can actually hear the chant, "Hail Satan!" Conservative Republicans will find this appalling. Those of us who believe in a God and a Satan have a hard time comprehending how Democrats could worship Satan in public like this. But this is just one more example of why it is not unreasonable for conservatives who are also true Believers to ask, "How can someone be a Democrat supporting such radicalism and still claim to be a Christian?" [Also view this Youtube video of a woman protesting in favor of abortion and screaming "Hail Sodomy."] This is what the Democrat Party represents and promotes today.

Christian Democrats?

While there will be many Democrats out there who may be Christians who would say, "Well, I don't agree with a chant that would hail Satan," as long as they continue to vote Democrat, they are supporting the liberal agenda. That also means they are indirectly supporting those Democrats who do worship Satan. Democrats who call themselves Christians ought to consider the fact that they are helping to promote evil with their votes. Part of being a true Christian is realizing when you're wrong and correcting wrong beliefs or wrong behavior. And then never going back to that behavior again. That is the meaning of repentance.

It's time millions of Democrats who are Christians take a good hard look at their Christian beliefs and compare them to liberal radicalism. This is not just a philosophical or theological question. It is a question that requires a long hard look in the mirror for all Christians who are registered Democrats.

It must be said here, although it should be obvious, that the Republican party cannot be equated to a Christian party. There is no such thing as a Christian political party. There are only Christian individuals. That being said, the Republican party tends to attract more genuine Christians than the Democratic party by an order of magnitude. Why?

Consider the following. These are the liberal rules from the liberal template in the last chapter. The behavior that is behind these rules is very repulsive to Christians. As you read these, ask yourself if these behaviors or beliefs are consistent with what the Bible teaches.

Use Every Crisis to Control People
Ignore Facts Contrary to the Agenda
Manipulate & Distort When Necessary
Rally The Liberal Forces (to misrepresent)
Use Repetition Ad Infinitum to Manipulate
Control The Media to Manipulate People with fake news
Use Celebrities to Manipulate People
Use Third Party Attack Entities
Use Personal Attacks if Nothing Else Works

Use Government Employees Illegally
Use Government Resources Illegally
Deny, Babble, Witch Hunt, Politicize
Weaponize the language
Weaponize the legal system with "lawfare" against opponents
Use Race to Divide & Conquer
Use Class Warfare to Divide & Conquer
Diminish the Value of Human Life
Promote abortion with euphemisms
Promote transgenderism and child mutilation
Use the FDA, USDA, and CDC to facilitate pandemics
Force untested and dangerous vaccines on citizens
Work closely with Big Pharma
Redefine The Meaning of Words to Confuse People
Promote Pacifism among people but control from the top
Preach Peace But Promote Violence
Make Everything Environmental if not racial
Establish Different (Low) Ethical Standards
Destroy family members
Destroy political opponents financially
Generate false stories with hideous themes against opponents
Ignore laws and regulations that deport illegal aliens
Promote policies that encourage illegal aliens to come
Oppose all efforts to secure our borders
Allow criminals and drug dealers to walk freely across the border
Offer to pay illegal aliens, give them housing, offer them welfare
Oppose voter identification so illegal aliens can vote
If all else fails, assassinate opponents through independent contractors, proxies, false flags or "suicide".

Who can look at this list, most of which is either outright evil behavior or dishonest and immoral behavior, and conclude that it is anything but anti-Christian? And anyone who would argue that these behaviors do not represent the core of the Democratic party is most definitely in denial.

> *The legitimate question for all Democrats today who claim to be Christians is this: How can you possibly be a Christian and support such a horrendous and evil agenda? The answer is "you cannot." Not according to the Bible.*

There is, of course, a branch of liberals who claim to be Christians, and they love to play the role of offended victims whenever this issue comes up. But if you think about it, radical liberals have hijacked every Christian theme.

The National Organization for Women argues we have no Christian or constitutional right to hinder women's rights, but it's okay to kill their unborn children. There are groups that promote immoral sex in the name of God's love. There are groups that push entitlement programs in the name of helping the poor even though it hurts the poor in the long run. There are groups that promote child sex and the distribution of condoms to elementary school children in the name of protecting the children from disease and death. All of these fanatics are liberals. In Jesus' day, these were the money changers in the Temple and the hypocrites of the day.

Self-defense is a fundamental Biblical concept that has been taught in ecclesiastical law as long as civilized men have lived. There are liberal groups that would take away a woman's right to protect herself with a gun, instead suggesting that she could protect herself from violent rape by spitting on her assailant or even "peeing on him." When liberals talk so crazy, you have to wonder why so-called "Christian Democrats" don't see the insanity that is so obvious to the rest of us.

The point is that radical liberalism hijacks Christian concepts to promote evil causes. The Democrat party is the arm and weapon of radical liberalism in America. Like a deadly cancer, liberalism is spreading, and if it isn't stopped quickly, it will consume the host. Just like cancer spreads into vital organs to kill, liberalism has worked its way into American Churches and the modern version of "American Christianity."

Liberalism and the Democratic party do not stand for Christian principles. On the contrary, liberals intend to destroy any and every sign of Christianity in America, and they have been diligently working to do just that for many years. What's amazing is that many Democrats who claim to be Christians are doing all this in Jesus' name. Sound familiar?

> *It is no coincidence that Donald Trump stands against all of these evil practices and will lead our country consistent with a biblical code of conduct. No claim is made in this book that Donald Trump is a genuine believer. The claim is that God appointed Trump according to Romans 13:1, and like it or not, Trump will be the 47th President and govern consistent with his moral compass, which runs parallel to a biblical code of good behavior and positive motives that serve the people. This is another reason this election is so momentous and will forever change America and the world.*

CHAPTER 17
THE DESTRUCTIVE EFFECT OF LIBERALISM
AMERICA'S TOTAL POLITICAL, ECONOMIC, AND SOCIAL DESTRUCTION

Liberal progressivism evolved after our Constitution. It has repeatedly failed all over the world. So why do we think it could be successful here in the United States of America? Allen West

The long-term cumulative effect of liberalism in America is terribly destructive. Clearly, the deeply entrenched liberal policies, laws, judicial precedents, regulations, and liberal agendas permeate our American way of life. As we've seen in the chapter on **Why There is No Turning Back**, all of this becomes part of a massive set of laws, cases, and regulations that cannot be undone. Even if everyone agreed, which they do not and never will, two hundred years of liberal brick and mortar cannot be quickly disassembled. The cumulative effect of liberalism is horrendously destructive to our precious freedoms.

Rewriting history is one of the most effective ways that Liberals are destroying America. Liberals have been working for decades to rewrite history, and they have been doing that on many fronts. Many liberal soldiers armed with Ph. Ds from liberal bastions have been diligently rewriting history books for use in the public schools. This has been a long-term project, but liberals always knew they couldn't destroy capitalism and a free America in a single decade. They don't even think in terms of decades. They think in terms of generations. Brainwashing entire generations takes time, but if you rewrite the history books, you have a very effective strategy to brainwash upcoming generations.

The authors of most history books used in public schools are clearly radical liberals. This is because many of the Ph.D.s coming out of our liberal colleges are liberal fanatics, but it also is the result of school administrators selecting books that suit their liberal effort to convert our children. Their anti-Christian bias and their hatred of God are often stunningly obvious.

A school district in Brevard County in Florida has been using a 9th-grade history text for three years that includes 36 pages dedicated to Islam and the prophet Muhammed, but not one page on Christianity. Not only does the book promote Islam, but it also suggests that Muhammed, not Jesus, is the true prophet. The book actually misrepresents Islam factually, stating that Islam is wonderful for women. A group called Citizens for National Security reported that over 80 textbooks are being used that promote Islam and denigrate Christianity. These books lie about Jihad and other beliefs of Islam. This is not just wrong, it is downright evil, and they're doing it to our children, to entire generations. It's hard to imagine that we have textbooks in our schools all over the country that have an agenda of promoting radical Islam with propaganda. But when you realize that liberalism seeks to destroy our American system as we know it, it makes sense.

Brainwash Entire Generations

The strategy to brainwash entire generations began with taking over the Education Departments at Colleges and Universities around the country. I know about liberal professors from personal experience. I got my B.A. in Economics and then went on to take one year of full-time education classes and an additional year of student teaching. Apart from two great thought-provoking professors, the others were right out of the liberal playbook. What these liberal professors taught me about teaching high school students can be summed up within the period at the end of this sentence. I went on to teach high school for two years before going to law school, and I was a good teacher, but that was in spite of those liberal professors, not because of them.

After a couple of decades of liberal professors brainwashing naive college students, those students went on to teach the next generation of kids in our public schools. What an unmitigated disaster that has been. Liberals are masters of long-term strategies.

Liberalism is an Elaborate Re-Education System

Liberal education does not stop in the public school system. Liberalism has one of the most extensive education and re-education systems in the world. It reaches out to children, young adults, parents raising families, single mothers, pregnant mothers living in poverty, senior citizens, and of course minorities. It extends to some of the most ingenious propagandizing the world has ever known. At times it is violent, but most of the time it is subtle.

Liberals have been unashamed of their bold use of the Federal government as a propaganda machine using our tax dollars to create commercials and programs that promote the liberal agenda. In years past, much of this was done quietly so Republicans wouldn't wake up, but lately, liberal methods have been in-your-face as they get bolder. The Feds have created huge marketing campaigns to encourage people to get into entitlement programs, and their campaigns have been very successful. The food stamp program, for example, has exploded in the past few years.

As a result of the extensive non-stop cultural, political, economic, and historical propagandizing by liberals, entire generations of Americans are now brainwashed with the idea that government has the answers to all their problems. Anything that is perceived to go wrong anywhere is immediately answered by cries for government solutions, new government laws, new government enforcement, more government employees or funding for more programs. As long as so many Americans have the belief that government is their God with the answers to all their problems, we will continue to slide toward darkness.

Destructive Liberal Consequences

Liberals have been very successful with the election of liberal politicians, who can then make new laws, vitiate good laws, and rewrite the future of America. Liberals have blitzed Republicans at getting out the vote and persuading uninformed voters in most of the heavily populated voter regions. Liberals also use their power to appoint liberal judges. Federal judges are appointed for life. Out of liberal judgeships come thousands of bad law twisting the meaning of the words in our Constitution.

Another front is the writing of regulations that implement laws and define the processes and the administrative remedies that allow liberals to control people. Since liberals have been in control the majority of time in the past 40 years, the creation of entire departments and the appointment of department heads and employees has largely fallen to the liberal camp. But even when Republicans have a majority in the House or the Senate and in the White House, they never disassemble the liberal monsters that were created under Democrat administrations. Republicans have been giving away the advantage of a majority even when they have it.

Americans should be asking, "How did our Republican leaders let this happen?" And another equally important question Americans should be asking is, "How did we let this happen?" If Republicans have lost control of America, Americans certainly have lost control of Republicans.

As a footnote to this discussion, what can we deduce about political science education in America? They are apparently not worth the money Republican parents are paying for their children's educations. Apart from the obvious liberal bias at our colleges and Universities, these schools have been issuing political science degrees to young Republicans who go on to become politicians or organizational leaders in the party, but who are so naive, they don't seem to understand Political Warfare 101. Liberals have been cleaning house.

Chaos Defaults to Evil

All liberals are not necessarily smart enough to develop incredibly powerful strategies, but here's the thing about evil. Evil strategies can evolve as circumstances dictate, and liberals often stumble into the perfect storm to promote another tenet of their agenda. For Republicans, it takes a good heart and good organization to consistently promote good, but liberals can promote their agenda with chaos. Chaos defaults to evil, not good. This is one of the reasons liberals make tremendous headway during times of economic and social chaos. ***Chaos always favors evil***.

Liberals have stumbled onto opportunities over the decades to capture entire government departments and agencies. And when Democrats stumble into an opportunity, they take full advantage of it. The IRS scandal is a good example. The IRS recently admitted that they targeted Tea Party organizations, and they admitted that it was wrong. Liberals quickly explain this away, just as they do every time one of their strategies is exposed. They play dumb, and they love to say, "Everyone makes mistakes."

And then they go from the defensive to the offensive by attacking Republicans for even suggesting that the IRS's motivations were politically motivated. Liberals can get away with murder, but if Republicans get caught, there is a relentless attack to destroy them and to highlight the mistake forever. But if Democrats get caught, we're supposed to turn our heads and ignore it.

Liberals Have An Army of Government Employees

But do not lose the bigger picture of what this IRS scandal reveals. It shows us that once liberals have dug deep into our system of government with tens of thousands of loyal employees marching to their liberal agenda, they will not be stopped. They will work from every angle to promote liberalism and destroy capitalism and freedom. Like termites that find their way into the darkest corners of a home and into the walls and ceilings and basement, and slowly but steadily eat away at the wood structure, liberals are constantly hard at work. They work night and day, 365 days a year (less paid Federal holidays), in every government agency, in every courtroom, in every school, and anywhere they can quietly promote liberalism.

Many Americans have expressed shock and dismay, and many have suggested this IRS scandal by Democrat employees is an isolated event! How incredibly naive! Most Americans think now that Democrats have been caught using the IRS to promote their political agenda, they will stop. Again, this would be naive. They may have gotten caught, but they will not stop. They are on a mission, and they don't know how to stop. They will just be more careful about getting caught.

There's another important reason liberalism is destroying our country. Republicans do not lay awake at night scheming to destroy their enemies like Democrats do. In fact, the vast majority of Republicans do not consider liberals their enemies. But make no mistake. Liberals consider Republicans enemies, and liberals are almost rabid with passion to destroy capitalism and the American constitution once and for all. For liberals, anyone who gets in the way becomes a target for destruction. For Republicans this is just politics. For liberals this is war.

The effect of liberalism has been devastating to America. Unless Americans take control soon, America will fall into darkness. Even if we survive, America's best days are not necessarily ahead of us.

CHAPTER 18

REPUBLICANS HAVE BLOOD ON THEIR HANDS
THEY CONTINUE TO COMPROMISE OUR MOST SACRED RIGHTS

They who can give up essential liberty to obtain a little temporary safety deserve neither liberty nor safety. Benjamin Franklin

In recent years America has been rapidly declining, and Republican leaders are not innocent bystanders. Far from it. Republican leaders, and especially moderate Republican leaders, have greased the skids and have helped keep liberal progress from getting derailed along the way. Republicans have become bosom buddies with Democrats on massive government expansion programs and plenty of legislation that has been chipping away at fundamental constitutional rights. Democrats could not have accomplished so much without Republican support in the Senate and in the House.

Republican leaders have fallen into a terrible trap for the unwary. The trap wasn't even set by Democrats. Republicans found this trap all by themselves. The trap is revealed in part by a famous Benjamin Franklin quote, "They who can give up essential liberty to obtain a little temporary safety deserve neither liberty nor safety." The Republican party has been compromising our constitutional rights one small compromise at a time for decades. While there are many good conservative Republicans working diligently to save America, based on past history and cooperation with Democrats, the Republican Party deserves neither liberty nor safety at this point. No wonder there is a powerful tea party movement. No wonder so many conservatives are leaving the Republican party to become Independents. Many feel the Republican party has betrayed the trust of conservatives, and they would be correct. But there are plenty of moderate Republicans across America who would argue that the Republican Party never was a "conservative" party. The discussion on that point would be more about relativism than the U.S. Constitution.

Here we are, almost 240 years after Benjamin Franklin wrote those famous words, and today, we are living with the consequences. Franklin could have been preaching to the Republican Party today.

Americans have been asleep for a long time, so they are generally unaware of the compromises. Most Americans don't care enough to participate in any meaningful way. This is why, throughout history, governments become too big, gained too much power, taxed the people excessively, and become bastions of fraud and corruption. The people don't defend their liberties, and their civil servants and politicians eventually do whatever they want. The result is never pretty. This is where America is today.

Republicans have stepped right into the trap of horse trading with Democrats to get their pet projects passed. Pork Barrel politics has become a way of life for Republicans, and guess who keeps getting screwed? Americans. But it's not just about pork, about a few pet projects. It's about trading with the enemy and giving away our constitutional rights. It's about trading the truth for a lie.

Washington, D.C., has become a corrupt playground where

politicians play high-stakes card games, and they're playing with our money.

Democrat: "*I'll give you that two hundred million dollar bridge project plus your new highway extension in return for your vote that life does not begin until the third trimester.*"

Republican: "*I'll see your hand and raise you by voting for your bill to make all semi-automatic guns illegal, but I want your vote against a deadline for pulling our troops out of Afghanistan.*"

Democrat: "*Done. By the way, why don't you and the little lady come over to our dinner party on Friday. The Fed Chairman will be there, and I know you've been trying to get an audience with him.*"

The game of American compromise in politics is repulsive to the vast majority of Americans, but notice that Americans do not hold their politicians accountable. Instead, they continue to let their politicians trade away their constitutional rights.

One of America's longest-seated Senators and well-respected Republicans with great seniority and power was Senator Ted Stevens. It wasn't until the end of his long career as a Republican leader that Americans began to see the grotesque Federal waste that he was responsible for. He managed to get billions of Federal tax dollars allocated for his Alaskan pet peeve projects, and Alaskans loved him for bringing home the bacon. Ted Stevens may have brought more money back to Alaska than all the gold ever mined in Alaska. Today, Stevens' legacy is summed up in this laconic phrase, "The bridge to nowhere."

Name a Republican who actually oversaw a reduction in the size of the Federal government. It hasn't happened in our lifetime, because the Federal government has never gotten smaller under any Republican administration in our lifetime. Even President Reagan, whom conservatives love and who might be called the greatest conservative President Republicans ever had in office, oversaw a massive expansion in the Federal budget. Arguments about the value of the military presence we had around the world, and the resulting fall in the Berlin Wall and the collapse of the Soviet Empire not withstanding, massive expansion in the Federal government is never good, because big is only the next stepping stone to bigger. We complain about how liberals grow government, but Republicans have been willing accomplices.

Name one Republican who oversaw a reduction in the rate of the government's increasing size. That might be tough. Politicians play games with us on the subject of government budgets. They love to claim credit for "reducing the size of government," but there's no such thing, at least in our time. What they are really doing is slowing the rate of growth. They're just lying to Americans. We are not amused.

Republicans who cannot get their special interest bills passed will regularly tack on Democratic packages to get the votes. This is now commonly recognized as the way American politics works. Americans' freedom and constitutional rights keep losing because too many simply accept the false notion that this is the way American politics is supposed to work.

Republican leaders tell us they must compromise, or they won't get anything done. It's that attitude that has put America on this roller coaster ride to hell. Years ago someone came up with the rhetorical question, "What would Jesus do?" The question has become a sarcastic way to make a point about doing what is right, but in the context of Republican compromises that have brought this country to the precipice of self-destruction, perhaps a few rhetorical questions will make the point.

What if Jesus had said, "Well, one itsy bitsy sin is no big deal," or "One or two little white lies never hurt anyone," or "Why not a little compromise with Satan? Everything would go so much smoother if I gave a little and Satan gave a little," or "I'll bet I could cut a deal with Satan so I don't have to die a gruesome death on a cross." Little compromises, eternal consequences.

Our Republican leaders have been horsetrading with our God-given and constitutional rights for a long time. They have given away our freedoms. They have compromised with the devil. Little compromises, eternal consequences.

The irony today in politics is that the Republicans are claiming that they can save America, but Americans don't believe that anymore. There's a good reason for that, and while most Americans may not be able to articulate exactly why they feel that way, I believe it is because they know in their hearts that Republicans have blood on their hands.

> *It is no coincidence that the majority of American voters believe in Donald Trump, and in what can only be considered a miracle, Trump has completely remade the Republican party and controls the direction of the nation's agenda for his second term. The power he wields as the 47th President with the Senate and House majorities and the U.S. Supreme Court majority is almost unprecedented, but it is uniquely powerful and absolutely necessary to save America from the darkness that shrouded it for so long.*

CHAPTER 19
HOPE IS NOT A STRATEGY
SOMEBODY PLEASE DO SOMETHING TO SAVE OUR COUNTRY

To sit back hoping that someday, some way, someone will make things right is to go on feeding the crocodile, hoping he will eat you last, but eat you he will. Ronald Reagan

If America stays on its current course, we are headed toward the destruction of American capitalism and the American freedoms enshrined in our Constitution. To suggest that our best days lie ahead without substantial evidence to expect a dramatic reversal in America would be incredibly naive, and there is little evidence to support the notion that there is such a reversal on the executive, legislative, and judicial fronts, and certainly nothing on the cultural and political fronts. To suggest that our best days lie ahead and not behind is wishful thinking, and we must not place the hope of America's survival on wishful thinking. There is far too much at stake.

I think too many good people are making a major tactical mistake today. They know the power of positive thinking in their own lives. It may have brought them through the toughest of times when all hope seemed lost. It may have helped them climb higher in life than many thought possible. There is no doubt that positive thinking and faith and hope are powerful tools for living. But positive thinking alone will not save a nation. Positive thinking will not erase a hundred years of bad case law, bad statutes and ordinances, bad regulations, and bad policies. Positive thinking alone will not reverse a half-century of moral and spiritual decline. Hoping upon hope that things will get better is not a strategy to save America.

The evidence is going the other way. Liberalism is gaining momentum. Some believe that we may have reached the tipping point, so that at least 51% of the voters are now entitlement voters who will elect liberals perpetually. If that's true, and if enough of these voters cannot be turned around very soon, then our nation is already lost.

President Reagan was incredibly positive and saw hope for the future of America, and it was his positive attitude that gave us all hope and endeared us to him. We love positive politicians. But he also did not hesitate to call out the bad players of the world, including American liberals and world leaders. Reagan had the courage to call out Gorbachev. No one else did. That's not going negative, that's standing against the lies and holding up the truth. Reagan knew you could not pretend everything was okay if it wasn't. His formula was simple. ***First, expose the lie and reveal the truth. Second, take positive action in the right direction.***

If Reagan had been standing on the deck of the Titanic as it began titling, he would have given the people exactly what they needed. He would not have given speeches while hanging onto the railing, saying things like, "Tomorrow will be brighter than today. Our best days are ahead of us, not behind." Instead, he would have buckled down to get women and children into life rafts. Of course, his positive attitude would still rule the day, and his hope in God would never waiver. But he was a realist with a positive attitude. He would have willingly sacrificed his life to save others on the Titanic, and he would have done so with a word of encouragement to the women and children he put into the rafts. Reagan was never in denial. He was a man with hope for a nation who became the most powerful leader in the world and used that power to effect change. Unfortunately, many of the positive changes Reagan made have since been reversed by liberals.

I believe if Reagan were alive today, he would say something like this:

> *My fellow Americans, our nation is on the brink of falling into darkness. The 11th hour is upon us, and this nation's salvation depends not on politicians who are the blind leading the blind, but on all Americans who want a brighter future, a future that reclaims our precious freedoms and God-given rights. It is time to raise a strong defense against liberalism. Together we must fight the lies, and we must fight the liberal agenda that seeks to destroy capitalism and America as we know it. Together we can save America. Evil is upon us, and our nation's salvation hangs on this moment in time with profound eternal significance. With determination and by God's grace and mercy, we can bring America back to greatness. But today we must speak the truth. Hope alone is not enough. We must expose liberalism for what it is. We must say, "Enough!" Americans must stand up and say, "We will no longer suffer politicians who tell bold-faced lies, who distort history, who use race and class to divide Americans, who manipulate the very people they claim to help." We must hold every politician accountable for his promises and for his actions. And character must matter once again in every politician. Until and unless Americans take that stand, America's future will not be brighter than the past. Americans*

must take their country back, or we will surely fall into darkness.

Is this not almost exactly what Donald Trump said many times in his speeches at rallies across America? I originally wrote that fictitious Reagan speech in 2013 in the first edition of *The War for America's Soul*, and that was two years before Trump first announced he would run for president. I had no idea Donald Trump would enter the race in the future, and I had no idea Donald Trump would say the things he now says, almost verbatim from that pretend Reagan speech.

It is no coincidence that Donald Trump has said these things and includes them in his core agenda for his second term. Do you see the amazing timing of the appointment of this man for this time? Can anyone doubt the miracle it was that he should become the 45th and 47th President of the United States, and that it should happen on the brink of America's total collapse?

Let's be positive. Let us live with hope and by faith. But let us be ready for these times. If we say America's future will be better than our past, we darn well better have an effective national strategy that is powerful, and we had better have the support of the majority of Americans, and we had better oust liberal Democrats and take control. Americans have to wake up and engage. They must want to know the truth, and they must want their freedoms back. There must be an effective strategy to defeat liberalism. We have had none of these things until now with the promises of Donald Trump. Even after implementing his agenda on all these things, we still have a lot of work to do for many years to reverse the tremendous damage Democrats have done to this country.

Americans have not yet stopped liberalism's violent war on

truth, and frankly, the defense has been sorely lacking. Americans apparently have not reached their threshold of pain, and until they do, they won't do enough to stop this insanity.

America is dangerously close to the point of no return. It's possible we have already crossed the line of no return, although I hope and pray there is still time to save our country. Feeble overtures to stand up against liberalism are doomed to failure. That has been the Republican defense for decades, and it has been a miserable failure. **With Donald Trump's election for a second term, there is now hope we have not had in several generations**.

Albert Einstein Understood Liberal Thinking

Albert Einstein said, "We can't solve problems by using the same kind of thinking we used when we created them." My adaptation of Einstein's insight would go like this, "We cannot hope to save America using the same kind of thinking that is destroying America."

Does anyone really think that the men and women who have been driving this country into the ground are suddenly wise enough to save us? It's an amazing irony, but the very politicians whose policies are destroying our economic power and worldwide influence refuse to admit that their policies have failed. Instead of recognizing disastrous failure, they double down. They get louder and more aggressive in pushing failed liberal policies. They want more government, more programs, higher taxes, and more intrusions into our personal lives. Yet these are the very ideologies that are destroying America. The inmates really are in charge of the asylum.

Lawyers and Politicians

As a lawyer, I witnessed what the liberal mindset can do. The same mindset is in our lawyers and politicians, and our politicians largely come from the legal profession. Our politicians have learned some evil tricks from their legal careers, and our liberal politicians practice these tricks religiously. Perhaps an example will best make the case.

I litigated cases against home builders who breached their contracts with homeowners. When confronted, a builder who was not building the home according to the contract and specifications would get very defensive about the quality of his work and would engage in lying, misrepresentations, and outright perjury. As part of his legal defense, he would go on the offensive and accuse his victim, the homeowner, of breaching the contract with various dishonest arguments. There would be months of written interrogatories, multiple depositions, various specious motions flying back and forth, and, of course, many court appearances up to the date of the trial. The builder and his attorney would create so much stress for the homeowner, and he would cost them so much money in legal fees, that many homeowners would either drop the lawsuit, or they would settle by compromising in a way that never made them whole.

One of the most insulting settlement proposals a builder in this kind of lawsuit would make every time is that he repair the construction defects. You can imagine my clients' first reactions when they heard that the same builder who screwed up their dream home was proposing that he now repair the mess he created. All my clients were incredulous. Their builder had misrepresented what he would do when they signed the contract, he made a mess of building their home, and then when they confronted him politely, he became very arrogant and aggressive. He hired an attorney and dragged them into an expensive and stressful lawsuit. He lied under oath on the witness stand. His attorney lied in the courtroom about the facts, and told boldfaced lies about them in the courtroom. And now this same builder would dare propose that he finish their home and repair the defects? None of my clients were amused.

Do you see the incredible parallels to how politicians practice today? The very politicians who are destroying our house, who lied to us, who insult us regularly, who have stolen our freedoms, compromised our precious Bill of Rights, taxed and regulated us to death, denigrated our Christian beliefs, attacked our traditional values, . . . these are the same politicians who now tell us they are going to save us. Einstein was right. They cannot save us. And conservatives are not amused.

The liberal answer to any problem is always more government and less freedom for the people. The government always gets bigger, and Americans' freedom always gets smaller. Beyond the horrendous economic and social damage that liberalism has done to America, there is the unmeasurable damage to the soul of America. Liberalism is destroying our great American culture and American values. The salvation of America is about much more than just economic and political salvation--it is about cultural and spiritual salvation for millions of Americans.

The challenges we face as Americans who want to take our country back are almost overwhelming. The problems are much bigger than most people realize, and we are much closer to our doom than the vast majority think. We must not sit around hoping and convincing each other that things are going to "get all better." They won't if we don't make it happen. Next time you hear someone say, "I believe our best days are not behind us, but in front of us," what will you say? Ask them what evidence they would cite to prove that America is turning around. They will have no evidence. Only hope. But hope alone will not save America.

Is there is a way to save America? I've painted a very gloomy picture in this book, but that's because the truth about America today is gloomy. I believe America can be saved, but it will not be easy. It will be harder than anything the American people have ever done before. In the next chapter I propose a three part strategy to save America.

While this strategy was originally published in 2013, I must say, it is no coincidence that the 47th President's agenda can be seen in this strategy to save America. Tell me God isn't at work!

CHAPTER 20

A STRATEGY
FOR THE SALVATION OF AMERICA

The ultimate tragedy is not the oppression and cruelty by the bad people but the silence over that by the good people. Martin Luther King, Jr.

I believe America's salvation will depend on three critical components, and all three must be in play simultaneously.

1. America's salvation will require a spiritual revival.

Unless there is a true spiritual revival in America, don't expect the supernatural salvation this nation so desperately needs. We are no longer like the Titanic headed for the iceberg. America is the Titanic after it hit the iceberg. Time is of the essence, and our salvation cannot be left to men alone. Good men do not have the power to save this country apart from God.

Does anyone really think that a Holy God, the very one who created us and blessed the founding of this great nation, would use His mighty power to save us as long as we continue to mock His character, deny His existence, and practice the most unholy acts of sin the world has ever seen? By His ordained rule that men shall have free choice, He has given us the freedom to destroy ourselves. He will not interfere if we choose sin and death. But if we repent, if we recognize that He is our God, if we acknowledge that our salvation is in Him alone, if we pray and seek Him, He may yet choose to save this nation. But we must turn from our path of destruction and seek Him. If we do not, nothing else will matter.

Spiritual revival is desperately needed, and it is the key to America's preservation. Without spiritual revival, we have already condemned ourselves, and we are lost. Only by the grace and mercy of God and His supernatural blessing can this great nation survive and thrive in the years ahead.

How will spiritual revival happen in America? This may surprise the Churches, but they have been tasked with the prime responsibility, and it starts and ends with prayer, the prayers of millions of Christians around America and around the world. The Body of Christ has an awesome responsibility to save this nation.

Politicians cannot start a spiritual revival. They can participate with Christians everywhere in prayer seeking God's help, but they will not be the start, nor do I expect politicians to be the power behind revival. We can hope and pray that Godly men and women will become politicians who can become leaders of the movement, but they are few and far between. True spiritual revival always begins with God's people, and so it will be in America.

2. <u>America's salvation will be found in the acceptance of what is true and the rejection of the lies that have destroyed the fabric of America.</u>

Lies and deception are at the root of what has driven this country so far down this path of self-destruction. For people who have been immersed in a culture of deception, it is often impossible to recognize the truth, at least until it becomes blatantly obvious.

Imagine a dark room with just enough light to see the people in front of you. The corners of the room are pitch black. You're told that the corners are full of danger and that you must rely on your guide to protect you. Your guide tells you to never go into the corners, lest you lose your life or get seriously injured.

Then one day a shady character gives you a small flashlight and encourages you to look into the dark corners yourself. He tells you what the corners contain, and it sounds all too fantastic, because it is the opposite of what your trusted guide has been telling you your whole life. At first you resist turning the flashlight on. After all, it would mean going against everything you have been taught to believe. Your whole life has been about interpreting events and people consistent with your belief system. You have validated your beliefs over and over again in your own mind. Your beliefs define you. What would you do if you suddenly discovered you lived in a totally different world?

But something has been nagging at you from deep within your soul, and you don't know what it is. So one day you turn the flashlight on and shine it into one of the corners of that dark room, but you turn it off quickly. You didn't see what you expected - scary things, dangers, monsters. You didn't leave the flashlight on long enough to see what was there because your mind was overwhelmed with the single thought that there were no monsters. It's almost too much to comprehend. So emotionally taxing is the thought that your whole life has been wrong, you can't bring yourself to turn the flashlight back on to see what really is in the dark corners.

Until one day you can no longer stand it. You shine the light into the darkness again, and what you see begins to change your life forever. You will never forget what is in the corners. You see things that you didn't know existed, things that fill your mind with excitement. The shady man is no longer the evil man your guide said he was. Your mind begins to expand with all kinds of possibilities, and you experience a surprising sense of freedom and hope. The truth can do that, and once you've seen the truth, you cannot unsee it.

The darkness represents the lies and deception of liberalism. It is the darkness that keeps the masses enslaved. But once light exposes the lies, you can never forget what you saw. Once you know the truth, you cannot forget it. Once you've tasted true freedom, you will never again be content with slavery.

America's salvation will not happen if people don't turn from the lies to the truth. America cannot hope to move away from darkness toward the light until its people comprehend the lies and understand truth. As long as liberals, both politicians and liberal voters, continue to live in the darkness, and as long as the majority of Americans live in the darkness, America is guaranteed to self-destruct.

America will not be saved if liberals continue to be a majority of the voting block in America. Therein lies the dilemma. The liberal voting block is growing steadily. Liberals have seen to it that their constituency continues to grow. It has been a long term strategy that is paying off for them, and it is quite simple. Here are a few of the elements of their plan to build a huge growing voting constituency.

1. Allow millions of immigrants into the country illegally, because illegal immigrants will automatically vote for Democrats for the rest of their lives.

2. Create massive entitlement programs, because this builds a dependent voting constituency that always votes for Democrats.

3. Expand government at every level, thereby expanding the dependent Federal employee population, which largely becomes another large Democratic voting block.

4. Take control of the national education system, rewrite the history books, and baptize entire generations into liberalism.

5. Take control of the national healthcare system, the entire medical profession, insurance companies, all American's personal

medical records, and the massive bureaucracy and taxation all this will involve.

These five strategies are only the tip of the bigger liberal plan, but one has to admit that Democrats have been incredibly successful with all five. The great victory they have achieved has involved incredible lies and deception to the American people for decades, and a lot of behind-the-scenes deception and manipulation by the worker bees. Their work has required liberal workers in the House and Senate, the White House, the Courts, Federal agencies, Unions, our education system, the mainstream media, and so on. These strategies alone have given them majority control of America.

A nation built on lies cannot survive in the long term. Unless we have an extraordinary awakening by the American people and their leaders, one which causes them to turn from living with lies, this nation will not survive.

This may sound a lot like spiritual revival, but Americans who recognize truth and the lies of liberalism certainly do not have to be born-again Christians. Some of the finest Americans I have met are not Christians. Truths about economics, personal motivation, freedom, constitutional rights, the interpretation of our founding fathers' true beliefs, the real history of the United States, the causes of injustice and crime - all of these truths transcend Christian lifestyles and politics. For the Christian, God may be the author of Truth, but what is true is true for every human being. America must find its way back to truth in order to survive and thrive again.

3. America's salvation will only be found in a return to the freedoms and rights protected by the U.S. Constitution.

Until the majority of Americans seriously want their fundamental Constitutional rights and privileges, we won't get them back. But even if they want these things, what a daunting challenge it will be to reverse decades of law, case precedent, and massive regulations. Even if Americans want to save America, can it really happen? Is it possible?

Here's the challenge of trying to return America to its rightful place. Our founding fathers built a very solid foundation upon which to construct and maintain an extraordinary structure. The foundation was so well engineered and so well constructed that it is fair to say there has never been a foundation in the history of the world like it. Many argue that the wisdom and foresight involved in the creation of America's foundation are so extraordinary, it could not have been the work of men alone. The argument is that this country was founded with the wisdom and blessing of God. George Washington certainly believed that. Whether that is true or not cannot be proven, but the wisdom and foresight of the founding fathers when they created the U.S. Constitution and laid the foundation of America cannot be disputed.

America today is a tall structure built on this foundation. The foundation remains solid, but the building is leaning to the side, and the higher the building gets, the more it leans. A building becomes unstable because it violates known engineering principles. The more it violates these principles, the more precarious the structure becomes. The higher the building, the greater the likelihood that one day it will simply collapse.

The only way America is going to get back to its constitutional foundation is by deconstructing the massive structure that is faulty. That means revoking or reversing millions of laws at every level of government, reversing or removing millions of case precedents, and wiping the slate clean on millions upon millions of regulations that are contrary to God-given freedoms, constitutionally protected freedoms, and burdensome regulations.

Many people today chit-chat about how to save our nation, and they will talk about reducing the rate of growth of the Federal government. That will not work. Others talk about reducing the size of the Federal government by 1% or even 5%. That will not save us either. If we are to get serious about saving America, I believe we are going to have to figure out how to reduce the size of the Federal government by very large percentages, perhaps 20% to 50%. It would be a daunting and overwhelming challenge, but as long as our government is so large and is so intent on dominating and controlling the people, we will never see the return of our freedoms and our constitutional rights and privileges. Government is the problem, not the solution. Therefore, we must reduce the government to its minimal size and with only the powers granted in the U.S. Constitution.

Is Help On The Way?

The answer is a loud "Yes" shouted from the mountaintops.

It is no coincidence that this strategy to save America is precisely Donald J. Trump's agenda to Make America Great Again! Do you still think it's all fortuitous and just the luck of the draw that put him back in the White House?

What are you going to do to help save America? You took the first and most important step, and that was to vote en masse for Trump and to give him a mandate to save America from the Democrats.

Congratulations to you and all of us who did our patriotic duty to vote for the best person for the job. But our job is far from over, right? We cannot fall back into the lackadaisical habits of yesteryear when conservatives and Christians left running the government and our education system to professional politicians.

May I recommend you develop your own personal plan to save America by working within one or more of these *Three Steps to Save America*?

1. Be Part of Spiritual Revival.

If you're part of a Church or if you are a Christian, consider rallying the troops to pray for revival like never before. Get permission in your church to start a new ministry called, "Spiritual Revival in America Now." Organize, manage, exhort, and spread the revival spirit. Pray for America. Pray for Americans. Pray for our leaders. Pray for God's protection over Donald Trump and his entire family. And don't stop praying.

2. Promote Truth and Defeat Lies.

You can promote truth and defeat lies by educating others, by facilitating the free flow of information, and by supporting those organizations that do spread the truth and fight the lies. Everyone can participate in this area. If you are a gifted teacher, writer, or speaker, you have a responsibility to spread the truth and help to re-educate Americans. You may not have those gifts, but if you love your country, talk to friends over coffee. Recruit others in this great battle for truth. Organize weekly meetings in your home where others can be educated and inspired. Invite teachers who can come to your home study and teach. Read, study, and share. Stand against the lies. Spread the truth.

3. Deconstruct Bad Laws, Court Decisions, and Regulations.

If you are a politician or a lawyer or judge, you can start by telling the truth yourself and never falling into the trap of compromising the truth. If you're a politician, don't let your colleagues lie in the Senate or the House. When they do, stop everything and stand up and hold them accountable right there. If you're a judge and a lawyer lies in your courtroom, stop him and lecture him about lying in your courtroom. Stop worrying about getting re-elected as a judge by staying on everyone's good side. Truth and justice are not cliches.

We must together start the long arduous process of getting rid of all those bad laws, regulations, and court decisions. That process will take many years, even decades, but it starts today with you and me.

Standing For The Truth Is Dangerous

There is risk in standing up for the truth. If you have the courage, you will pay a price in an America dominated and controlled by vengeful liberals. Anyone who stands for the truth in these difficult times where the truth is hated so much, will be persecuted. But if we don't stand, our country will fall.

Great basketball coaches who take over struggling teams that have lost their way will typically say to the players, "We are going back to the basics." And the coach will have them go back to the fundamentals that made them great at one time. They find themselves working harder than they've ever worked, but it's what they have to do to survive and become great again. This is true for basketball, football, boxing, and any sport.

Like many great athletic teams, America lost its way, and now it's time to go back to our roots. We must learn to think and behave like our founding fathers. We must have the same kind of independent and clear thinking they had when America was founded. It will not be easy to capture that kind of thought process again, but we must if we are to survive and become great again.

I do believe it is possible for America to survive and to shine brightly in the world again, but if that's going to happen, we need a miracle. America must be reborn.

I think God just answered our prayers. It's no coincidence that against all odds Donald J. Trump is back as our 47th President. Thank you God!

APPENDIX: HOW CAN PEOPLE BE BLIND TO THE TRUTH?

How can people be blind to obvious black and white truths?

How can someone deny the simplest and yet clearest truths in politics and life, and how can they run with blatant lies as though they are gospel truth?

There is an answer, and it's clear from the Bible, although you might have to read multiple verses to really begin to see what God has told us long ago. For this reason, I want to share these verses to demonstrate how so many people today in America can be so blind to the obvious and deny the truth that is so clear to most people. When it comes to these verses, if you have an argument, realize it's not with me—it's with God.

Matthew 6:33

But seek first the kingdom of God and his righteousness, and all these things will be added to you.

Matthew 13:13

This is why I speak to them in parables, because seeing they do not see, and hearing they do not hear, nor do they understand.

Matthew 13:15

For this people's heart has grown dull, and with their ears they can barely hear, and their eyes they have closed, lest they should see with their eyes and hear with their ears and understand with their heart and turn, and I would heal them.'

Matthew 15:14

Let them alone; they are blind guides. And if the blind lead the blind, both will fall into a pit.

Luke 4:18

The Spirit of the Lord is upon me, because he has anointed me to proclaim good news to the poor. He has sent me to proclaim liberty to the captives and recovering of sight to the blind, to set at liberty those who are oppressed.

John 3:19

And this is the judgment: the light has come into the world, and people loved the darkness rather than the light because their works were evil.

John 8:12

Again Jesus spoke to them, saying, "I am the light of the world. Whoever follows me will not walk in darkness, but will have the light of life."

John 8:44

You are of your father the devil, and your will is to do your father's desires. He was a murderer from the beginning, and has nothing to do with the truth, because there is no truth in him. When he lies, he speaks out of his own character, for he is a liar and the father of lies.

John 9:25

He answered, "Whether he is a sinner I do not know. One thing I do know, that though I was blind, now I see."

John 12:40

He has blinded their eyes and hardened their heart, lest they see with their eyes, and understand with their heart, and turn, and I would heal them.

John 12:48

The one who rejects me and does not receive my words has a judge; the word that I have spoken will judge him on the last day.

John 14:15-17

"If you love me, you will keep my commandments. And I will ask the Father, and he will give you another Helper, to be with you forever, even the Spirit of truth, whom the world cannot receive, because it neither sees him nor knows him. You know him, for he dwells with you and will be in you.

1 John 2:11

But whoever hates his brother is in the darkness and walks in the darkness, and does not know where he is going, because the darkness has blinded his eyes.

John 9:39-41

Jesus said, "For judgment I came into this world, that those who do not see may see, and those who see may become blind." Some of the Pharisees near him heard these things, and said to him, "Are we also blind?" Jesus said to them, "If you were blind, you would have no guilt; but now that you say, 'We see,' your guilt remains.

1 Corinthians 2:14

The natural person does not accept the things of the Spirit of God, for they are folly to him, and he is not able to understand them because they are spiritually discerned.

1 Peter 2:9

But you are a chosen race, a royal priesthood, a holy nation, a people for his own possession, that you may proclaim the excellencies of him who called you out of darkness into his marvelous light.

Ephesians 5:8

For at one time you were darkness, but now you are light in the Lord. Walk as children of light

Zephaniah 1:17

I will bring distress on mankind, so that they shall walk like the blind, because they have sinned against the Lord; their blood shall be poured out like dust, and their flesh like dung.

Acts 26:18

To open their eyes, so that they may turn from darkness to light and from the power of Satan to God, that they may receive forgiveness of sins and a place among those who are sanctified by faith in me.'

Psalm 119:18

Open my eyes, that I may behold wondrous things out of your law.

2 Corinthians 4:6

For God, who said, "Let light shine out of darkness," has shone in our hearts to give the light of the knowledge of the glory of God in the face of Jesus Christ.

2 Corinthians 4:3-4

And even if our gospel is veiled, it is veiled only to those who are perishing. In their case the god of this world has blinded the minds of the unbelievers, to keep them from seeing the light of the gospel of the glory of Christ, who is the image of God.

2 Corinthians 11:14

And no wonder, for even Satan disguises himself as an angel of light.

Deuteronomy 29:4

But to this day the Lord has not given you a heart to understand or eyes to see or ears to hear.

Isaiah 35:5

Then the eyes of the blind shall be opened, and the ears of the deaf unstopped.

Isaiah 42:16

And I will lead the blind in a way that they do not know, in paths that they have not known I will guide them. I will turn the darkness before them into light, the rough places into level ground. These are the things I do, and I do not forsake them.

2 Peter 3:3

Knowing this first of all, that scoffers will come in the last days with scoffing, following their own sinful desires.

Isaiah 37:23

"'Whom have you mocked and reviled? Against whom have you raised your voice and lifted your eyes to the heights? Against the Holy One of Israel!

Psalm 146:8

The Lord opens the eyes of the blind. The Lord lifts up those who are bowed down; the Lord loves the righteous.

Jude 1:18

They said to you, "In the last time there will be scoffers, following their own ungodly passions."

Romans 1:28-32

And since they did not see fit to acknowledge God, God gave them up to a debased mind to do what ought not to be done. They were filled with all manner of unrighteousness, evil, covetousness, malice. They are full of envy, murder, strife, deceit, maliciousness. They are gossips, slanderers, haters of God, insolent, haughty, boastful, inventors of evil, disobedient to parents, foolish, faithless, heartless, ruthless. Though they know God's decree that those who practice such things deserve to die, they not only do them but give approval to those who practice them.

Romans 8:7

For the mind that is set on the flesh is hostile to God, for it does not submit to God's law; indeed, it cannot.

Romans 11:25

Lest you be wise in your own sight, I want you to understand this mystery, brothers: a partial hardening has come upon.

Romans 8:7-8

For the mind that is set on the flesh is hostile to God, for it does not submit to God's law; indeed, it cannot. Those who are in the flesh cannot please God.

Deuteronomy 28:29

And you shall grope at noonday, as the blind grope in darkness, and you shall not prosper in your ways. And you shall be only oppressed and robbed continually, and there shall be no one to help you.

Colossians 1:13

He has delivered us from the domain of darkness and transferred us to the kingdom of his beloved Son.

1 John 1:6

If we say we have fellowship with him while we walk in darkness, we lie and do not practice the truth.

Psalm 82:5

They have neither knowledge nor understanding, they walk about in darkness; all the foundations of the earth are shaken.

Isaiah 42:7

To open the eyes that are blind, to bring out the prisoners from the dungeon, from the prison those who sit in darkness.

2 Thessalonians 2:12

In order that all may be condemned who did not believe the truth but had pleasure in unrighteousness.

Isaiah 42:18

Hear, you deaf, and look, you blind, that you may see!

Ephesians 4:17-19

Now this I say and testify in the Lord, that you must no longer walk as the Gentiles do, in the futility of their minds. They are darkened in their understanding, alienated from the life of God because of the ignorance that is in them, due to their hardness of heart. They have become callous and have given themselves up to sensuality, greedy to practice every kind of impurity.

Isaiah 43:8

Bring out the people who are blind, yet have eyes, who are deaf, yet have ears!

2 Peter 1:9

For whoever lacks these qualities is so nearsighted that he is blind, having forgotten that he was cleansed from his former sins.

Ephesians 6:11

Put on the whole armor of God, that you may be able to stand against the schemes of the devil.

Isaiah 29:10

For the Lord has poured out upon you a spirit of deep sleep, and has closed your eyes (the prophets), and covered your heads (the seers).

1 Corinthians 1:18

For the word of the cross is folly to those who are perishing, but to us who are being saved it is the power of God.

Hebrews 4:7

Again he appoints a certain day, "Today," saying through David so long afterward, in the words already quoted, "Today, if you hear his voice, do not harden your hearts."

Ephesians 6:10-18

Finally, be strong in the Lord and in the strength of his might. Put on the whole armor of God, that you may be able to stand against the schemes of the devil. For we do not wrestle against flesh and blood, but against the rulers, against the authorities, against the cosmic powers over this present darkness, against the spiritual forces of evil in the heavenly places. Therefore take up the whole armor of God, that you may be able to withstand in the evil day, and having done all, to stand firm. Stand therefore, having fastened on the belt of truth, and having put on the breastplate of righteousness, and, as shoes for your feet, having put on the readiness given by the gospel of peace. In all circumstances take up the shield of faith, with which you can extinguish all the flaming darts of the evil one; and take the helmet of salvation, and the sword of the Spirit, which is the word of God, praying at all times in the Spirit, with all prayer and supplication. To that end, keep alert with all perseverance, making supplication for all the saints.

1 Peter 5:8-9

Be sober-minded; be watchful. Your adversary the devil prowls around like a roaring lion, seeking someone to devour. Resist him, firm in your faith, knowing that the same kinds of suffering are being experienced by your brotherhood throughout the world.

1 John 4:13

By this we know that we abide in him and he in us, because he has given us of his Spirit.

1 John 2:15-16

Do not love the world or the things in the world. If anyone loves the world, the love of the Father is not in him. For all that is in the world—the desires of the flesh and the desires of the eyes and pride in possessions—is not from the Father but is from the world.

2 Timothy 2:26

And they may come to their senses and escape from the snare of the devil, after being captured by him to do his will.

Acts 28:26-27

"Go to this people, and say, You will indeed hear but never understand, and you will indeed see but never perceive. For this people's heart has grown dull, and with their ears they can barely hear, and their eyes they have closed; lest they should see with their eyes and hear with their ears and understand with their heart and turn, and I would heal them.

America The Last Days

The Slaying of a Great Nation

All is Not Lost

Chuck Marunde, J.D.

INTRODUCTION

Experts of all kinds love to forecast America's future by analyzing our past as well as current events, and there's certainly no shortage of experts. They come from Wall Street to tell us where the stock and bond markets are going. In New York and Washington D.C. there are political experts, who prefer to call themselves consultants, on every street corner with as many opinions.

The President has consultants, and of the 535 members of the Senate and House, they all have multiple consultants. Our military branches and our national security agencies all have consultants backed up by massive intelligence staffs.

The main street media has consultants to guide their agendas and to broadcast their prognostications as talking heads. CEOs in America have consultants. The Pope has consultants, as do the mainline Protestant denominations. Everyone wants to know what the future holds for America and for the World.

Here's the problem and my concern. Nearly all the so-called "experts" render their opinions entirely from a secular perspective to the exclusion of any biblical component in their analysis.

INTRODUCTION

Don't jump to conclusions, because this is not a book on theology, and it won't be in the "Christian Book" category. I want you to be aware of the gap between what you are being told every day of your life and what you are not being told that is so critical to a true or comprehensive understanding of America. You won't hear what I share in this book anywhere else, at least I've not seen this kind of explanation, and I think it is very likely that this perspective will change your entire view of the your future and the future of America.

Let's make sure we are defining terms so there is no misunderstanding. The definition of secular is "the exclusion of everything religious or spiritual."

A large percentage of the experts render their opinions from a worldview that says there is no God at all, and a lesser percentage do so with a passionate hatred for God and Christians. Is it not obvious that such a bias will color their agendas and their opinions? Of course it will, but it's much worse than that.

These experts who forecast politics, the financial markets, and International affairs from a secular perspective are wrong far more than they are right. Perhaps one dramatic example of failed secular forecasting will make the point.

We were told by the Princeton Election Consortium, where some of the finest political consultants can be found, that in the 2016 election "Hillary Clinton has a 99 per cent chance of winning the election over Donald Trump." [Source: Clinton to Win]

It's hard to imagine being any more wrong than that. To this day Hillary Clinton and her cohorts cannot believe she lost. You can see that from their expressions and the language they use even three years after the election. In their minds a Trump Presidency was just not possible, not even remotely. Even news anchors at the major networks would burst out laughing when asked if they thought Donald Trump had a chance of getting

INTRODUCTION

elected President. In my lifetime of watching politics for the past half a century (I'm 65 as I write this), I've never seen such arrogant mocking that turned out to be so wrong.

They were so convinced his presidency was impossible and unlikely, their only response after he was elected was that he was not a legitimate President, and he must be removed. The problem was they had no way to legally remove him, and you know how the impeachment turned out.

My point is that these experts who predicted a Hillary Clinton win are some of the best and sharpest minds America has to offer. They had the resources, financial power, and network of multi-billion dollar PACs, at least 5 of the 6 largest media companies, plus most Universities, Think-Tanks, billionaires around the world, the trillion dollar military-industrial complex, and the leadership and control of most of the leadership at our intelligence agencies and Federal agencies. Their interpretation of America and their forecasts of our future were 100% secular.

During President Trump's first term in office, it appeared we were witnessing the implosion of the Democratic Party, which clearly has been guided on devastatingly wrong expert opinions by thousands of the best of the Democratic leadership in America, and that in spite of their impressive resumes and powerful resources.

The Democratic party seemed to stage a resurgence when Biden claimed the presidency, but it was little more than a fleeting lifeline for the beleaguered deep state. We also have ample evidence that millions of votes were fraudulent, so when the democrats reclaimed the White House, it was actually on very thin ice.

Now that Donald Trump is going to reclaim his rightful place as the 47th President, the deep state is about to experience what it truly means to have a stake driven through the heart of a vampire, banishing its grip on power once and for all.

INTRODUCTION

Their persistent secular thinking has not worked out, and that may be the understatement of the century. This may be the clearest proof yet that neglecting the spiritual perspective will, in time, lead to inevitable disaster. You cannot analyze these complicated issues strictly from a political science perspective and hope to possess wisdom. I'm not suggesting you must be a Christian to understand the world in which we live, but ignore God and the spiritual realm, and you'll suffer a huge deficit of knowledge and wisdom that will hinder your ability to understand the future.

Without a spiritual perspective your forecasts of the future will be woefully inadequate. Do you want to know the future? Then pay attention to what the Bible says about the future.

Imagine a man playing golf for 18 holes and believing there is no such thing as gravity or wind or sand traps. Let's say he just doesn't believe those things even exist, and he has no interest in hearing from anyone who wants to persuade him that they do. If he is playing against someone who does believe in gravity and paying attention to windage and sand traps, who would you bet on over the long term? Who would have a better grasp of the golf course? Who would be better equipped to forecast the end of the game?

Expert consultants who don't believe the world has a spiritual realm are like the golfer who refuses to acknowledge gravity and wind and sand traps. The world has certain realities, and refusing to acknowledge them means operating out of a vacuum of knowledge and inevitably from a lack of wisdom.

The real world is Earth with laws of physics, laws of human behavior, and there is a Heaven and a Hell, a God and a Satan. There is good and there is evil. Deny the reality of the world we live in, and any vision you have for America's future will rest on dangerously incomplete information.

INTRODUCTION

This book bridges the vast divide between those who speak only from the secular side and those who speak only from the theological perspective. Granted, there are a few excellent books that would seem at first blush to bridge the gap, and I'm speaking of books written by Christians who have great knowledge and experience and live and breathe the world of politics and business.

These are excellent reads, but they lack any truly helpful spiritual analysis, and I'll tell you why. None of them apply the wisdom or prophesies of the Bible to America's future in a meaningful way. In their defense, that is not the intended purpose of their books on politics, business, and foreign affairs. Their books focus on the secular perspective, although these authors acknowledge God. However, if you leave God and his written prophesies out of the equation of the future of the world, understanding the world will be virtually impossible.

I want to emphasize that this book is not primarily a book about religion or theology. It is about the world we live in, and in particular about America and where we as a nation are headed. This book makes the argument that in the long term America is in decline, and America is in its last days. This does not mean that a Trump presidency will not lift America to fulfill his MAGA theme. The MAGA theme is enthusiastically embraced by all of us who are patriotic and love the truth and hate lies and deception, but the MAGA movement is a short-term movement. How many years, no one can say. My argument in this trilogy is that we will see many good things happen in the coming several years, and that God heard our prayers and is giving us a reprieve from the evil that has been taking over the world. Realize, however long the MAGA movement helps to raise all the boats with a rising tide across the world, the world still will end according to God's prophecies clearly spelled out in the Bible. There is a coming 7-year tribulation and Armageddon is a real world war that is coming in the

INTRODUCTION

future. In the Bible America is NOT standing with Israel at the very end in God's final judgment. The Bible makes it very clear that Israel stands alone without a single ally, so America is not there at the end. We also know that prophesy makes it crystal clear that evil takes the world down a horrible path to hell, so we can be certain America does not miraculously escape God's judgment and the tribulations of the world.

I believe the evidence of this is beyond a reasonable doubt, and the way I conclude that is by doing something other political analysts have not: Along with the secular knowledge we have acquired about politics, business, and human behavior, I include the history, the prophesies, and the wisdom in the Bible in my database of information and research for a complete analysis of America. Any approach that only includes a secular perspective and leaves out the spiritual will be woefully inadequate to understand where America is headed.

You may be thinking that there are many preachers and teachers of the Bible who have written and taught extensively on the signs of the times and America's future. That would be true, but again there is a wide gap between their most excellent theological knowledge, and practical applications in today's world of politics and business.

In other words, their spiritual insights are great, but if they do not help us answer the difficult questions of our time about living in America and what we should expect in our future, then we are left feeling like we are adrift at sea. And this is precisely how most Americans are feeling today—lost and without a compass.

You see, preachers have spent their lives in the Bible and in the study of theology. I have the utmost respect and admiration for their service, but what the vast majority of good preachers know about politics and business could fit on the head of a pin with room for another million atoms. Of course, a man of faith

INTRODUCTION

preaching the Word of God would logically say that his calling is to preach the Word in season and out of season and not to involve himself in politics and business. I understand the argument, which is to say I'm not being critical of them at all. They are doing precisely what they believe they are supposed to be doing.

The corollary is also true. While there are many sincere, honest, and very knowledgeable men and women writing and talking about the state of America's politics and business, what the vast majority of these people know about the specific end times prophecies spelled out in the Bible in the context of today's current events could also fit on the head of a pin with room to spare.

In other words, the best books and the best of the talking heads forecasting America's future are either entirely secular (and anti-God), or so theological that they leave a giant gap between the average person's understanding of spiritual matters and the real world where Americans live and work every day.

On both sides, there are people who range from reasonable thinkers on one end to off-the-chart deranged on the other end, with everything you can imagine in between. No wonder people joke about the dysfunction of the U.S. Government, and when it comes to Congress, joke that the inmates are in charge of the asylum.

I admit that there are a handful of smart theologians who are able to put today's current events into a proper Biblical context and describe the future scenario with great accuracy, although no one knows the precise timing of such events. These gifted people are still on the religious side of the tracks so to speak, so few people outside the Christian community are hearing their incredibly important messages and how they connect their forecasts with current events. The sad news is there may only be two dozen such teachers in the entire country. I can name most of them.

Unfortunately there are all kinds of religious heretics out there

INTRODUCTION

selling their wares with unbiblical and bizarre prophetic theories. That confuses the daylights out of the average American who is not well grounded in doctrine and cannot discern the fakes from the genuine watchmen.

Do not think for a minute that I am under any false notion that I am smarter than any of the amazing men and women on both sides of the analysis of America's future. But this I would say. I share a perspective that includes the wisdom of both sides and one that has taken me 50 years of observation and study.

What unfolds in this book is a logical and reasonable analysis of America and its future that does not abandon one side or the other, or one worldview to the exclusion of all others. That alone makes this book unique, and it is my humble opinion that if you want the most accurate and the wisest of views of America's future, you must include worldly knowledge and Godly wisdom.

If you want to know exactly what the Bible says will happen in the last days, ask a pastor who is grounded in Bible prophesy. If you want to know what is going on in the world of politics and business, ask an expert in politics and business. But if you want to understand the state of America now in the context of our political and business environment, and if you want to begin to comprehend what the future holds for America, you must bridge the gap between secular knowledge and Biblical knowledge.

I can't promise I can harmonize various bodies of knowledge to be able to accurately forecast our future, but I do hope to prompt you to bridge that gap to view America's future through a clear lens, rather than the rose colored glasses the politicians want you to wear. As you know from the title of this book, it is my strong conviction that we are in a very dangerous place right now, and the future is not what "they" claim it will be.

There are three chapters in this book that will stretch your mind if you are teachable. The three chapters that will rock your life-long paradigm about the future of America are *The Psychology*

INTRODUCTION

of Liberalism, What God Says About Narcissism and Psychopathy, and The Trajectory of America's Final Days.

In *The Psychology of Liberalism* you'll be surprised to learn how professional psychologists describe the people who are destroying America today. You may even be shocked at how precise the profile of very dangerous people is the precise profile of America's leaders today. You will never look at our leaders the same again after reading this chapter.

In the chapter entitled *What God Says About Narcissism and Psychopathy* you'll see that the radical liberals of today were described in the scriptures two thousand years ago. The description is uncanny as you'll see, and God has very specific plans for their minds and their future.

And in the chapter entitled *The Trajectory of America's Final Days* you'll get a very articulate forecast of future events spelled out in the scriptures and connected to actual events in America today. Instead of seeking to tickle your ears with false hope for tomorrow, I will tell you what God says he is going to do. So far, God has never been wrong.

If you only read three chapters in this book, read these three. The way you think about American politics, conservatives, liberals, and where this country is headed in the immediate future will change forever.

I promise you that after reading this book, you will have a clear understanding of what is happening in America and why, and you will know where America is headed.

I can't predict how much time we have left before God steps on the accelerator, but we can thank God for appointing Donald J. Trump the 47th President of the United States.

CHAPTER 1
THE GREATNESS OF AMERICA
AND THE PRECIPICE OF DARKNESS

America was the greatest nation the world has ever known. America was a force for good, the world evangelist of freedom, and the most powerful military force in history. We saved the world from the clutches of an evil dictator, Adolph Hitler, and we oversaw the collapse of the Soviet Union, and the destruction of the Berlin Wall.

With almost 1,000 military installations around the world shielding nations from wannabe conquerors, there has never been such a powerful and generous nation as the United States. The American economy and military are powered by the free enterprise system that is uniquely American. We are a country that was founded upon an absolute right to personal freedom, and a courageous faith in the One True God. It was this amazing American freedom and faith driven by the motivation of great rewards that made America so great.

America has given trillions of dollars to less fortunate peoples on every continent, and American non-profits have provided aide to millions of people suffering from the devastating consequences of hurricanes, earthquakes, floods, and tsunamis.

America became the first world power to embrace the Christian faith and design its governmental foundation upon the freedoms granted by God, which is abundantly evident in our founding documents and in the lives and words of our founding fathers. There is no doubt that this nation has been used by God to promote good and defeat evil all over the planet.

I could go on and on about all the good things America has done since its founding, and the amazing generosity of its people. I could write a treatise about all the great things America has done, but you already know about our greatness.

And you know by the title of this book, I have a different mission here. Reminiscing might boost our serotonin levels and elevate our moods for a time, but now is not the time for sipping on champagne and reminiscing with naiveté. America is in an end-of-days crisis.

We ought not to be re-arranging the deck chairs on a tilting Titanic. There was a more fundamental and greater danger looming on the Titanic, and right now in America while many argue surface issues, there is a much deeper disease threatening the survival of America.

Now is a time of great urgency, and there is little time left. I know it's popular for politicians and motivational speakers to say, "I believe our future is brighter than our past," or words to that effect. The top political consultants advise their clients to be positive and paint a rosy picture of the future if they want to get elected. In order to get elected radical liberals today make all kinds of promises they know they cannot keep, including massive giveaway programs and promises ad infinitum. They know that by appeasing the entitlement mentality, they will get re-elected to office.

I'm here to paint a picture of the state of America today, and the prospects for our future with cold hard facts and my opinions based on history and current events. It's not a pretty picture, but I'm not running for office, so I don't have to lie to you.

I can tell you the truth. How novel is that these days? I have no hidden agendas, and let's be honest, no one who self-publishes a book makes any serious money. I must have something to share with you that motivates me passionately, or I wouldn't bother.

I do, and I hope this book helps you understand that radical liberalism and the evil forces behind liberalism have already taken our country down a long dark path, and the total destruction of America is nearly complete. We might see what we would call a short term comeback, but it's too late to make a big comeback over the long term. The politicians, pitchmen, and salesmen who are telling you otherwise all have hidden personal agendas, and they are either sincerely wrong, or they are intentionally lying to you.

America is in its last days, but do not misunderstand me, because this most certainly does not mean we should give up. We must stand to the last day for what is right and true. We cannot let America fall into darkness and let our children and grandchildren become enslaved by deranged evil psychopaths and narcissists. We need to face reality and not be naive any longer.

Thank God we are seeing the beginning of an awakening in America. Evil is suddenly getting exposed like never before, and there's some kind of new found interest by people all across the world in discovering the truth about a lot of things. Never have we seen this kind of awakening.

America's greatness is past history, and nearly all our institutions and nearly all government and business systems, all educational systems at every level, our healthcare system, our military machine, our largest tech companies, and our own national intelligence agencies have been irretrievably poisoned by liberalism and by its driving force, which is evil itself. Do not be fooled by the deceivers. The end for America is on our horizon now and rapidly approaching. We have little time left.

Let me dispel any misconceptions up front. I do not pretend to have any special dispensation or vision. I write only as a man with a lifetime of practical experience and observations that go back half a century. There's nothing mystical about my thoughts or conclusions. I hope only to help awaken those who have been too long in a deep slumber. Please consider what I say with common sense and a heart in pursuit of the truth.

It took liberal Democrats a century to destroy this country, and it is thoroughly infected at every level. Do not think that after a century of poisoning the executive, legislative, and judicial branches of our government, and after a century of poisoning the people, our culture, our Churches, and our way of life in every possible way that suddenly everything can be turned around and made right. Neither you nor I have a magic wand that can reverse a century of devious destructive work.

Radical liberal Democrats are the driving force that is destroying America, and the closer we get to the end, the harder they press the accelerator, driving us toward total destruction with a madness that they apparently do not comprehend themselves. They seem to have no clue that they are committing suicide themselves and that they are sending their own children and grandchildren on a tragic course.

The undeniable truth is this: America has lost its way. This is perhaps the greatest tragedy in all of human history. A once great force for good is now a divided force dominated and controlled by evil. The poison known as radical liberalism is killing its host.

While the reality that I share sounds quite disparaging, I will also share the positive news and what we can do to defend ourselves and our great nation, and ultimately how we can live a good and victorious life. All is not lost, but it will be if we do not wake up and act accordingly.

Isn't that really the core message of America from its founding —that freedom from slavery is not only possible, but in the spirit of our founders it will be achieved even in the face of evil opposition. We may be living in the Valley of the Shadow of Death, but there is hope and light ahead, and we will be victorious.

C.S. Lewis captured the danger of mentally sick politicians when he wrote this:

> Of all tyrannies, a tyranny sincerely exercised for the good of its victims may be the most oppressive. It would be better to live under robber barons than under omnipotent moral busybodies. The robber baron's cruelty may sometimes sleep, his cupidity may at some point be satiated; but those who torment us for our own good will torment us without end for they do so with the approval of their own conscience.

CHAPTER 2
AMERICA IS A BATTLEFIELD
WITH DEAD AND WOUNDED EVERYWHERE

If good Americans are to understand how to respond to liberalism today, they must first understand liberalism. This is critical, but very few Americans understand liberalism. Why is this understanding so critical?

Special forces never go into the theater of battle without knowing their enemy intimately. In fact, they know everything that can be known about their enemy on each mission, including their enemy's location and travel patterns, their cache of weapons and supplies, and their support and communications systems. In addition, their intel includes information about their friends and family, their sleeping habits, health issues, psychological profile, their Internet activities, their email communications, and their idiosyncrasies.

All possible escape routes of their enemy are known, and no stone is left unturned during the planning phase. They also have their own retreat plan backed up by plan B and plan C. In other words, special forces go in well prepared to attack and defend themselves under any possible scenario. They do not plan, train and prep to fail.

You and I don't think of liberals as our enemies, but radical liberals sure think of you as their enemy if you are a conservative, and if you are a Christian multiply their abhorrence for you by ten. You are not just someone they feel they need to oppose: They truly see you as an enemy they must destroy. This is difficult for us to understand, because it's hard for a reasonable mind to comprehend the radical liberal mind. We don't think like they do, so it is nearly impossible for the untrained mind to anticipate their behavior.

You may not need to know liberals as well as special forces know their enemy targets, but the better you understand the liberal mentality, the better prepared you will be to enter the theater of political and spiritual warfare. And there is a threshold of knowledge and understanding you must achieve, or you will have no clue how to defend yourself.

Said another way, you need to know your liberal opponents if you hope to avoid total defeat and the abolition of all your constitutional rights and freedoms in the years to come. Do you think you really have the option to sit back and do nothing and let the liberals take it all away from you and your children and grandchildren? That's what past generations thought, and that's precisely why we are in this nightmare scenario now with America on the precipice of its final demise.

We call the WWII generation the "Greatest Generation," and they did save the world, but when the men and women came back from the war, they ignored the great threat that was just getting a foothold in America. They went to work, got married, had children, and worked for 30 years at General Motors or the railroad. Some went into business for themselves, and some went to work on their parents' farm. They were hard working, good people, but they were incredibly naive to the danger that was already creating a massive infrastructure to take America down.

In their defense, it would have been almost impossible for a healthy and normal mind to comprehend what was happening. You would have to lie awake at night imagining what evil people would do to destroy your freedoms and America, and virtually no normal person would do that. The greatest generation was focused on taking care of their families, serving in their communities, and making something of their homes and farms. Those who were lying awake at night and plotting were the radicals who wanted to take all these things away from good Americans and enrich themselves.

Unfortunately, our generation has been equally unaware. Apparently it is part of the human experience to wait until one reaches the threshold of pain before one wakes up and starts asking questions. It would appear Americans have reached their threshold of pain, or at least a significant percentage of us have. Now we are asking questions and demanding answers. In other words, we are in pursuit of the truth.

Americans Are Incredibly Ignorant of The Liberal Agenda

Most conservatives are astonishingly ignorant about liberals, how they think, how they became liberals, what their true agenda is, and how to have a conversation with them. Very few understand what works and what doesn't work in dealing with liberals. The vast majority (perhaps 98%) of Americans have no idea how to stop the liberal nightmare destroying our country!

Those who tell us they know how to stop liberalism and who run for congress or the senate don't actually know. The evidence proving that is history itself unfolding during our lifetimes. None of the politicians have put a dent in slowing down the destructive force known as radical liberalism. For decades I have watched sincere politicians just become cogs in the massive bureaucracy designed and managed by liberals and their hidden agendas. I feel like I'm watching kindergarteners sharpening their number 2 pencils to go into a battlefield where the enemy consists of highly trained soldiers well equipped to destroy and kill.

This is why I wrote this book. This book will show you who liberals are and how to deal with them. I use clear understandable language, and I'll show you what makes liberals tick, and what their intentions are. I'll reveal to you what drives them with such passion to pursue their hidden agendas at any cost. You'll discover bits and pieces of these thoughts from other books and independent journalists, but you won't find the unvarnished truth like this. I will write and speak in plain and unambiguous language anyone can understand. I will explain exactly what makes radical minds work and what their hidden beliefs and agendas are.

I will combine what we can learn from the best minds in psychology and match that wisdom with the best theological minds in what many of us call the "last days". I will show you how to do battle with liberals and win.

You are in this war whether you realize it or not. You cannot sit on the sidelines and watch while others fight for your freedoms and stand against the lies and deception of the evil powers under the management of radical liberals. Yes, you could sit by and just watch, but I'm telling you the days of the spectator are over. You will become a casualty if America falls. We all will.

You Are Hereby Called to Service. Consider This Book Your Draft Notice.

How many times have you or a friend said, "We are living in crazy times?" There's no doubt about it; we are living in crazy times, and we are seeing things we never imagined we would see —unbelievable and irrational human behavior. What surprises most people today is that the people who are acting deranged are bold enough to accuse you and me of being insane. Who would have thought the insane would one day be the ones calling the normal people insane?

I've been observing deranged liberals for over a half a century now. I don't know why, but I developed an intense interest in trying to understand human behavior and the irrational behavior of liberals at the age of 14. I'm 65 years old now, and I am deeply thankful that my father brought me into the world of politics at an early age. I only wish my Democratic friends who abhor being associated with radical liberals but still call themselves liberals, had 50 years of intense personal observation under their belts. They would suddenly see with eyes wide open.

As a boy I loved growing up in Alaska and hunting and fishing and living off the land. I would take my dog and my 22 pistol and explore the woods behind our cabin from morning 'till night. It was a wonderful way for a boy to grow up. Of course, I didn't know how good I had it, because I had no standard of comparison. Now I do.

We lived in an area that was unincorporated with no organized local government. That meant no property taxes, no municipal or state income taxes, no zoning restrictions, no building restrictions, no assessments, no bond issues, and no local government. I didn't know what a bureaucrat was in those early years. I grew up truly free.

No one could foreclose on our property, which was free and clear, and no one ever tried to take our guns away with any laws or regulations. No one ever thought of crushing our freedom of speech, and no one got in our face about our beliefs. I was young and innocent, so I thought that's how life would be for the rest of my life. How little did I know about the future!

Everyone who lived in remote Alaska at that time had to be independent. I never questioned why I had to cut and split wood. If we didn't have at least 10 cords of firewood every winter, we would freeze to death. We all knew that without ever discussing it.

If dad and I didn't get enough moose, caribou, Dahl sheep, Salmon, and Cod before winter set in, our entire family would starve to death. There was no welfare office, no food stamps, and no one from any government to save us from the harsh realities of living in Alaska. I never questioned that. I didn't know there was such a thing as victimhood or welfare or entitlements. It was much later in life that I heard about such dysfunctional thinking, and I had some difficulty comprehending why anyone would want to be a victim or a second or third generation welfare recipient. Why would anyone want to roll over and just play dead for the rest of their lives?

My father taught me how to think and how to analyze problems and seek practical solutions. I think my father was a genius. He was a graduate of the School of Engineering at Purdue University, and there wasn't a subject he couldn't discuss intelligently and in great detail. As a boy I would sit quietly for hours listening to his conversations with other men who would come over to talk politics, economics, and International affairs. We didn't have a T.V. or radio station, so that was my entertainment, that and laying on the living room floor browsing the J.C. Whitney catalogue looking at auto parts and tools and gadgets.

My parents never had to tell me I was a boy. I automatically gravitated toward boy things. If you had told me then that someday we would have 100 genders instead of only two, I would have thought you were crazy.

Apparently my father anticipated what was coming. Long before it happened he saw a society of liberals who would go to any length to take away his freedom and his fundamental constitutional rights. He abhorred government excess, government bureaucracies, unfair taxation and burdensome regulations, and he had little patience with the fools who promoted such programs. So he escaped to Alaska and homesteaded 30 acres when that was still possible. He cleared some trees and built a little cabin with a few thousand dollars and his own sweat.

Then he invited my mother to come to Alaska and marry him. Thank God she did. Technically he was my step-father, but I've always thought of him as my real father. We hunted and fished and mostly lived off the land. My father was a smart man, a man of integrity, but he was independent and just wanted to be left alone.

But even in remote Alaska in the '60s and early '70s, we could not get away from liberals who had a host of deep unresolved psychological issues which they constantly projected on the rest of us with their anger and personal attacks. Their solutions always included government programs to save all the victims they could identify in society, starting with us and all the little people.

My first exposure to the dichotomy between humble and hard working conservatives and arrogant and loud liberals was in that little remote Alaskan town. Even though this was over 50 years ago, I can still view it like a video in my head as though it were yesterday. Why do I remember it so well? Because it made a big impression on me as a 14 year old boy.

Her name was Millie Terwilliger. She was the town liberal and head of the local Democratic Party. I can't forget her holier than thou attitude, her arrogance, and how she was so loud in telling the rest of us how government programs were for our own good. The liberalism just oozed out of her demeaning countenance.

Something you'll learn if you study this subject of liberalism enough is that the radical liberals are typically narcissistic, sociopathic, or psychopathic. I'm very sorry to be so blunt so soon in this book, but it's true. Study the definitions in the DSM and examine their behavior, and you can't ignore the match. I'll explain this in detail in the next chapter entitled The Psychology of Liberalism, and you don't want to miss that chapter.

My hope in this book is that I will be able to share with you over 50 years of observing liberals and studying their beliefs and their behaviors, and putting it in context so you can understand this crazy world we live in. When you understand radical liberals, your whole life of trying to understand their irrational behavior and their politics in America will suddenly come into focus, and you'll no longer feel frustrated and defenseless. The greatest source of stress is uncertainty and confusion. I'll help clear those up for you.

CHAPTER 3
THE PSYCHOLOGY OF LIBERALISM
YOU ARE THEIR MORTAL ENEMY

Radical liberals do not think like mentally healthy persons, because they are not. Radical liberals suffer from serious psychological illnesses, which are identified in the DSM (Diagnostic and Statistical Manual of Mental Disorders). Experienced mental health professionals describe these personality disorders in books, professional journals, and in hundreds of Youtube videos.

Of course, I'm not talking about non-radical average Democrats who are honest and sincere people, even if they are unwittingly on board with the irrational and deranged agendas of radical Democrats. As a percentage of the Democratic population, the radical Democrats are surely a very small percentage, but they are in control of the direction of the party and it's policies. That means the largest percentage of Democrats are not radical, and it also tells us that the vast majority of these Democrats are deceived by their own leaders.

I don't know any non-radical Democrats who are in favor of the entire radical Democratic agenda, and I would add that the vast majority of Democrats in America are not even aware of the full DNC agenda or the implications of the radical agenda. Here is the tip of the iceberg of the radical agenda:

Abortion (even after delivery), voting in American elections with no accountability or proof of citizenship, voting by illegal aliens, voting multiple times by the living, voting by the dead, tampering with voting machines to control the outcome, the entire LGBTQ+P agenda, the full panoply of lesbian and homosexual rights, transgenderism, support for the idea that there are 100 genders, shredding of the U.S. Constitution and the Bill of Rights, re-writing of American history on major subjects like slavery and the KKK, elimination of God-given and constitutional rights to privacy and the right to due process as well as the judicial construct that one is innocent until proven guilty, unlimited government power, secret black budgets controlled by a select few in government not including the congress or senate or the President, openly attacking America's law enforcement, particularly police officers and encouraging vicious physical attacks on our officers as well as false accusations of racism to discredit them and take away their authority on the streets, denying war veterans proper medical care by continuing corrupt VA practices than literally endangers veterans' lives, environmental extremism and worshipping nature, supporting and excusing corrupt politicians who use their government positions to make millions of dollars in fraudulent transactions, the dehumanization of people and the elevation of animals and microscopic species equal to or above humans, approval of CIA involvement in MK Ultra and human experiments and drug trafficking and human trafficking, support for the vast pedophilia network in the U.S. and Internationally [Don't tell me the Democratic leadership in America is opposed to pedophilia. They protect all the billionaires and famous and wealthy people in their liberal network who have been accused or suspected of being involved in coordinating or participating in the pedophilia business. Do you doubt the deep state of the evil empire? Just look at how all these evil people like Hillary Clinton just keep getting away with unbelievable crimes year after year. They are protected, and guess who is protecting them?] total confiscation of all guns and ammunition owned by citizens, multi-billion dollar fraud with non-profits to promote political agendas, using U.S. intelligence agencies as weapons against conservatives, spying on the same, using entire segments of society and lying to them intentionally for decades to get their vote, and the list goes on and on.

Parenthetically, I want to share that every single item in this list has been verified and proven. Do not think there is any fluff or conspiracy talk in this list of liberal causes, because there is not. I have followed the trail of evidence for literally 50 years, and 20 years of that as a lawyer, so I understand how to objectively view evidence and filter out the inadmissible evidence, the hearsay, and the unreliable documents. I have diligently followed the bread crumbs my whole adult life. It is not the purpose of this book to prove by a preponderance of the evidence that all these things are true. Many others have done that on each of these items, and that evidence is easily accessed. It's important that we stay on track with the narrow theme in this book if you are to understand how truly sick the radical liberals are.

My point of creating this long list is that these horrendous evils are all supported by radical liberal Democrats, and they endorse every single one of these radical agenda items, but your average American Democrat who is not in a DNC leadership role, does not support most of these, and many do not support a single one of these radical ideas. This is why I often say, and I'll say it again here:

Good citizens who are hard working and love America who were raised Democrat and still are Democrats as adults have been abandoned by the Democratic Party, and their party has been hijacked by radicals. Such good citizens need to realize they are being lied to and deceived, and if they want to live consistent with their deepest beliefs and their faith, they ought to leave today's Democratic Party as quickly as they can.

Haven't you wondered how some of these crazy radicals could lie so much with a straight face, and not only with a straight face, but with apparent total sincerity? Many of them have no compunction at all looking right into the camera and telling bold faced lies that we all know are lies. These people tell lie after lie, and their constituents seem to care not. But the lying is the tip of the iceberg. The depravity behind the lying is almost beyond anything we can imagine.

This book is about America and specifically the implosion of America's greatness (and the consequences for you and me), so I want to take a look at the leaders of America—our politicians. They have been leading our country on a fast track to hell, and the question is how did that happen, and why?

I understand that a book that delivers a positive message about how Americans will overcome these radicals and become great again for decades to come would be much more popular than a book that tells you the cold hard truth. But if I'm right, then don't you want to know? Who wants to live in the dark with a false hope for the future? Maybe it's time to take the red pill.

How many times have you or a friend said recently, "Have these people in Washington D.C. gone crazy?," or words to that effect? To a normal and rational human being, sometimes it does seem like the world has gone crazy, or that our leaders in America have gone crazy. Let me help you out there.

Many of our radical Democrats have, in fact, gone crazy, and I'm about to explain why that is true on a clinical level.

I can tell you that having watched politics very closely for 56 years (I'm 70 now and have been watching since I was 14), I have never seen the insanity I am seeing today, and I'm not the only one. You'll hear this from rational conservatives and Christians all over the country. We know something is terribly wrong, and it's never been this insane and this irrational. As a footnote, I want to say that when I was 14 years old, our generation was much more mature than the teens of today. Not only were we more mature emotionally, we were more practical and had a solid grasp of the good character values that are needed for a productive life. We had to work hard to pull our weight. I took care of all my own needs since the age of 14, including clothing, transportation, school, and later college. I earned the income to do all of that by getting jobs without the help of my parents. I had to learn how to make wise decisions on my own. I don't share that to boast, but to make a valid point that in decades past we were far more mature and equipped to support ourselves much earlier in life than the current generations.

I find it more than fascinating that almost no one in the media wants to touch this subject with a ten foot pole. It is politically incorrect, and unless you are willing to walk around with a target on your chest, it is best left alone. I believe it is important to understand the times in which we live, and we need to try to understand these irrational people and why they behave the way they do.

You don't have to have a Ph.D. in psychology or psychiatry to get a fundamental understanding of what we are facing. Professionals have been sharing their knowledge and wisdom for decades in the DSM, books, seminars, and videos. It's all there if we will just open our eyes and learn. There is plenty of data out there, more than enough medical and psychiatric studies, clinical trials, and surveys. It is the accurate interpretation of knowledge that brings us wisdom, something sorely lacking on the liberal side of the equation.

I've learned that mental health issues and spiritual issues are at the core of the problems in America, and I want to give you some information that will help put much of what is happening in its proper context. Believe me, when you understand how psychologists describe the profile of radical liberals today, you'll be surprised, especially because it does become obvious once you know these things, and once you know the truth, you can never forget it.

The tragedy for America and you and me, and our children and grandchildren, is that very sick people have gotten control of the reins of leadership in this country. They suffer from a variety of mental illnesses, but primarily from personality disorders that clinical psychologists who specialize in personality disorders classify as anti-social, narcissistic, sociopathic, or psychopathic.

Let's look closely at these personality disorders, and keep radical liberals you know in mind. While psychologists like to classify personality disorders into tidy categories, they admit that there is a lot of overlap between them.

> The Antisocial Personality Disorder is characterized by a pervasive pattern of disregard for the rights of other people that often manifests as hostility and/or aggression. Deceit and manipulation are also central features. In many cases hostile-aggressive and deceitful behaviors may first appear during childhood. These children may hurt or torment animals or people. They may engage in hostile acts such as bullying or intimidating others. They may have a reckless disregard for property such as setting fires. They often engage in deceit, theft, and other serious violations of standard rules of conduct. When this is the case,

Conduct Disorder (a juvenile form of Antisocial Personality Disorder) may be an appropriate diagnosis. Conduct Disorder is often considered the precursor to an Antisocial Personality Disorder.

I've heard a psychologist say that the psychopath and sociopath are not defined separately in the DSM, but are considered subcategories of the antisocial personality disorder.

People with Narcissistic Personality Disorder have significant problems with their sense of self-worth stemming from a powerful sense of entitlement. This leads them to believe they deserve special treatment, and to assume they have special powers, are uniquely talented, or that they are especially brilliant or attractive. Their sense of entitlement can lead them to act in ways that fundamentally disregard and disrespect the worth of those around them.

There are several outstanding videos by professionals describing the several types of narcissists, and these videos are so good, I highly recommend you watch them. Dr. Ramani specializes in narcissism, and she has produced many helpful videos on Youtube. She does not specifically discuss politicians as I do here, but if you listen to her descriptions of narcissists, you'll say these descriptions fit the leaders of the Democratic Party to a T. You cannot deny that after watching her videos.

I also highly recommend Dr. Les Carter's Youtube videos on narcissism. Dr. Carter does not talk about politics either, but you'll think your watching training videos for the DNC.

Definitive statistics are unavailable as to how many Americans suffer from narcissism, but estimates range from 6% to 10% to 30%. No one has accurate data, so everyone is guessing, but I would tend to see the personality disorders at the higher end of the estimates. Just consider your own experiences, and narcissism is probably the biggest character flaw in Americans today. It has been baked into our culture by radicalism for decades.

Psychologists tell us that narcissists will never go to a psychologist or any counselor. They also tell us that even if one did go, he or she would feign victimhood so well that your average psychologist would not diagnose him or her as narcissistic. So we simply don't have good stats on the percentage of the population that suffers from narcissism.

Just listen to our national politicians. Can you tell me with a straight face that nearly all of them are not narcissistic! What have we done in this country? How did we elect such dysfunctional leaders? What a tragedy for our nation.

Personality Inventory for Psychopathy The Psychopathic

Personality Inventory (PPI-Revised) is a personality test for traits associated with psychopathy in adults. The PPI was developed by Scott Lilienfeld and Brian Andrews to assess these traits in non-criminal populations, though it is still used in clinical populations as well.

The analysis of the initial 160 items in the psychological study revealed 8 factors:

1. **Machiavellian Egocentricity (ME)**: A lack of empathy and sense of detachment from others for the sake of achieving one's own goals
2. **Social Potency (SOP)**: The ability to charm and influence others
3. **Coldheartedness (C)**: A distinct lack of emotion, guilt, or regard for others' feelings
4. **Carefree Nonplanfulness (CN)**: Difficulty in planning

ahead and considering the consequences of one's actions
5. **Fearlessness (F)**: An eagerness for risk-seeking behaviors, as well as a lack of the fear that normally goes with them
6. **Blame Externalization (BE)**: Inability to take responsibility for one's actions, instead blaming others or rationalizing one's behavior
7. **Impulsive Nonconformity (IN)**: A disregard for social norms and culturally acceptable behaviors
8. **Stress Immunity (STI)**: A lack of typical marked reactions to traumatic or otherwise stress-inducing events

Do you see how these are clearly connected with the behavior patterns of radical liberals today? Everyone is afraid to talk about this, but I am not. This description could be an overlay template on the profile of the Democratic leaders in congress today.

Professor Robert Hare is a criminal psychologist, and the creator of the PCL-R, a psychological assessment used to determine whether someone is a psychopath. For decades, he has studied people with psychopathy, and worked with them, in prisons and in society.

> These people lack remorse and empathy and feel emotion only shallowly. In extreme cases, they might not care whether you live or die. These people are called psychopaths. Some of them are violent criminals, murderers. But by no means all.

I will add, many have gone on to become politicians. You can probably name several off the top of your head right now.

Dr. Hare developed what is now the master list of personality traits of the psychopath, and here is that list:

1. glib and superficial charm
2. grandiose (exaggeratedly high) estimation of self
3. need for stimulation
4. pathological lying
5. cunning and manipulativeness
6. lack of remorse or guilt
7. shallow affect (superficial emotional responsiveness)
8. callousness and lack of empathy
9. parasitic lifestyle
10. poor behavioral controls
11. sexual promiscuity
12. early behavior problems
13. lack of realistic long-term goals
14. impulsivity
15. irresponsibility
16. failure to accept responsibility for own actions
17. many short-term marital relationships
18. juvenile delinquency
19. revocation of conditional release
20. criminal versatility

Doesn't all this begin to answer some big questions you've had for years? You might even consider making your own private list of politicians who clearly have the profile of a psychopath. Such a list can help you predict with a very high degree of accuracy how they will behave in the future and what agendas they promote.

Who would ever have imagined that politics would attract so many narcissists, sociopaths, and psychopaths? I would venture to say no one, and certainly not me. Had you described to me 50 years ago the behavior of the radical Democrats who are running our country today, I would have thought you were making it all up. I would never have imagined that our country would be run by the insane and deranged. And I would never have anticipated that the American voters would sit by and do nothing to stop the insanity. I honestly would have thought you were describing some kind of dystopian fiction novel.

Trump—The Catalyst That Triggered Deranged Liberals

It would seem that President Trump has been a catalyst that broke all the barriers of sanity for the uber radical liberals in America. In plain language, they have gone from ridiculous, irrational, and sick before Trump was elected to off-the-rails insane and deranged and out-in-the-open demonic after Trump's election.

Radicals have gone ballistic and stepped up their attacks on America during Trump's first term, and it is the most obvious turn toward evil we have ever seen. They are no longer holding back. They are desperate and have pulled all the plugs to destroy Trump and America.

The most wanted terrorist in the world was a man named Abu Bakr Al-Baghdadi. We had him but let him go. He was caught and imprisoned by the U.S. military, and released by George W. Bush in 2004. Subsequently, Al-Baghdadi went back to his terrorist roots and became the world leader of a new group of terrorists called ISIS.

When you follow the chain of evidence and testimonies of top military leaders, you learn that ISIS was created under the Bush and Obama administrations and Hillary Clinton played a key role as Secretary of State in securing the creation and propagation of ISIS.

The evidence has been well documented that he plundered, raped, and killed. He kept many sex slaves and tortured, serially raped, and murdered Kayla Mueller. This man was unquestionably one of the most evil people on the face of the earth.

Al-Baghdadi was recently in the headlines again. He was killed by U.S. special forces in Syria by the order of President Donald Trump. Actually, he killed himself and his children with a bomb when our forces found him. What a reprehensible human being! Righteous people do not necessarily rejoice at anyone's death, but they are glad the world is rid of such an evil man. His history is summarized in Wikipedia:

> Baghdadi was directly involved in atrocities and human rights violations conducted by ISIL. These include genocide of Yazidis in Iraq, extensive sex slavery, organized rape, floggings, and systematic executions. He directed terrorist activities and massacres. He embraced brutality as part of the organization's propaganda efforts, producing videos displaying mass crucifixions, sex slavery and executions via hacking, stoning, and burning.

I'm sorry to have to share such graphic history here, but you're about to learn why I had to explain how evil Al-Baghdadi was. What I just described to you about him is all true and is documented history. Factually there is no doubt about Al-Baghdadi's evil past. But how do liberals describe him after his death?

> Abu Bakr Al-Baghdadi, austere religious scholar at the helm of the Islamic state, dies at 48" Joby Warrick, The Washington Post, October 27, 2019.

This wasn't the only liberal defense of Al-Baghdadi. There were others, including a journalist who goes by the name of Max Boot who had to retract a sentence in an article he wrote that shows the deranged thinking of liberals. He wrote, "The assertion that Baghdadi died as a coward [as President Trump had said] was, in any case, contradicted by the fact that rather than be captured, he blew himself up."

The liberals in the media make a hero out of an insane and evil man, and at a minimum they defend this terrorist. What does that tell you about liberalism? Such thinking comes from a deranged mind, and deranged is the perfect word here.

This exact scenario was played out again with the U.S. taking out another long time terrorist from Iran by the name of Qassem Soleimani. This evil man was responsible for 600 American deaths, and it is estimated he was responsible for tens of thousands of murders around the world as a terrorist commander for decades. I don't need to go into great detail on his long terrorist history, but once again after Trump took this evil man out, the liberal Democrats raced to Saleimani's defense. The liberal talking heads in the media have gone berserk defending Saleimani. Whose side are they on? Not yours, and not America's.

If you are a Democrat, and you still call yourself a liberal, I strongly urge you to run from the label liberal, because you are associating yourself with radical liberals who are deranged, and running this country into the ground as fast as they possibly can.

The phrase "Trump Derangement Syndrome" was coined by someone, and it is quite apropos. Liberals were planning Trump's impeachment before he was sworn in as president, and they have not stopped. They broke all kinds of laws creating the Russian Collusion, and after $32 million, about 500 depositions, and over two years of a grossly biased and determined independent prosecutor who had no legal authority to even be appointed and commence an investigation because there was no evidence of a crime, and with a staff of 19 Democrat attorneys supported by 40 FBI agents, along with intelligence analysts, forensic accountants and other staff, all determined to impeach President Trump even though they had no evidence. They ultimately had to admit they had not a single shred of evidence of any Russian collusion with

Trump. The actual collusion it turns out was by the Democrats and their operatives who illegally surveilled President Trump.

Don't forget, Trump and his administration cooperated fully with the Mueller investigation, giving them tons of documents. Even with all that cooperation, Mueller found nothing, despite the liberal media's two year rampage against Trump pretty much every day of the week.

Intelligent conservatives who know true history and economics and politics have learned to put up with uninformed arguments by sincere Democrats (and republicans), but the crisis for America today is not coming from uninformed sincere Democrats. The real crisis in America is the vicious attack by deranged radical liberals who are not just uninformed, they are astonishingly arrogant, and they are blatantly evil and proud of how they conduct themselves.

This is why sincere and honest Democrats need to completely separate themselves from the radical liberals of today. The radical liberals of today in America are evil, and that evil is seen clearly in their agendas and in the way they vote. What is their agenda?

They have no conscience whatsoever when it comes to the murder of 61 million babies since Roe v. Wade in 1973. They have no qualms about illegal aliens voting, because those votes go to Democrats. They apparently lose no sleep over criminal illegals murdering good Americans despite being sent back across the border many times. Today's radical liberal hates America's economic system called free enterprise, and they love socialism, despite its evil beginning and it's repeated disastrous failures throughout history. Radical liberals don't believe in the U.S. Constitution or the Bill of Rights. They believe government is the answer to all our problems, and they believe that personal rights must be subservient to the state.

People who are psychopathic prey ruthlessly on others using charm, deceit, violence or other methods that allow them to get what they want. The symptoms of psychopathy include: lack of a conscience or sense of guilt, lack of empathy, egocentricity, pathological lying, repeated violations of social norms, disregard for the law, shallow emotions, and a history of victimizing others.

I want to walk through this process of considering how liberals are often psychopaths, and I want to do this very carefully and accurately. So I want to describe the behavior of a few very public radical liberals. Let's consider the personalities and behavior of Bill Clinton, Hillary Clinton, Anthony Weiner, Barak Obama, James Comey, John Brennan, Nancy Pelosi, Adam Schiff, Alexandria Ocasio Cortez (AOC), Chuck Shumer, Harry Reid (retired Senator), Al Gore, Gavin Newsom, George Soros, Jeffrey Adam Zucker, and Mark Zuckerberg.

What do all of these people have in common? I'm going to describe a personality profile which fits all of these radicals.

Arrogant, unforgiving, demanding, self-righteous, grandiose visions of self, grandiose notions of what they can accomplish with little connection to reality, no remorse, never entertain thoughts of their own wrongdoing even when they do something blatantly wrong, will lie without hesitation, manipulative, severe control freak, will use people for their own agendas without any concern whatsoever for the harm they cause their victims, believe they know better than anyone how things should work, sincerely feels they can make better decisions for the rest of us than we can for ourselves, believes they are special—more special than anyone else, have no boundaries or limits for themselves either legally or morally but are quick to set boundaries for everyone else, are hypocrites of the highest order, feign insult when they are caught doing wrong and will viciously attack anyone who catches them or accuses them, and they do not perceive that they have political opponents—they

have enemies who must be destroyed if they stand in their way.

Does not this profile sound exactly like our national political leaders on the radical side? Of course it does! Seriously, it doesn't take a rocket scientist to see Pelosi, Schumer, Schiff, and the others in this sick psychological profile.

Psychologists estimate that between 6% and 10% of the American population suffers from narcissism, and then there are the sociopaths and psychopaths. Another estimate I think is more accurate is that as much as 30% of our population suffers from narcissism.

The challenge is that the mental health industry has no data on how many suffer from these terrible personality disorders. Psychologists admit that those with narcissism refuse to see counselors. Period. If you've ever been married to a narcissist, you know they never do anything wrong, and anything and everything that has gone wrong is always your fault, not theirs. They never ever need to see a counselor or psychologist, because there is absolutely nothing wrong with them and never has been.

Welcome to the culture of Washington D.C., the narcissism capital of America.

Allow me to put this in perspective for you. The leaders of our great nation in Washington D.C. certainly have a much higher incidence of narcissism, sociopathy, and psychopathy than the general population. Don't even doubt me on this. If you were to go to D.C. to do research on this topic, you would do better to try and find politicians who were normal, because you have to start with the proposition that nearly everyone there suffers from a serious (not mild) personality disorder. Think I'm exaggerating?

One of the preeminent works on narcissism is a book entitled Narcissism and Politics by Dr. Jerrold M. Post, a Psychologist and Professor at Cambridge University. He felt this sentence was so important, he included it in the first sentence of the Preface to his book:

> **If one were to strip from the ranks of political figures all those with significant narcissistic personality traits, those ranks would be perilously impoverished.**

I estimate that as many as 70% of Democrats at the Federal level in the congress and in the senate suffer from narcissism, sociopathy, or psychopathy. Again, it's easier to name those who suffer from personality disorders than to name those who do not.

Narcissism has become so prevalent in America that the American Psychiatric Association (APA) considered eliminating the narcissistic personality disorder (NPD) from the Diagnostic and Statistical Manual of Mental Disorders (DSM), because some argued it is the new normal.

This book emphasizes the sickness of radical liberals or progressive Democrats, but are there sick politicians on the Republican side or on the Independent side, too? Of course there are, but the percentage is not nearly as high, and you don't even have to look very deep to find the evidence for that. The absolutely insane behavior is in the real news every single day and is coming from the Democratic side by a margin of 10 to 1.

I am assuming you have a connection with real news and not fake news. If you are what has been called a "low information" voter and all you watch is CNN, MSNBC, and ABC, and you actually believe their constant stream of propaganda and lies, you may have trouble getting past this chapter.

I suspect that you know exactly what I'm talking about, and that you can see the logic of what I'm saying. Don't take my word for the descriptions of these personality disorders and how damaging they are to victims—just watch the hundreds of Youtube videos by professionals who describe all of this.

When I suggest that 70% of the radical Democrats in Washington are suffering from serious personality disorders, I'm speculating on the percentage, but I'm not speculating on the profiles or the affect that these people have on their victims. All that has been long established in the mental health industry. I'm just putting this in the context of our political crisis, which psychologists are reticent to do, since the DNC is not their client or their study target. Psychologists are also bound by their own code of ethics, which prohibits them from publicly analyzing people they have not personally observed. They also can not reveal client confidentialities because of privacy laws and the doctor-patient privilege.

Why do we need to study this subject and seek to understand such human behaviors? Because we need to stop saying naive things like, "I don't understand how they can do what they do and go on as if nothing is wrong?" We need to understand what works and what doesn't work with these fools.

And we need to stop being their victims!

CHAPTER 4

WHAT GOD SAYS ABOUT NARCISSISM AND PSYCHOPATHY

OLD ILLNESSES, NEW NAMES

We looked at the secular view of mental illnesses in the last chapter, including the anti-social personality disorder, narcissism, sociopathy, and psychopathy. We now have clear categories and labels with profiles for each of these illnesses. This "science" has dramatically advanced in recent years to define these constructs with surprising precision. Psychologists and psychiatrists are quite proud of themselves, and to some extent, they should be. Many of their studies have helped us to better understand mental illness, and to a lesser extent how to treat mental illness.

But there really isn't anything new under the sun, and the Bible described these illnesses literally thousands of years ago. These are not new mental issues or newly discovered psychological profiles. They are as old as man. Let me give you a big hint right now. These illnesses find their roots in the fall of mankind, in his fallen flesh, the lust thereof, and even before all of this, in the fall of Lucifer himself, who was the very first narcissist and psychopath in all of God's creation.

I'll bet you never thought of Lucifer as the first narcissist and the first psychopath in the Universe. I'm also certain that today's psychologists never thought of Lucifer when they developed their profiles, but when you read the profile of the narcissist and the psychopath, you now will probably say something like, "My goodness, I never even thought about this before, but these profiles are exactly the profile of Satan himself."

Lucifer Was The First Narcissist In Eternal History

Of course, we do need to address the issue of mental illness which is not the result of sin. Can Christians suffer from a mental illness? The answer to that question is yes. There are genetic defects, and there are chemical imbalances, and body organs can and do fail to function properly. There are diseases that attack the body with grave consequences leading to mental incapacity of various degrees. There are also mental illnesses that are caused by physical trauma, so a person could have brain damage as the result of an injury.

My focus in this book is not on any of those categories or anyone who suffers a mental illness as a result of a genetic defect, a disease, or an injury. It should be apparent that my focus in this book is exclusively on the radical Democrats who are clearly and obviously very sick people and who fit well within defined DSM parameters. These are people whose sin is made apparent every day of the week, and they boast of their evil practices.

In other words, we can easily connect the dots from their blatant gross and public sins with their mental insanity. They cannot and do not claim a genetic defect, a disease, or a physical injury. As the Bible says, they have no excuse for their sin, which has led to their mental illnesses, which I will show you is described clearly in the Bible.

With that, let's get back to considering the behavior and personality disorders of the radical Democrats at the Federal level in America. Let's look at the definition of the antisocial personality disorder as defined by the DSM and professional psychologists who specialize in this disorder:

The **antisocial personality disorder** is characterized by a pervasive pattern of disregard for the rights of other people that often manifests as hostility and/or aggression. Deceit and manipulation are also central features. In many cases hostile-aggressive and deceitful behaviors may first appear during childhood. They may engage in hostile acts such as bullying or intimidating others. They often engage in deceit, theft, and other serious violations of standard rules of conduct.

What a stunning and apropos description of liberal Democrats! But wait, it gets better, or should I say worse? I also shared Dr. Hare's master list of personality traits of the psychopath in the last chapter, and here's a quick review of that list which I shared in the last chapter:

> glib and superficial charm grandiose (exaggeratedly high) estimation of self need for stimulation pathological lying cunning and manipulativeness lack of remorse or guilt shallow affect (superficial emotional responsiveness) callousness and lack of empathy parasitic lifestyle poor behavioral controls sexual promiscuity early behavior problems lack of realistic long-term goals impulsivity irresponsibility failure to accept responsibility for own actions many short-term marital relationships juvenile delinquency revocation of conditional release criminal versatility

This is the modern vernacular of psychology, and many of us have gotten comfortable with the DSM descriptions. So now let's go directly to the Bible to see how God describes such behavior and people. To be accurate and careful in proper interpretation, I'll take verses in context one at a time starting with this first important verse:

> **For the wrath of God is revealed from heaven against all ungodliness and unrighteousness of men, who by their unrighteousness suppress the truth. Romans 1:18 (ESV)**

This verse tells us God's wrath is coming against such sin, and while America is not specifically named, if the shoe fits perfectly . . . let's put it on. But this can refer to any nation that becomes as evil as Sodom and Gomorrah. What could cause God's wrath to come upon America? Remember the list of what radical Democrats believe and what is essentially the DNC platform?

This list describes what the Democrats have made of America by hook and by crook over the last few decades. We'll look at this modern description of their beliefs and behavior, and then we'll look at what the Bible says about such behavior and how God tells us he will respond.

> Abortion (even after delivery), voting in American elections with no accountability or proof of citizenship, voting by illegal aliens, voting multiple times by the living, voting by the dead, tampering with voting machines to control the outcome, the entire LGBTQ+P agenda, the full panoply of lesbian and homosexual rights, transgenderism, support for the idea that there are 100 genders, shredding of the U.S. Constitution and the Bill of Rights, re-writing of American history on major subjects like slavery and the KKK, elimination of God-given and constitu-

tional rights to privacy and the right to due process as well as the judicial construct that one is innocent until proven guilty, unlimited government power, secret black budgets controlled by a select few in government not including the congress or senate or the President, openly attacking America's law enforcement, particularly police officers and encouraging vicious physical attacks on our officers as well as false accusations of racism to discredit them and take away their authority on the streets, denying war veterans proper medical care by continuing corrupt VA practices than literally endangers veterans' lives, environmental extremism and worshipping nature, supporting and excusing corrupt politicians who use their government positions to make millions of dollars in fraudulent transactions, the dehumanization of people and the elevation of animals and microscopic species equal to or above humans, approval of CIA involvement in MK Ultra and human experiments and drug trafficking and human trafficking, support for the vast pedophilia network in the U.S. and Internationally, total confiscation of all guns and ammunition owned by citizens, multi-billion dollar fraud with non-profits to promote political agendas, using U.S. intelligence agencies as weapons against conservatives and against citizens, spying on the same, using entire segments of society and lying to them intentionally for decades to get their vote, and the list goes on and on.

Let's look at exactly how God responds to the depths of this kind of depravity in any nation.

For although they knew God, they did not honor him as God or give thanks to him, but they became futile in their thinking, and their foolish hearts were darkened. Claiming to be wise, they became fools, and exchanged the glory of the

immortal God for images resembling mortal man and birds and animals and creeping things. Romans 1:21-23 (ESV)

God will not give his glory to another, so not honoring God is very offensive to God, and to not give thanks is to not acknowledge where our blessings come from, also very offensive to God. As a result of the sin they practice and their behavior and beliefs, God made their thinking futile and their hearts dark. Whether you argue their foolishness and blindness is a natural result of their sin, or it was a direct result of God's wrath doesn't matter to us for purposes of this analysis. What does matter is that they became fools with dark hearts. Notice that these same people claimed to be wise.

I give you radical Democrats. Does that not describe them to a T? Of course, it does. They have become fools with the most outlandish and insane agendas imaginable, and yet they claim themselves to be wise, wiser than all the rest of us, claiming they have the right to control us and determine how we should live.

Therefore God gave them up in the lusts of their hearts to impurity, to the dishonoring of their bodies among themselves, because they exchanged the truth about God for a lie and worshiped and served the creature rather than the Creator, who is blessed forever! Amen. Romans 1:24-25 (ESV)

What is one of the proudest agendas within the Democratic Party? Apart from abortion, it is the promotion of homosexuality, transgenderism, and of course, there is the LGBTQ+P community, and don't forget the P stands for pedophilia.

Notice in Romans 1:24 that God gave them up in the lusts of their hearts to impurity, to the dishonoring of their bodies among themselves. Do you see how sin that God identified in the Bible is so prominent among radical Democrats? How could anyone possibly ask for God's wrath more than they have been doing? But the verses aren't finished describing them, and we are told why God's wrath is coming upon them.

> **For this reason God gave them up to dishonorable passions. For their women exchanged natural relations for those that are contrary to nature; and the men likewise gave up natural relations with women and were consumed with passion for one another, men committing shameless acts with men and receiving in themselves the due penalty for their error. Romans 1:26-27 (ESV)**

If there was any uncertainty in your mind that God was talking about sexual immorality, Romans 1:26 and 27 states that God gave these people over to dishonorable passions in which women exchanged natural relations for unnatural, and men did the same.

For all those radical liberals pretending to be Christians who claim that God is perfectly fine with homosexuality, tell me please how these verses could not be more unambiguous in the prohibition. God hates sexual immorality, and that cannot be explained away by anyone except those whom God has given over to a depraved mind.

If you might have thought God was just a little upset with the thinking and behavior of radical liberals, think again. He already told us he gave them over to futile thinking and to darkened hearts, which of course would have tragic consequences for anyone if that were the end of it. But that is far from the end of God's wrath against such evil people.

> **And since they did not see fit to acknowledge God, God gave them up to a debased mind to do what ought not to be done. They were filled with all manner of unrighteousness, evil,**

covetousness, malice. They are full of envy, murder, strife, deceit, maliciousness. They are gossips, slanderers, haters of God, insolent, haughty, boastful, inventors of evil, disobedient to parents, foolish, faithless, heartless, ruthless. Though they know God's righteous decree that those who practice such things deserve to die, they not only do them but give approval to those who practice them. Romans 1:28-32 (ESV)

My goodness, does not this detailed list of behaviors sound like the radical liberals of today in America? If you haven't been watching or reading real news, you might not realize how accurate this list is. This list of today's depraved behavior was written by the Apostle Paul in about 58 A.D., but it could have been written today to describe the DNC agenda. Do you now understand that this sin is not something new under the sun?

Notice that what secular unbelieving psychologists call mental disorders, God calls sin. Do not miss this point. It is perhaps the single most important truth in this entire book that you've got to internalize if you are to understand what is happening in America.

In this modern era when man thinks he is solving old problems with new technologies and human genius and artificial intelligence, the truth is he is only restating centuries old problems for which the Bible long ago told us the causes and the cures.

Many Christians today believe that we are in the last days, and that the rapture is imminent. They argue there are two primary reasons for such a belief, and they are compelling reasons. First, all the Biblical prophesies of thousands of years that must happen prior to the rapture have all happened as we entered the year 2020. That alone is a pretty big clue.

Second, the sin that is described in the Bible in the very last days is prevalent in America today everywhere, as well as the rest of the world. In addition to the verses we already examined, consider these verses:

> But understand this, that in the last days there will come times of difficulty. For people will be lovers of self, lovers of money, proud, arrogant, abusive, disobedient to their parents, ungrateful, unholy, heartless, unappeasable, slanderous, without self-control, brutal, not loving good, treacherous, reckless, swollen with conceit, lovers of pleasure rather than lovers of God, having the appearance of godliness, but denying its power. Avoid such people. 2 Timothy 3:1-5 (ESV)

Welcome to America circa 2020.

Narcissism and psychopathy started first with Lucifer who fell from Heaven in his rebellion and sin. He then spread his arrogance and pride, his lack of empathy, his hatred, his manipulation, his deception, and his evil agenda throughout the human race. Lucifer thought he could become completely independent of God, and remember that was the temptation he brought to Eve in the Garden, that she could know what God knows and become independent of God. Arrogance and pride at that level is described today as narcissism and psychopathy.

Today that same sin that we can trace to Lucifer and then to the Garden of Eden in the fall of man, and throughout history to the great flood of Noah's time and all the way to today in America reigns supreme in America among our nation's leaders and particularly among radical liberal Democrats.

Today the secularists call it narcissism with variations of that profile, but God called it what it is—sin. The result of that sin was to destroy their minds and God gave them over to the depravity they so desired.

The result is the coming wrath of God Almighty upon this

nation. This is why we can say with such certainty that America is not going to rise from the ashes to become the greatest nation on earth for the next one hundred years. America is doomed, because the Bible tells us God's wrath is coming for the very sins we celebrate as a nation.

CHAPTER 5
LIBERALISM IS DESTROYING AMERICA
FEW LIBERALS COMPREHEND THEIR DESTRUCTIVE ROLE

Liberalism is destroying America, but many democrats who like to say "I'm a democrat, and I'm not ashamed to say I'm a liberal," do not realize how the meaning of liberal has evolved since they first became a liberal democrat.

Today's Honest Rational Democrat is Not A Liberal

Let's be absolutely clear who I'm writing about in this book. I'm writing about today's liberals, who are extreme liberals or radical liberals, or as you will see later, they like to call themselves progressive democrats. I will use the word in today's vernacular. In other words, when I use the word "liberal" I am referring to the liberals of today who are radical liberals.

Most democrats in America are not radical liberals, so if you are a rational democrat and not an extreme left winger or radical, than understand I am not writing about you in this book. You are not a liberal in today's America, and it's important that you understand that and stop calling yourself a liberal.

Many democrats today who are sincere and honest people (as

opposed to the deranged extremists on the left today, like AOC, HRC, Adam Schiff, Nancy Pelosi, Pete Schumer, Reverend Sharpton, Rachel Maddow, Gavin Newsom, and George Soros, are using a definition of liberal that was used back in the days of JFK, not today's definition.

If JFK were alive today, he would be one of the most conservative politicians of the day, and remember he was a classic democrat of the '50s and '60s. You've heard it said that yesterday's democrat is today's republican. That's largely true, but I'll go one step further.

Today's republican is more like yesterday's socialist than yesterday's democrat, and democrats were not originally hard core communists. The radicals of the left are the leaders of the democrat party today. It's really amazing how far our politicians on both sides have willingly dragged our country to the precipice of total destruction.

Let's consider some of the ways JFK was a conservative. JFK was a proponent of reducing taxes to boost the economy, the opposite of today's democrats. He believed in hard work and independence, the opposite of the entitlement and victimhood psychologies that are foundational for all liberal programs today.

JFK was going after criminals in the drug trade and the mafias in Chicago and New York. He was adamantly opposed to Cuba's socialist and communist agenda, had plans to curtail the CIA's far reaching powers that topple governments and even presidents, and JFK was planning to strip the Central Banks and the Federal Reserve of the manipulative financial domination they held over America's hard working middle class.

Many historians believe these are the very reasons he was assassinated. That makes more sense than a lone patsy gunman who was immediately murdered before he could testify. Since then we have seen the same template used many times: a loner with serious mental issues goes on a shooting rampage and immediately before he can testify, he is promptly shot and killed, or suicided later. When you learn to read the signs, you recognize a patsy who was set up.

JFK essentially made enemies of the most powerful people on the planet, people with money and with influence everywhere, even in America's intelligence apparatus. My point in this paragraph is not to review JFK's assassination conspiracy, but to emphasize that America's greatest democrat, JFK, had a whole list of conservative and righteous goals, none of which have survived the liberalism of America. Lee Harvey Oswald was such a patsy.

JFK's political agenda included going after powerful forces destroying America, and while not all of these enemies were liberal democrats, the large majority of those who were his enemies were liberals in his own democrat party, starting with his VP, Lynden Johnson. Presidents ought to be aware of VP's with ambitions of their own.

It's unfortunate that our political system rewards VPs when their President is assassinated. What a motivation, especially when Presidents have a bad habit of selecting a VP who was a political enemy for decades in order to unite the party! Can you imagine the President meeting with his Vice-President and knowing that "this man would benefit greatly if I was assassinated, and essentially all his dreams would come true—power, money, control, fame. By operation of law, he becomes the most powerful and influential man in the world. All that has to happen is for me to die somehow."

My point is that the democrats today who call themselves liberal are not today's liberal democrat. They may be democrats of JFK's day, but not today. The democrat party was highjacked over the past two decades by radical liberals, who prefer to call themselves "progressive liberal democrats." The leaders of the progressive democrats are radical liberals, and they have highjacked the democrat party.

With the stealth of the devil himself, this radical left-wing of the democrat party slowly took over their party agenda, their leadership, and the democrat's policies in congress and in the senate. The decent democrats of the older generation who still call themselves liberal are anything but liberal today—they just don't know it.

Liberalism today is nothing like the liberalism in America four and five decades ago. Today liberalism is extreme, radical, full of seriously deranged people who have lost touch with reality, the rule of law, honesty and integrity, and reasonableness. Liberalism today has crossed the line from any kind of reasonable political philosophy to an irrational and sick psychopathy, and based on any decent human standards or Christian standards, today's brand of liberalism is evil. Period.

Liberalism in America Today is Evil

Let me unpack this idea that liberalism today in America is evil and far beyond anything yesteryear's democrats envisioned. Liberalism is destroying America, and here is a brief summary explaining why this is so important for all of us to comprehend. I can't cover all liberal policies, but I can touch on main agenda items.

- <u>Abortion</u>. Since Roe v. Wade in 1973, over 50 million babies have been aborted, or let's just say it, murdered. This is incomprehensible. What evil is in the hearts of liberals to murder 50 million human beings, and then they rejoice over Roe v. Wade and it's progeny. This is satanic, and anyone who rejoices in these murders is truly deceived. This cause has been at the foundation of liberalism long before Roe v. Wade. To emphasize how evil this liberal agenda is, consider the exposure by Veritas that the abortion fanatics have been selling the body parts of the babies after they are put to death. To a Christian, this is an evil that is incomprehensible. Abortion is the pride of liberalism.

- <u>No Borders & Illegal Aliens</u>. This is a grave danger to America's entire political system of democracy, but few Americans realize the danger. It's easy to understand how grave this danger is when you learn that at least 70% of all immigrants vote democrat. Illegal immigrants vote democrat, even if the democrat is a radical liberal. They don't make any distinction, because democrats invite them in without any restrictions and give them leniency even for those illegal aliens who commit felonies. It was Hillary Clinton who said she wanted to completely eliminate borders and immigration. That would mean an increasing voting percentage for liberals, and the total end of any Republican president in the U.S. This is also why liberals do not want voter ID cards. They want illegal votes, because those votes always go democrat. This kind of dishonesty and total lack of respect for the U.S. Constitution and integrity in voting is so hard for good honest people to understand. How can liberals be so blatantly evil?

- <u>Entitlements</u>. LBJ as President created massive entitlement programs managed by none other than Federal agencies that keep growing, and he began the creation of a monster, Federal obligations that are financially impossible to fulfill. This nation has more debt than it can service, and the unprecedented default of Treasury bonds in on the horizon. Many states, including California ($1 trillion) and Illinois have unfunded pensions that will someday leave retirees without pension checks. U.S. Congressmen and U.S. Senators have spent decades bringing America to the precipice of total collapse with entitlement programs of all kinds. Many retirees are waiting for the day when they are told their social security retirement checks cannot be sent because the trust fund has insufficient funds. As you probably know, President Obama increased our National Debt more than all presidents before him combined. What a powerful way to destroy America, and yet Americans sat by and let him do it. Liberals love entitlements and debt because it helps them control the people and destroy America. And let there be no doubt about their goal of destroying the greatness of America. You could not possibly put together a better plan to do exactly that.

- <u>Victimhood</u>. This is a big one, because the mentality of victimhood reverberates throughout nearly every liberal agenda and program. It is a virus that has infected the minds and hearts of liberals to the point that they cannot think without thinking about victims. To a democrat, everyone is a victim, unless they are a victimizer. America is guilty of horrendous sins against Indians, against blacks, against hispanics, against the Japanese, against Asians, against anyone who is not white, against illegal aliens, against Transgenders, against the LGTBQ community, and all white men are racist pigs. No one in poverty has any responsibility for their situation, because they are victims, period. Drug addicts are not responsible for their drug addictions, because they are victims. Women are victims. Children are victims. Illegal aliens are victims. Criminals are victims. Need I go on? Victimhood is a sick philosophy that is destroying everything that built America.

- <u>Big Government</u>. What is the solution for all those who want an abortion, all illegal aliens, everyone who is entitled, and everyone who is a victim? The answer is always the same for liberals—government programs, and the bigger the better. And let's not pussyfoot around here. The bigger the failure of Federal and State programs to solve everyone's problems, the greater the need to throw more money at the problem. Tell a liberal that their multi-billion dollar program is a tragic failure, because it did not help those they promised it would, but actually created more problems and did the opposite of what they said it would do, and they will immediately and without any embarrassment, tell you the reason their massive program did not succeed is because the program needs more money, a lot more money. The answer is always bigger government, more programs, more taxes on the people to run these programs. The metrics consistently tell us that the programs never work. Apparently no one is listening.

I'm barely scratching the tip of the iceberg on liberal issues that are grotesque failures, but failure has never stopped liberals from doubling down. When their programs fail miserably, you would think they would have an aha moment and begin to wake up, but no, they do not. Instead they double down by insisting that their program would have worked, but we didn't throw enough money at it. Their program needs a lot more money and must be much bigger, and then we'll all see how right they were.

But they are never right about massive government programs solving all our problems. Do I even need to remind you of Obama's and HRC's disaster of disasters, the Obama "Affordable Healthcare Act." Bold-faced lies got it approved by the public and politicians, and there was manipulation with insurance companies. What a massive failure. The truth is, after the Act was law, was that you could not keep your doctor. Premiums didn't go down, they went up. It was anything but affordable! This is liberalism today at it's best, and it is disgusting, and it is evil.

When you begin to understand the secret agendas of evil which are foundational to the entire liberal agenda, you realize that their programs are not really about the people at all. Their decades long campaign to brand the democrat party as the party of compassion is one of the greatest deceptions of this century.

Liberals are not about helping people, they are about helping themselves. When a liberals tells you they are going to help you, run as fast and far as you can, because the liberal translation is

I'm going to lie to you, convince you I'm you're best friend who is here to help you, and then I'm going to secretly stab you in the back, take all your money, take all your freedom from you, and trick you into supporting me and voting for me again and again.

Liberals are destroying America, and if we don't defend ourselves and our freedoms, they will finish what they started.

CHAPTER 6
LIBERALS MURDERED 66 MILLION BABIES
THEY CELEBRATED ROE V. WADE

Since the single most evil decision to slaughter human beings in history, Roe v. Wade in 1973, over 66 million babies have been aborted in the U.S. and over 1.7 billion worldwide. [Source: NumberOfAbortions.com] This is incomprehensible to a normal and decent human being.

What depravity lives in the hearts of liberals to murder 66 million human beings in the U.S. and 1.7 billion worldwide? They literally rejoice over Roe v. Wade and it's progeny. They are not just happy about murdering babies, they are giddy.

Adolph Hitler authorized the murder of between six million and 14 million Jews and the world cannot forget. Hitler has been condemned innumerable times over the seven decades since WWII ended, and his atrocities have become the standard by which all others are measured, although he was not the most prolific murderer in the world.

Many politicians talk a big game, but there were seven who committed their agendas to action. When it comes to murdering human beings, these men stand above all others in history. I would call the men on this list the seven most evil men to have ever lived:

- Mao Zadong (responsible for 26 million deaths)
- Adolf Hitler (responsible for 17 million deaths)
- Leopold II (responsible for 15 million deaths)
- Joseph Stalin (responsible for 10 million deaths)
- Hideki Tojo (responsible for 5 million deaths)
- Nickolas II (responsible for 3 million deaths)
- Saddam Hussein, (responsible for 2 million deaths)

Very soon radical liberals through their greatest victory, which is abortion and Roe v. Wade, will have murdered more human beings in the U.S. alone than Zadong, Hitler, Leopold II, Stalin, Tojo, Nicholas II, and Hussein . . . combined!

Abortionists may already have exceeded these murderous despots if the number murdered by Hitler is closer to six million than 17 million. No one really knows the exact numbers, but no one really knows how many more babies have been aborted either.

Every single day in the United States there are more than 3,657 abortions, and 152 abortions every hour.

As I first typed the numbers of babies murdered and realized the extent of the murderous results of Roe v. Wade and how the mass murders compared with the most evil men in history, I had to pause and just stare into space.

I felt like the wind had been knocked out of me. I felt deeply saddened, shocked, and heartbroken for all the precious lives lost. I had to hold back the tears, because I was in a public restaurant. My mind couldn't seem to comprehend the enormity of the slaughter.

Liberals in America murdered 66 million babies and liberals rejoice, congratulate each other, celebrate with parades and other outrageous public spectacles, and Democrat sheep around the country step in line to say nothing in defense of the precious lives of the unborn, all of whom were uniquely created by God with eternal souls.

> *As my research continued, I realized it's actually much worse than the Google stats would tell us. The worldwide count of babies murdered by abortion exceeds . . . 1.7 billion. Murder by abortion accounts for more deaths than all world despots in history, more than all wars in history, and more than all natural disasters and pandemics in history. My God, what has America done?*

This all shocks the conscience and breaks the heart. But they, meaning radical liberals who love abortion, have no remorse in their hearts at all. None whatsoever.

This is evil, and anyone who rejoices in these murders is truly sick. This cause has been at the foundation of liberalism long before Roe v. Wade. To emphasize how evil this liberal agenda is, consider the exposure by Veritas that the abortion fanatics have been selling the body parts of the babies after they are put to death. To a Christian, this is an evil that is beyond anything we would have thought possible.

With New York in the lead, many states have enacted laws allowing abortions right up to the moment of birth, and some have allowed the mother to end her baby's life after birth.

Yet, abortion is the pride of liberalism. It is their shining victory, and they are so darn proud of Roe v. Wade. Someday Justice Blackmun and the other Supreme Court Justices who voted to approve these murders will answer to God. So will all the radical liberals who have supported, funded, and celebrated these murders. I would not want to be in their shoes on the day of judgment.

There is Good News

The good news is that in his first term as President, Donald Trump appointed conservatives to the U.S. Supreme Court, and since then the Supreme Court actually overturned Woe v. Wade. This was a shock to everyone, and a great cause of celebration by the majority of Americans who consider life to be precious and abortion to be murder.

Trump has made it clear in his campaign for his second term that the Federal Government has no right to be involved in any way with abortion decisions and that states should be sovereign in this area. While Trump is not taking a stand against abortion, he is right in taking the Federal Government out of the picture.

It is no coincidence that Donald J. Trump has won a landslide victory as the 47th President of the United States. If you don't see God's hand in his appointment, you are not seeing what is obvious to the rest of us.

CHAPTER 7

LGBTQ+P AND SEXUAL PERVERSION

HOMOSEXUALITY, TRANSGENDERISM, PEDOPHILIA AND HUMAN TRAFFICKING DEFINES LIBERALS

LGBTQ stands for lesbian, gay, bi-sexual, transgender, and queer. You've seen many of these queer people. They dress in brightly colored outfits or stripes, and some are nearly naked but grossly overweight, and others wear hats too embarrassing for a man of discretion to describe.

If their dress at parades and in front of CNN cameras isn't bizarre enough, their behavior is so bizarre, I don't even know how to describe it. As if this whole scenario isn't "other worldly" strange enough, they've been adding more letters to LGBTQ as more freaks pile onto the largest perverted movement of the century. More letters? That's right. Wait for it...

Do you want to try to guess what LGBTTQQIAAP stands for? I'll save you the mental stress. It stands for lesbian, gay, bisexual, transgender, transsexual, queer, questioning, intersex, asexual, ally, and pansexual.

Perhaps you thought they were done adding initials? Far from it. There's another sub-group of radical liberals who have increased the acronym to 26 letters, but no one can remember all 26 letters in the same order, so others are insisting that it remain simple as an abbreviated acronym. It appears their branding will be done with their mainstay LGBTQ+ with the + sign indicating there are more initials and groups represented.

Are pedophiles part of this panoply of perverts? It would appear they are, although many deny this. There are many articles and videos that prove this, but I'll just reference one here from the online news source called NowTheEndBegins.com. Here's a quote from this article published January 18, 2020:

> **We have been warning you over and over again that the LGBTQ+ Movement is actively working and campaigning to 'destigmatize adult-child sex' at a furious rate and at very high levels. Pedophiles advocacy group called B4U-ACT is holding their annual workshop on April 18th, to 'raise awareness' and support for pedophiles who are now calling themselves MAPs, which stands for Minor Attracted Persons. [Source: NowTheEndBegins on Pedophilia]**

I know, this all sounds so surreal, doesn't it? But you don't have to stretch your mind very much. Just think about what has been promoted at Disney, Hollywood, on Facebook, and Google (the largest purveyor of pornography in the world). What has the main street press covered up? What do politicians get away with in D.C.? What is that deep and dark underworld that we all know exists, and which continues to thrive, and which no one in our government will stop? The answer, of course, is:

Pedophilia

Does the name Jeffrey Epstein awaken uncomfortable feelings for you? Have you ever considered that Epstein made billions from other billionaires, millionaires, politicians in positions of power, government leaders, and those networked in the business and financial worlds? For very large sums of money, Epstein flew them on his private jet (nicknamed the Lolita Express) to his private island where the unspeakable happened regularly.

I don't want to go into too much detail, but understand that pedophilia comes with other baggage, like kidnapping, human trafficking, sexual rape, sexual and physical torture, human sacrifice, the torture of babies and young children so their blood will spike with adrenaline as they scream in pain and fear and so their torturers can drink their blood in a Satanic ritual.

Are you angry yet? Are you beyond disgusted with liberalism? I hope so, because I am, and what is so frustrating is that no one in the U.S. government will investigate and prosecute these evil people! Why? I hope you know. The U.S. government, our intelligence agencies, and our Department of Justice is full of . . . you guessed it—radical liberals (progressives) who don't see anything wrong with pedophilia and all these associated crimes. Many of them appear to be caught up in their own world of sin and blackmail.

Many whistleblowers and victims have come out to testify that the CIA was involved in drug trafficking going back to the days of Bill Clinton as Governor of Arkansas. They even made a movie about it. There are many reliable people who insist that the CIA is the largest drug dealer and drug transporter in the world. There are also many who have gone public on the abuse they suffered under the CIA's MK Ultra Project. Cathy O'Brien is one such victim, and her testimony is very credible. You can watch her testimony on Youtube. If you don't have any knowledge about the CIA's involvement in the mind control projects, I recommend you do a Youtube search for "MK Ultra", and you'll get quite an education.

It is all so disgusting and repulsive, and it's hard to comprehend that this is what liberals have done to America. Honestly, how does any decent Democrat today still stand with these radical Democrats? As I've said elsewhere, radical liberals have highjacked the Democratic Party, and it seems mainstream Democrats are completely oblivious to this reality. If they understood, they would leave the party in a heartbeat.

By the way, don't forget radical liberals are calling themselves "progressives" today. It sounds more polite than liberal or radical liberal or left wing nutcase. That doesn't change a thing as far as I'm concerned. They are still evil.

Progressives are also perverted. They are destroying America as we know it. They are part of a larger movement—an evil movement to destroy all that is good and true. It's truly sad that we have had to go this far down into darkness before people start waking up.

My argument in this book is that it is too late for America. I wish it were not, but it is. We cannot recover the most important and precious things we have lost, because it is not things we lost, but the hearts and souls of human beings.

CHAPTER 8
LIBERALS DESTROYED OUR EDUCATION SYSTEM
FROM KINDERGARTEN TO IVY LEAGUE UNIVERSITIES

The radical liberal agenda took over the entire American education system decades ago. They did this with a multi-prong attack, which is their strategy on every front.

First, they slowly took over the teacher curriculum at colleges and universities around the country. Remember that one of the old war strategies is to focus on long-term goals to take over major industries and sectors. Their timeline is not years or even decades, but generations. They are exceedingly patient and will to devote their lives to a cause that will not bring ultimate victory in their own lifetimes.

The communists and the Saul Alinskys of the world (and the deep evil state) knew they could not simply take over the education departments at teacher colleges overnight. It would take decades, and they did it.

There was a time when teachers in the U.S. were well equipped with an extensive knowledge of American and world history, English grammar, mathematics, and their speciality subject. The focus was on preparing young minds for productive contributions to society in their chosen careers and in their personal lives, too.

But once radical liberalism began implementing a strategy to take over the America education system, they drilled down with great intensity to take control of the entire curriculum and the teaching staffs at every school and college classroom in the country.

Two characteristics that radical liberals have that the vast majority of conservatives have not had in this hundred year war for America's soul (I urge you to read my book, The War for America's Soul) includes extraordinary patience that exceeds their own lifetimes.

The two most powerful warriors are patience and time. Leo Tolstoy

The radical liberals' multi-generational patience to achieve their goals, and their commitment to the cause no matter how long it takes has been a powerful war strategy for liberals. This has been an amazing contradiction in American culture, because everything they have been inculcating in American children in schools, on T.V., in Hollywood and in entertainment has been impatience and entitlement. But below the radar, they believe in patience and long-term planning. In other words, they have been laying the ultimate traps for the unwary.

First, they developed a plan to gain total control of the education departments of America's universities. This would mean inserting Professors into Universities who were themselves radical liberals and who were passionate about promoting radical liberalism by evangelizing and recruiting for the liberal cause.

The teacher curriculums would be developed to thoroughly brainwash students who would eventually become teachers and professors themselves. All this took decades, but they did it. By the time I went through the teacher curriculum to become a high school teacher myself in the 1970s, they had already taken control at nearly all American Universities. The professors in the education department with liberal fools, and their lectures had very little content that would prepare someone like me to be a good teacher.

I'll never forget the nonsense 90% of the professors espoused every single class. They never talked about practical methods to reach students and teach them the three Rs. Instead they engaged us in the classrooms with discussions about "becoming" and about "self-realization" and other esoteric and nonsensical philosophies that took up a lot of time but had no benefit to anyone.

That's been a part of the plan. Distract everyone from the real focus of preparing young minds for a productive future. Evil does not want a future full of productive healthy minds. It wants minds of mush who have no clue what truth is, cannot stay focused, and whose minds have been reprogrammed to lead them and everyone they influence for life to to on a journey that leads anywhere but toward what is true and right, and especially leads anywhere but in the direction of discovering the true God.

No wonder students are not learning anything to prepare them to lead productive lives today. If you haven't studied the incredible collapse of the American education system, you may not realize how deep and wide the radical liberals have worked to destroy the American education system.

Second, they literally re-wrote history books, expunging everything that was inconsistent with their world view, and promoting everything that was. But it was really much more devious, because they distorted history with their manipulation, deletions, and lies. They pushed a philosophy and a theology that twisted young minds with what must be called what it really is—brainwashing.

CHAPTER 9
LIBERALS SHREDDED THE CONSTITUTION
PRIVACY IS COMPLETELY GONE AND THEY'RE COMING FOR YOUR GUNS

Thanks to liberals we can say goodbye to most of our most precious constitutional and God-given rights, such as:

- our right to freedom of religion,
- our right to freedom of speech,
- the right to keep and bare arms,
- the right to privacy,
- the right to due process and an opportunity to be heard,
- the unfettered right to one's own personal and real property with the bundle of rights that come with such property,
- the right against illegal personal search and seizure without due process,
- protection from the seizure of private property and realty without unconstitutional takings and just compensation,
- the fundamental legal right to the presumption of innocence until proven guilty,

- the right not to be taxed excessively and especially without representation,
- the right to exercise our precious right to one-person-one-vote, which has been nearly destroyed by liberals' aggressive promotion of outright fraudulent voting by dead people and multiple voting of the living, and voting by illegal aliens (once again, liberals have absolutely no shame),
- the right to think the way I want to without being assaulted and viciously attacked by the radically insane,
- The right to say "him" or "her" or "male" or "female" and the right to believe that God created only two genders, not 100,
- The right every American was born with—the right to be treated equally with every other American, and not be attacked because I'm a white male by those calling me racist when they are actually the racists,
- The right as a white man to be considered as having equal rights with blacks, hispanics, and Indians,
- The right to an honest state and Federal government that doesn't lie, steal my money and waste it, and spy on me and my family with high tech equipment I helped pay for, and
- The right to NOT have to pay two other families to live on welfare generation for the third generation, killing myself with insufficient retirement and no medical insurance coverage while those I support through a massive welfare and entitlement system live without financial stress and get all their medical and dental covered.

Thank you liberals for destroying as many God-given rights as you can possibly destroy. Let's face it, this list could go on and on, but the incredible damage liberals have done and continue to do to you and me and to America is almost unbelievable if we didn't see it so obviously.

When you start to think about all that radical liberals are doing to us and our great country, it starts to get you angry. They are truly bad and evil people, and they are running our country.

What are you going to do about that?

CHAPTER 10
LIBERALS DESTROYED THE AMERICAN CHURCH
THEIR HATRED FOR CHRISTIANITY AND GOD IS LEGENDARY

I realize it's a bold claim that liberals destroyed the American church, but here's how I connect the dots. American churches, especially mega-churches, have strayed far outside the Biblical reservation of sound doctrine, and that is largely a function of the DNC platform year after year, until now when their platform is so radical and so evil, it is beyond hope. The people in these mega-churches are essentially Democrats in their beliefs.

Granted, there are many causes for pastors of mega-churches preaching heresy today, and many causes for large congregations to turn to heresy. Such pastors seem focused on fame and fortune to the total exclusion of the Gospel of Jesus Christ. Based on their messages and on their lavish personal lifestyles, one would struggle to align their lives with the Bible.

Seriously, a $50 million dollar private jet, a private airport, a massive mansion (and multiple homes), and personal collections of art and other possessions! Add to that sermons that constantly promote the heresy known as the "prosperity doctrine," or the "health and wealth gospel," and it just doesn't take a graduate of

Master's Seminary to think these mega-churches have derailed and gone off a giant cliff in Peru.

And the congregations are just doing what the Bible said they would do in the last days:

For the time will come when they will not endure sound doctrine; but after their own lusts shall they heap to themselves teachers, having itching ears. 2 Tim 4:3

These mega-church pastors are not as sharp as they think they are, and not as sharp as many in their congregations think. They are simply playing their roles as "vessels of wrath" to fulfill end times' prophesies. What they and their followers think is great is actually a sign of the coming of the fiery wrath of a righteous God.

What you ask, is the connection between liberalism and the destruction of the American church? That's actually an easy question to answer, although sometimes the answer to a question doesn't become obvious until you hear the answer.

Liberals, as you must know by now, hate God with a passion that is beyond comprehension. I wrote extensively about that in my book, The War for America's Soul. Anything and everything they can do to turn people away from even the idea that there may be a God will appeal to them. How do mega-church pastors and tens of thousands of members (and millions online) get so far astray? They are willing victims of the liberal notion that you can become your own god.

You see, when you decide that you can determine your own destiny, which is at the core of the prosperity doctrine preached at most mega-churches, you are saying you are in control of everyone on earth, all circumstances on earth, and every business and every government agency that may impact your goals. You are saying that whatever "you can dream, you can achieve," but there's one problem with all of this. You are not God. You are not in control.

I fully realize that their response to this would be something like, "No, we aren't suggesting we're in control of all those people and institutions. We're saying that there is power in positive thinking, power in dreaming, and that a man or woman with vision can achieve whatever they can dream."

Right, and your dream must have power over people and institutions, or you could never guarantee that anyone could do what you have done and achieve your goal of being wealthy and having all you want, which does not include sadness, illness, or any other negatives that destroy or detract from fame and fortune. In other words, you must become God to do all of that and maintain absolute control of the world. In other words, to claim that you and you alone can determine your destiny is to play God.

The theology of liberalism has highjacked American churches, meaning it has raised false pastors and just like the Bible says, people will gather teachers who will tickle their ears.

What has been so shocking of late has been the public defection of mainstream Christian leaders and pastors to the dark side of heresy and apostasy. People we trusted, including many we thought were well grounded in Biblical doctrine, have been defecting in droves. Apart from the obvious heretics who have been heretics for their entire careers, others who we thought were mainstream, like Pat Robertson, have surprised us by endorsing long time heretic and prosperity con artist Kenneth Copeland.

And who among Fundamental Evangelical Christians did not think Pastor Rick Warren to be a wonderful Godly leader in America? Pastor Warren has gone off the deep end with his ecumenical approach to endorsing all kinds of heretics, including his best bud, the Pope. The current Pope is anything but Christian and has said so many anti-God things lately, it is nothing short of shocking. He recently said there is no hell. What? The list of doctrinal problems with the Pope is far too long to review here.

Pastor Andy Stanley, son of famous Pastor Charles Stanley, has gone astray, misleading tens of thousands in his mega-church. After Billy Graham's passing, we learned he never did believe in the inerrancy of the Bible, that he gave the invitation cards from his crusades to local Catholic churches for recruitment, and that he was a long time associate of cults around the world, even claiming them as friends and endorsing their religious beliefs via Graham's ecumenical approach to religion.

Long after his big crusades, many are now realizing it was Graham who started the cheap salvation movement by inviting people to say the words and then falsely telling them they are saved. Billy Graham was best friends with Nixon, the Pope, Muslim leaders, and many evil people who preached gospels other than the gospel of Jesus Christ. Graham never challenged their un-Biblical and un-Godly doctrines and practices. Instead, he endorsed them, one after another.

Bill Graham was perhaps the first mainstream preacher to accept and practice radical liberalism into his doctrine and beliefs and practices. It was the beginning of a massive infection of evil in American Christianity.

Once liberalism is invited into any organization, it infects and spreads like a virus, and ultimately if it is not radically expunged, it destroys from the inside out, and then morphs into a completely different organization, one that promotes the very causes the church stood against. It is a classic strategy of Satan to turn a church from serving Christ to serving satan's evil purposes.

CHAPTER 11
LIBERALS DESTROYED THE NEWS MEDIA
THEIR EVIL AGENDAS TAKE PRIORITY OVER THE TRUTH

It's an amazing thing, but radicals took over the main street media decades ago. Today all main street media T.V., radio, newspapers, and other news outlets are owned by only six corporations, and all six are liberal. The only news network that some people still think is conservative is FOX.

One argument is that the media is an arm of the Democratic Party. Another argument is that the Democratic Party is an arm of the media. Some have legitimately argued that there is a much bigger liberal force, and the Democratic Party and the media are simply puppets of that larger liberal force. I cannot connect all the dots for you with any precision or certainty, but I will say that it is apparent there is some greater force at work.

Of course, we could say the foundational force is evil or satan. Granted, that's beyond doubt at this point. But is there a world organization that dictates what will be done and not done across national boundaries and to heads of state and CEOs of corporations and the Central Banks?

That's hard to prove at this stage of America's decline, but it's hard to imagine that a bunch of disorganized liberals full of hate could slay the greatest nation in history. Nancy Pelosi, Adam Schiff, AOC, Harry Reid (retired), Jerry Brown, Barak Obama, and Bill and Hillary Clinton are not capable of destroying America. It took much more power and money and a massive network.

If there is an authority from on high, it is probably not one organization. It may be a combination of what has been called "the deep state," and "the cabal," and "the Illuminati". It is more likely a combination of loosely connected government leaders, corporate leaders, financial leaders, and wealthy billionaires.

The one common thread or powerfully networked form of communication for all of this is the main street media. Their power to control the news you get, to feed you lies, to burry the truth, to manipulate and to brainwash is unparalleled, especially when they can draw upon the resources of the CIA and our national intelligence agencies. It is well known that the CIA has many people working in media. All of this is part of liberalism, and once again all a part of dishonesty to Americans.

CHAPTER 12
LIBERALS DESTROYED THE U.S. GOVERNMENT
THEY HAVE INFILTRATED THE CONGRESS, THE SENATE, AND EVERY AGENCY

Liberalism has goals that requires a continually growing government power over the people. For the radical liberal Democrats in the U.S. Senate and House, their service is not defined by humble service to their constituents. Not at all. Not even close.

Their service is defined by their personal goals, which focus on fame and fortune, and includes prestige and power. Power is like a drug for those who acquire it, and living in luxury has a driving addictive force that grows as a politician gains power and influence.

As I have shared elsewhere in this book, a psychologist with the CIA once stated that their recruitment efforts preferred those who had sociopathic tendencies. This makes sense since a CIA field agent is trained to lie, cheat, and steal, and to violate the law and people's constitutional rights, and to do all of this without remorse for an entire career.

I think we could say exactly the same thing about those whom the national Democratic Party wants to recruit. They definitely prefer sociopaths, or better yet psychopaths to lead the party into the future. I explain more of the psychology of radical liberalism in the chapter entitled The Psychology of Liberalism. That may be the most important chapter in this book.

As Ronald Regan said, "Government is the problem not the solution." That is true, but liberals turn that upside down by a philosophy that states, "Government is the solution to all our problems." That is a lie straight out of hell.

What is the solution for all those who want an abortion, all illegal aliens, everyone who is entitled, and everyone who is a victim? The answer is always the same for liberals—government programs, and the bigger the better. And let's not pussyfoot around here. The bigger the failure of Federal and State programs to solve everyone's problems, the greater the need to throw more money at the problem. Tell a liberal that their multi-billion dollar program is a tragic failure, because it did not help those they promised it would, but actually created more problems and did the opposite of what they said it would do, and they will immediately and without any embarrassment whatsoever, tell you with a straight face that the reason their massive program did not succeed is because the program needs more money, a lot more money.

The answer is always bigger government, more programs, more taxes on the people to run these programs. The metrics consistently tell us that the programs never work. You might be tempted to think liberal Democrats don't understand the failure of their programs, but they certainly do.

Liberals fully know their programs will fail if their programs are defined as they publicly sell them, but they have a completely different agenda, one hidden from the public and their constituents.

The Democratic Party has promised blacks for decades that they would help them get jobs, competitive salaries, and live in a society where they do not have to suffer from racism. They have done an amazing sales job in the inner cities of Chicago, Detroit, Los Angeles, and New York, clinching the black vote by over 90% in election after election.

After decades of failures, and what is turning out to be manipulation to gain votes, America is seeing a whole new side of the Democratic Party. If you haven't seen the solid historical evidence presented by Dinesh D'Souza in his books and documentaries, you definitely would be well advised to do so.

What he has done that no one else has done is go back into history to show clearly and beyond a reasonable doubt that it was Democrats who were slave owners, and it was Republicans who won the freedom and the vote for black Americans. Not Democrats. Democrats fought Republicans on slavery and freedom for blacks.

As Dinesh D'Souza points out, it was Democrats, not Republicans who founded the Klu Klux Klan. Democrats have re-written the history books and brainwashed Americans starting in elementary school to turn their relationship with blacks completely upside down.

Why? Because they needed the black vote, and they got it with their lies. For decades. And now they've been courting the illegal alien vote so they can stay in office and stay in control indefinitely by tipping votes in their favor forever. Illegal aliens vote Democrat every time, so without any remorse, without any conscience, these Democrats want no borders and want illegal aliens to come into the country en masse so they can have a permanent voting majority. This political philosophy is evil on so many levels, I wouldn't know where to start.

Radical liberals have re-written their evil history right out of the text books, and they have continually and persistently told the public, with plenty of help from their media arm, the story they wanted us to believe.

I think one of the surprises in all of this is that we can be so thoroughly fooled, how history can be re-written, and how generations can be brainwashed. That is what shocks me. You would have to admit that such an agenda is nothing less than horribly evil.

Bigger government gives these liberals more power over the people. A larger military presence around the world gives them billions in slush funds to reward the right people and gain the network support they need. Better funded intelligence agencies gives them more control over Americans' personal information, all the better to control them. By virtue of their powerful positions and control of trillions of Federal dollars, bankers and Wall Street kiss up to them and will do anything for them, as will Hollywood and the entire music industry.

The larger the Federal and state governments, the greater their unbreakable control over the people. And that's exactly what they want. Bigger government is the key to their success in a hundred ways, and their constituents do not matter. The U.S. Constitution doesn't matter to them. Neither does justice. All they care about is power, control, fame and fortune.

I give you the liberal Democratic leaders of today. Beware, they will lie to your face and tell you they plan the exact opposite of what they intend. In the end, you are not their constituent. You are their victim.

CHAPTER 13
LIBERALS DESTROYED THE AMERICAN JUSTICE SYSTEM
WHEN LIES AND MANIPULATION AND HIDDEN AGENDAS RULE THE COURTS

I was a lawyer for 20 years, first as a JAG in the USAF and then as a civilian attorney. I made hundreds of court appearances and hearings, and I prosecuted and defended in many military and civilian trials. To say that the justice system is broken would not be front page news for most Americans, but I would take it a step further. Our justice system is not just broken, it has been destroyed by liberal philosophies.

I witnessed an enlisted member of the USAF with a perfect 12 year record get prosecuted for rape, dishonorably discharged, and sent to Leavenworth prison with a felony conviction, and all this even though he was clearly innocent based on all the evidence presented in the military trial. And by the way, he was black.

The woman who accused him of rape admitted on the witness stand that she was a Las Vegas prostitute, that she was a regular drug user, and that she had accused eight other men of rape during her career as a prostitute.

I heard all of this testimony first hand as I sat in the trial as an observer. She also had numerous inconsistent statements, which would normally have caused the jury to conclude the defendant was innocent.

In a military trial, the jury consists of officers on the base who are themselves charged with prosecuting all crimes within their own units. They charge, and they do not defend. They are told by base commanders that someone must go down when there is a crime, and they don't care who goes down as long as someone becomes that statistic for the record.

I was told by our JAG commander, Colonel Michael Lumbard, that we needed to exceed our previous year's statistic of 52 court martials. Our officer performance reports were not based on esprit de corps, or integrity, or great officer performance, but on pure statistics. The Colonel would review the spreadsheet of statistics when it was time for officer performance reports.

So when this exemplary black enlisted service member was wrongly convicted of rape, I met with the major in charge of the prosecution. I told him, "Sir, you realize an innocent man with a perfect military record was just convicted of a felony, and his life destroyed. After he finishes his five year prison sentence at Levenworth, you know he will be lucky to get a job as a janitor in some podunct town."

I'll never forget the major's response. He sat back in his chair and put his feet on his desk, clasped his hands behind his head and chuckled and said, "Well, we did our job. Ha. Sometimes you win, and sometimes you lose."

That is what made me separate from the USAF.

As I went back into civilian law practice, I found the ethics of lawyers no less disgusting. The vast majority, and I do mean the vast majority, care nothing about truth and justice. They care about money and prestige.

This is all part of the liberal thinking that has taken over our country. And guess who the judges are at the benches? They are the same men who stood on the other side of the bench for most of a career lying and distorting the facts and the application of the law. Where is the wisdom?

I retired from law practice because I was having no positive effect. Neither attorneys nor judges care an iota about truth and justice, and the times I argued that the truth is important, everyone's eyes in the courtroom, including the judges, glazed over. No one cares in our justice system anymore.

Welcome to a justice system that has marinated for decades in a radical liberal society.

CHAPTER 14
LIBERALS DESTROYED HOLLYWOOD AND NASHVILLE
THE MOVIE AND MUSIC BUSINESSES ALL FELL TO LIBERALISM

It's not news to you and me that Hollywood went liberal a few decades ago. Remember the list of sins I compiled that represents the radical liberal agenda? Here is it again as a reminder:

Abortion (even after delivery which is actually murder), voting in American elections with no accountability or proof of citizenship, voting by illegal aliens, voting multiple times by the living, voting by the dead, tampering with voting machines to control the outcome, the entire LGBTQ+P agenda, the full panoply of lesbian and homosexual rights, transgenderism, support for the idea that there are 100 genders, shredding of the U.S. Constitution and the Bill of Rights, re-writing of American history on major subjects like slavery and the KKK, elimination of God-given and constitutional rights to privacy and the right to due process as well as the judicial construct that one is innocent until proven guilty, unlimited government power, secret black budgets controlled by a select few in government not including the congress or senate or the President, the dehumanization of people and the elevation of animals and microscopic species equal to or above humans, worship of the environment, approval of CIA involvement in MK Ultra and human experiments and drug trafficking and human trafficking, support for the vast pedophilia network in the U.S. and Internationally, total confiscation of all guns and ammunition owned by citizens, multi-billion dollar fraud with non-profits to promote political agendas, using U.S. intelligence agencies against conservatives and against citizens, spying on the same, hiring intelligence contractors to create fictitious crimes to illegally attack political opponents, using entire demographic groups, and lying to them intentionally for decades to get their vote.

Hollywood subscribes to all of these. Hollywood went off the deep end long ago, and they have been shoving their radical theology in our faces all this time. I have little patience for Hollywood, and for that reason I'm not going to make a lengthy list of their movies, but I think you probably could do that yourself if you hold to family values, to what is right and good, and surely if you are a devoted Christian.

The music industry has been on the same parallel path with Hollywood, only many musicians have openly admitted in interviews that they gave their souls to Satan in a ceremony, and as you know, many have shows and videos which are openly satanic.

One of my early favorites for her music and her great videos was Shania Twain. I first became aware of her about 25 years ago. Over the years I have enjoyed some of her music and some of her videos. She always seemed like a family oriented woman, especially when you know her early family history and how hard she worked without any entitlement mentality.

I recently had the pleasure of visiting my three adult children who all live in Las Vegas. We went to a Shania Twain show at Caesars. Of course the show was entertaining with quite a light show and loud music that pounded into my chest. And Shania sang many of her greatest hits. All good.

But near the end of the show, she suddenly started joking about drinking and gambling and how good such things were. Of course, she was playing her Vegas audience, right? The crowd cheered.

But here's where Shania went off the rails entirely, as if she wasn't already. She had a song in which two men sat at a table set up to look like a restaurant with candles and an obvious romantic scene. I suspected they were playing the part of two homosexuals, but then they kissed, and the crowd went crazy with giddiness. Shania continued her love song and smiled as big as she could as the crowd showered her with their admiration and approval.

What is Shania doing? She's playing along with the radical liberal culture that pays her so well. She sold out to the liberal cause. This is why I say Hollywood and Nashville sold us out. Liberalism is an evil virus that infects all that is good and poisons it and everyone who plays their part to promote it.

CHAPTER 15
LIBERALS WILL SINK THEIR OWN SHIP TO DEFEAT YOU
THEY CANNOT LET YOU WIN, EVEN IF IT MEANS THEIR OWN SUICIDE

Liberal solutions are the death of America, and much worse. They are the death of freedom, our constitutional rights, our God-given rights, morality, honesty, integrity, faith, religious freedom for Christians, privacy, and financial prosperity.

There is nothing good and righteous that comes out of liberalism. Liberalism is rooted deeply in evil itself, and when you begin to grasp that, everything about liberals and their liberal solutions begins to make sense.

Liberal solutions always involve the government as the ultimate savior for all the victims in America, and they truly cannot help it, but they see victims everywhere. Radical liberals are so driven by their own dysfunctional reality, they sincerely believe that their programs must be approved no matter the cost.

I may say this more than once to make sure this gets through, but radical liberals, aka progressive democrats, will sink their own ship if they have to in order to stop conservatives and especially Christians. They will sacrifice everything for themselves, for other Americans, and for their own children and grandchildren, and if that means taking the ship down, they will do it with a passioned insanity that boggles the mind of a normal person with a healthy mind and heart.

Why would radical liberals sacrifice themselves along with everyone else just to make sure conservatives and Christians do not win the war? Because they are very sick, and that sickness finds roots deep inside their souls. They are evil. Don't ever forget:

Radical Liberals Will Sink Their Own Ship and Sacrifice Everyone

Let's take a lesson from history. We can learn a lot from history In the beginning, and I do mean the beginning, way back in the Garden of Eden, who sunk his own ship with every human being on it just so God wouldn't win? Of course, God did win and wins in the end, but that's another story. Lucifer decided he wanted to become independent of God and become God himself. In his pride he became the first radical liberal with bold-faced lies, manipulation, and deceitful message delivery.

Lucifer was up against Almighty God, and he was desperate to assert his agenda in the Heavens and on earth. He found himself in a serious crisis, and he wasn't winning, so he came at God from another direction. He went after God's greatest creation, mankind. He wasted no time, either, and immediately promoted his liberal agenda in the Garden of Eden, first to Eve and then to Adam, and to all the generations to follow.

Lucifer sank the ship for the entire human race with the sin he got Eve and Adam to commit against God. But don't miss the fact that first Lucifer committed that sin himself. The sin that felled the human race wasn't eating a fruit from a tree. That was symbolic of the sin committed by rejecting God, becoming one's own God by being independent of God and going one's own way.

Lucifer took everyone down on the ship (the entire human race), and he knew full well he was on the ship, too. Compare the liberal agenda to Lucifer's own strategies, and you're eyes are going to suddenly be wide open, and you will feel like you just woke up from a long slumber. The truth does that to a person. The truth sets you free, but it also wakes you up to reality, and that can be painful.

Victimhood Seeking Government Solutions

It is astonishing to mentally healthy people, but the truth is liberals see victims everywhere. This intense victimhood mentality is at the core of who they become as adults. How do people become radical liberals with a deeply ingrained and sincere belief that victims are everywhere and deserve to be made whole?

Have you ever asked yourself that question? Have you ever done the research to find out what creates such deranged behavior, like the kind we see at protests and marches by liberals, and the kind we see from the radical liberals in congress and in the senate?

The Source of Mental Psychopathy

Most liberals have come out of a personal experience from their own childhood that hard wired them as victims. You'll learn more about that from mental health professionals in the next chapter. Because liberals see victims everywhere, they also see bogeymen everywhere, the bad people who are responsible for all the victims.

Radical liberals have emotional switches that get flipped on by specific events or specific phrases. This is astonishingly similar to a master hypnotist who uses an event or words or a song to flip the switch inside a person who has been pre-programmed. It's as though the person under the hypnotic trance has an emotional or mental switch, and once it gets flipped, they go into their automatic and pre-programmed mode. They act out. That's precisely what liberals do at the triggering event or something someone says. An emotional switch gets flipped on, and they can go berserk, depending on the severity of the pain associated with the neurological connection.

Perhaps a simple example will be helpful.

I recently posted a comment on social media about a controversial issue in my rural town in Washington state. My post was quite simple, "I hope other Christians will join me in prayer on this important issue, because I believe there is a lot of spiritual warfare on this." That seems like a fairly innocuous statement to me. Who would be bothered by that somewhat passive statement? Well, some statements can set a liberal off on a wild rage, even when you would think it wouldn't set anyone off.

Shortly thereafter a response was posted by a woman who went into a rant about how I should know that God is not a privileged white man. What? I was amazed at such deranged thinking, because I had never said anything about God being a privileged white man. My statement in its entirety is what I shared above.

This is another example of liberals skipping forward in their mental programming to their key talking points, and "privileged white man" is stuck near the top of their brainwashed psychotic minds. The woman's response to my post may actually have been demonic, and I only mention that because I had mentioned the need for prayer. Who knows where the dividing line is between psychotic liberal and demonic. It's hard to tell, especially when you see someone at a protest screaming irrationally, their face contorted, and their fists clenched as though they are in great pain. You know what I'm talking about. You've seen some of these deranged people on the news or on Youtube videos.

If you are an older white male, did you know that you are the cause of all our nations's woes, and you are to blame for all the bad things that happened to all the victims in America? You must make amends, but since your sins are so egregious, you can never finish making amends to all your victims, according to liberals you must be punished for the rest of your life. There is no forgiveness for you. You should learn to grovel and be mocked forever. You are condemned according to radical liberals.

This is the tip of the liberal mind. Because this kind of thinking is so deeply rooted, or should I say neurologically wired into the liberal mind, all their solutions must address victimhood, and the victims must be made whole.

Of course, the alleged and true victims can never be made whole. If you spent the rest of your life groveling, begging forgiveness, and giving every dollar you earn to recompense the "victims" in society, you will never do enough according to the liberal theology.

Here's the clincher. If the so-called "victims" got free housing, free land, free transportation, free food, free healthcare, free drugs at clinics for the addicted, and if they got monthly checks because they are victims in some fictitious class of protected victims, they can never be made whole. All that giving simply reinforces a fundamental defect in their motivations—it reinforces their belief that they are victims, that they are entitled to all these things from people like you and me, and they are being programmed to believe that dependence rather than independence is good, that being a lazy bum is honorable compared to working hard for a lifetime, that they never have to become responsible for their own decisions because they live by blaming others.

Liberals are living an incredibly unhealthy life. Of course, many liberals are very wealthy, and they have everything they could ever want, and they can do anything they want because of their wealth. But the Bible warns us against the dangers of wealth and how it can lead us into "many a pang." Life is not about who can acquire the most possessions, and they bring us no contentment in life, except on a very temporary level.

This means the liberal solutions must always come from government or through taxpayer sponsored programs. Taxes must be taken from you and me, and put into government programs to help your victims. Let's not get into how much of every dollar the government takes from you to actually reach the so-called victims. After all, there is the need to pay for massive government buildings, utilities and infrastructure, employee salaries plus government benefits and retirement contributions.

Liberal solutions never include help or participation by Churches or the faith community, unless the Church actually is a cult or heretical. They never include discussions about personal responsibility. Personal responsibility and independence are anathema to liberals.

When you dig deep into liberal thinking and solutions over the past 40 years, you find a deep seated aversion to the fundamental rights and freedoms that normal people refer to as "inalienable rights" or "God given rights." Why is that?

First, true liberals hate God with an incomprehensible passion. Second, true liberals have an agenda that requires total control over all people. All their solutions are intended to facilitate their agenda, which is an evil agenda. That agenda has many tentacles, but near the top of that agenda is a one world government, a one world currency, and a government that is 100% secular with humanistic practices, artificial intelligence (not God centered intelligence), and complete control over all citizens.

Their idea of the perfect world is one in which they (the elite) live in the lap of luxury and unlimited wealth, and in which they are in total control. They aspire to fame and fortune even if they have to force their fame upon you and me just like dictators around the world force people to adore and worship them. This is what liberals' ultimate agenda is, and the path to that final "happy" place for them is strewn with the pain and suffering of the ordinary people like you and me.

They only pretend to like you, and they pretend to work to promote your best interests. The truth is, they abhor you because you're in the way to the heaven they intend to create on earth.

Massive Liberal Failures

Just in case you're not a history buff and you haven't been watching liberal programs for the past 50 years like I have, and in case you haven't been connecting the dots, here is an abbreviated list of some of the liberal programs that liberals have forced down Americans' throats. I would point out that all of these programs were incredible disasters for Americans and for the groups the liberals sold on these programs, but . . . what most people miss entirely is that these programs have accomplished precisely what liberals intended.

In other words these programs all had hidden agendas to serve the elite liberals, not you and me, and most certainly not the less fortunate they claimed their programs would help. How the liberals have used minorities like blacks and Hispanics is a long history of lies and deception.

Liberal solutions, even for the poor and less fortunate, always increase the liberals' power, their control over Americans, and for many liberals allows them to get filthy rich off their government connections and the fraud many of them have committed. Most democrats (and republicans) get paid about $175,000 a year in congress, and yet many of them retire with a net worth in the tens of millions, and some in the hundreds of millions. A few, like Bill and Hillary, may have become billionaires, although their only employer was the United States government.

Of course, they typically have off shore accounts and multiple LLCs and untraceable entities to launder their cash and hide their fraud and wealth. The Clintons were bold enough to use the Clinton Foundation to steal billions from the victims in Haiti. It's hard to even imagine how anyone could be so cold and greedy.

Let's look at a short list of the massive failure of liberal programs in no particular order:

- Obama Care, known by the incredible lie as the Affordable Care Act
- In the Sixties urban liberalism was invigorated by LBJ's Great Society attempt to complete the American welfare state. This second phase of liberalism was built around the needs and agenda of racial minorities and public-sector unions. The public-employee unions became the organizational core of the new Democratic Party in New York City.
- Inner city programs of all kinds
- Obama spent the most taxpayer money in U.S. history. He created the most debt in U.S. history. He presided over the most people on welfare, food stamps and disability in U.S. history. And he produced pathetic growth. Obama is the only president to never produce a single year of 3 percent economic growth.
- Chicago is a totally democrat controlled city and has been for decades, and they have the highest murder rate in America.
- California fires, which have killed many people in the last few years and destroyed hundreds of homes, are the direct result of liberalism. Megan Barth recently noted that, "Obama-era regulations produced excessive layers of bureaucracy that blocked proper forest management and increased environmentalist

litigation ... Leftist politicians and judicial activists would rather let forests burn than let anyone thin out overgrown trees, or let professional loggers harvest usable timber left from beetle infestation, or selectively cut timber."
- The unbelievable failures of Los Angeles, San Fransisco, San Diego, and Seattle, all cities controlled by liberals for decades, have high crime rates, record setting homelessness, out of control drug problems, needles all over the streets, and human defecation on the curbs and sidewalks.
- Liberalism's experiments with socialism have all failed in every nation they were tried. Venezuela is only the most recent disaster.
- Liberals have had a tight grip on California for decades, and middle class Americans have been escaping California in record numbers, because of ridiculous taxes, regulations that appear to be designed to put businesses out of business, insane laws that drive business owners and citizens out of the state, and what is nothing short of political insanity by the four ruling families of California for the last half a century: Browns, Newsoms, Pelosis, and Feinsteins.
- Jimmy Carter's liberal revolution was a textbook example of failure in International politics. Many have written books and articles delving into his liberal failures.
- Need I point to Detroit and the total meltdown it experienced after decades of liberal control? Do you remember seeing photos of the empty run-down homes and auto plants? Thank you liberals for another example of what liberal programs do over many years.

- I cannot mention liberal failures without mentioning Secretary of State Hillary Clinton's failure at Benghazi. She was responsible, and then she had the gull to say, "What difference does it make?" No conscience at all. That's the state of mind of radical liberals.
- President Obama increased our Federal Debt more than all previous presidents combined. That is nothing less than shear insanity, especially because there was no progress in the economy or International politics after he was done with us and our money.
- President Obama delivered $150 billion U.S. tax dollars to Iran terrorists on pallets in the dark of night. What patriot would ever do such a thing?
- Lynden Baines Johnson oversaw the greatest military failure in U.S. history thanks to his liberal thinking, however, it must be admitted that both parties have members who are responsible for the constant state of war we have experienced our entire lives.

Liberal solutions, if enacted, will kill your dreams, your happiness, and your life as you know it. This is why you must understand liberals and how they think. If you do not, you will never see your destruction coming until it is too late, and maybe it is already too late for America. Maybe not.

CHAPTER 16
THE TRAJECTORY OF AMERICA'S FINAL DAYS
WHAT IF YOU KNEW THE END WAS NEAR?

It's popular for politicians to give speeches in which they proclaim America's future will be brighter than it's past, that there is a promising future for all Americans, one full of hope and health and prosperity, with a car in every garage and a chicken in every pot.

> There is no cause for worry. The high tide of prosperity will continue. Secretary of Treasury Andrew Mellon, September 1929
>
> Stock prices have reached what looks like a permanently high plateau. Yale Economist Irving Fisher, October 16, 1929

All we've heard in America during the Trump administration is how great the economy and the stock market are doing, and while that's been true, that doesn't mean it will continue. Historically just before a market top, all the so-called "experts" are telling everyone it is time to buy, buy, buy.

Politicians do the same thing by making wonderful promises, and whether they can keep their promises, or whether their promises actually will help people seems to be totally irrelevant.

Why do they make such shallow promises on both sides of the isle? Because that gets them elected, and it gets them re-elected. It always has. People love to hear positive messages of hope, especially when everything around them is going from bad to worse. In fact, the worse things are, the more these positive lies work. People love to be told their futures will be much better than the life they are living now. Who doesn't love a message of hope?

Of course, the deception here is that these very politicians who preach a message of hope so they can get elected and re-elected have no intention of actually helping the voters with anything. They have entirely different agendas. The business of politics is no longer a career that attracts hard working independent people who want to serve others and serve their nation. Politics has become a career that primarily attracts the greedy and power hungry narcissists of our day. It has become a career path to not only power and fame, but also to great wealth. Almost all U.S. Congressman and U.S. Senators who entered office without wealth are able to retire as multi-millionaires, and some have net worths in the hundreds of millions. This should not be so prevalent or likely on a $175,000 a year salary plus benefits.

Of the very small percentage of politicians whose hearts are in the right place, they either have no idea how to actually make the changes that will help people (even if they sincerely think they do), or they realize after a short time in office that they will never have the power to overcome the liberal machine that controls substance and process in Washington D.C. Let me add to this, there are a handful of congressman and senators who are good, who do know how to solve our problems, but they are up against vast opposing forces in both parties, so they cannot turn the tide either.

We can understand why both honest and dishonest politicians all preach a message of unrealistic hope for the future. For politicians what counts is not the truth, and certainly not whether they can keep any of their promises. It's hard to understand for the rational mind, but these narcissists don't feel any obligation to keep their promises, and the narcissistic personality feels no guilt and no empathy for the voters they lie to. You read in the Chapter on The Psychology of Liberalism that these liberals can be quite persuasive and charismatic, but their hearts are as cold as ice.

And here's the kicker. Voters are so naive, they don't care or they don't pay any attention to the lies and broken promises. As long as their politician makes the same unrealistic promises next time, he or she will be re-elected like clockwork. Sometimes I need to pinch my arm to see if I'm still living in America. I feel like I'm a resident in an insane asylum run by the deranged.

Let's face it, everyone needs hope to live and thrive, but what if your hope was disconnected from reality, and contrary to the most relevant and powerful evidence we have ever had? In that case, preaching a positive message with lies about what the future holds is not good. In fact, it is horrible. It's a terrible disservice with very destructive consequences in the long run.

We need to live with hope and there is a positive message we can all grab ahold of, but what we don't need to do is base our lives, our plans, and our futures on lies and deceit and manipulation by people with hidden agendas. Hope based on lies is tragic, but hope based on that which is true, even difficult truths, is the way we all should be living.

What the politicians and the talking heads are leaving out of their analysis of the times we are living in is the spiritual realm. You can talk politics, geo-politics, International law, economics, banking, and everything under the sun until you're blue in the face, but if you leave out the spiritual component, you are leaving out the true cause of evil, and you would be leaving out the greatest insight we can have regarding future events. No analysis is complete without the spiritual or Biblical component. In this next section, I'll include the spiritual component.

America's Destruction

Here's the hard core truth, and I'm sorry to be the bearer of such news, but America does not become great again in the long term. America does not recapture it's glory as the greatest and most powerful nation on earth in the long term. America has lost it's prestigious position as the world leader of righteous causes, as the world leader in spreading truth and freedom, and as the world leader in demanding justice and fairness for all peoples in all nations.

Do not jump to conclusions I have not made here. I specifically used the phrase "long term" to emphasize I'm talking about the long term and not the short term. President Trump is helping America become great again in the short term, but that will not last.

A time is coming in the near future when America will suffer total annihilation and be completely destroyed! I know all of this to be true, and now let me share how I know this with such certainty. No one knows the timeline, but we are precipitously close to the end, and this is how we can know.

The Bible tells us precisely what will happen to the world in the coming years. In thousands of years the Bible has been correct 100% of the time with hundreds of specific prophesies. It has never been wrong—not once. God cannot lie. For this reason alone, we ought to sit up and take the Bible prophesies about our present generation seriously.

You don't have to be a Christian to know that 1+1=2. When Bible prophesy is correct 100% of the time for thousands of years, we ought to ponder the possibility that the next prophesies are likely to come true also.

First, let's take a look at the state of the nation briefly, and then we'll look at what Bible prophesy can tell us about America's future.

There's an amazing description of the state of America in the Bible. Notice the uncannily accurate description of the leaders of the Democratic Party of today, their behavior and their beliefs, starting in Romans 1:18. Not only are their horrendous sins described, it also warns us of the coming of God's righteous wrath.

How Americans have somehow made God's coming wrath totally irrelevant and unimportant is a mystery. Almost no one wants to talk about it, preach about it, or even acknowledge it. These verses would say, "Wake up Americans. You're nearly out of time, God's wrath is coming soon, and eternal condemnation and separation from God is forever." Read these verses from Romans Chapter 1 written nearly 2,000 years ago.

> For the wrath of God is revealed from heaven against all ungodliness and unrighteousness of men, who by their unrighteousness suppress the truth. For what can be known about God is plain to them, because God has shown it to them. For his invisible attributes, namely, his eternal power and divine nature, have been clearly perceived, ever since the creation of the world, in the things that have been made. So they are without excuse. For although they knew God, they did not honor him as God or give thanks to him, but they became futile in their thinking, and their foolish hearts were darkened. Claiming to be wise, they became fools, and exchanged the glory of the immortal God for images resembling mortal man and birds and animals and creeping things. Therefore God gave them up in the lusts of their hearts to impurity, to the dishonoring of their bodies among themselves, because they exchanged the truth about God for a lie and worshiped and served the creature rather than the Creator, who

is blessed forever! Amen. For this reason God gave them up to dishonorable passions. For their women exchanged natural relations for those that are contrary to nature; and the men likewise gave up natural relations with women and were consumed with passion for one another, men committing shameless acts with men and receiving in themselves the due penalty for their error. And since they did not see fit to acknowledge God, God gave them up to a debased mind to do what ought not to be done. They were filled with all manner of unrighteousness, evil, covetousness, malice. They are full of envy, murder, strife, deceit, maliciousness. They are gossips, slanderers, haters of God, insolent, haughty, boastful, inventors of evil, disobedient to parents, foolish, faithless, heartless, ruthless. Though they know God's righteous decree that those who practice such things deserve to die, they not only do them but give approval to those who practice them. (Romans 1:18-32 ESV)

Is it not astonishing how this description sounds like it was written for the DNC and radical liberals today, the LGBTQ+P community, the abortionists, the Globalists, most of our politicians, the millennial socialists, and the sick people in Hollywood and the main street media?

These following verses could have been written by someone today to describe America:

But understand this, that in the last days there will come times of difficulty. For people will be lovers of self, lovers of money, proud, arrogant, abusive, disobedient to their parents, ungrateful, unholy, heartless, unappeasable, slanderous, without self-control, brutal, not loving good, treacherous, reckless, swollen with conceit, lovers of pleasure rather than lovers of God, having the appearance of godliness, but denying its power. Avoid such people. [2 Timothy 3:1-5]

How can Americans be so blind to God's coming wrath? The short answer is that too many Americans have become the fools the Bible speaks about, full of lust, greed, and seeking to be their own independent gods. We have plenty of examples of God's wrath in history, but I guess it's more comfortable to just ignore history than to face the reality it reveals.

> In the days of Noah, God destroyed all mankind in the Flood, except for eight people (Gen. 6-7). Several generations after Noah, He confounded men's language and scattered them around the earth for trying to build an idolatrous tower to heaven (Gen. 11:1-9). In the days of Abraham, He destroyed Sodom and Gomorrah, with only Lot and his family escaping (Gen. 18-19). He destroyed Pharaoh and his army in the sea as they vainly pursued the Israelites to bring them back to Egypt (Ex. 14). He poured out His wrath against pagan kings such as Sennacherib (2 Kings 18-19), Nebuchadnezzar (Dan. 4), and Belshazzar (Dan. 5). [Dr. John MacArthur, Commentary on Romans]

There's no question that America is the Sodom and Gomorrah of the day, the Babylon of sin in the world, and there's no doubt God's wrath is coming. But what does the Bible tell us about America in the last days? Are politicians on the right path when they say America will once again gain its world prominence and Americans will prosper and live happily ever after? Or is there a dark side to our future that we ought not ignore?

We should never ignore what the Bible says. That has never worked out for anyone. So let's briefly look at what the Bible says about these things.

> Look at the fig tree, and all the trees. As soon as they come out in leaf, you see for yourselves and know that the summer is already

near. So also, when you see these things taking place, you know that the kingdom of God is near. [Luke 21:28]

Leading up to Jesus statement in Luke 21:28 is his explanation of what events will occur just before his return. There are several places in the Bible that tell us what events will occur before the rapture. When we pull the verses together, here is what we see:

- False Christs and false prophets arise. Fulfilled.
- There will be wars and rumors of wars. Fulfilled.
- Nation will rise against nation and kingdom against kingdom. Fulfilled.
- There will be increases in famines, pestilences and earthquakes. Fulfilled.
- Lawlessness and immorality will rule. Fulfilled.
- The love of many will grow cold. Fulfilled.
- Christians will depart from the faith giving heed to doctrines of demons. Fulfilled.
- Men will be lovers of self, lovers of money, unholy, proud, boasters, blasphemers, unloving, disobedient to parents, unforgiving, slanderers, without self-control, brutal, traitors, headstrong, lovers of pleasure rather than lovers of God and unthankful. Fulfilled.
- There will be a number of celestial signs that must be completed. Fulfilled.

Here's where this gets interesting. All of the prophesies or the signs we have been given that must occur before the rapture, that is before the return of Jesus Christ to take all the believers out of the world and to Heaven, have already occurred, and we are no longer waiting for something to happen on the calendar. This means the rapture could happen anytime now.

It's hard for modern day Christians to comprehend the historical significance of this day. Christians have been waiting for more than 2,000 years for all the prophesies to unfold like this. They have been diligently watching the signs for many centuries, but in all these years past they knew that the signs had not all been fulfilled, so they continued to look to the future for the rapture, knowing it could be decades before we finally were in the last days.

We are now in the last days by virtue of the fulfilled signs and prophesies, and as Jesus said, "Look at the fig tree . . . when you see these things taking place, you know that the kingdom of God is near."

We are actually living in the days that all the Old Testament and New Testament characters longed to see with great anticipation. They looked to the rapture to be reunited with their Savior more than any other single thing in this life.

Noah, Abraham, John The Baptist, The Apostle Paul, King David, Mary and Joseph, they are all in Heaven now, but can you imagine what they would say right now if they could speak to us. I imagine, they might say something like this:

> Dearest brothers and sisters, do you not recognize the times? Do you not realize that you are living in the last days, the very days that we longed for our whole lives? For generations we talked excitedly about the Lord's return. We told our children about the signs of the last days, and how they could know the rapture was imminent, and they told their children. Yet we never saw it as you will see it. All the signs have been fulfilled, and you are so close. Do not be distracted by the things of this world. Get ready for Christ's return. Prepare your heart. You will see him soon, and it will happen suddenly and many will be surprised.

We are in a unique time in history, because on this side of the rapture we can see events beginning to unfold that are only going to happen after the rapture. In other words, we can look across the divide of time from today before the rapture to see the beginning of events that will only occur after the rapture and during the tribulation. These are events that are prophesied to happen during the seven year tribulation. It's as though we are looking to the horizon to see the unfolding of events that reveal the end is at hand. Do you realize we are at a vantage point right now that no Christians have ever been in? This is another huge indication we are living in the last days.

Here are events that have already happened, and events that are yet to happen after the rapture and during the nightmarish seven year tribulation.

PROPHESIES OF ISRAEL FULFILLED BEFORE THE RAPTURE

1. The Jewish people will be regathered from the four corners of the earth (Isaiah 11:11-12).
2. The state of Israel will be re-established (Isaiah 66:7-8 & Ezekiel 37:21-22). May 14, 1948
3. The Jews will once again re-occupy the city of Jerusalem (Zechariah 8:4-8). June 7, 1967
4. The land of Israel will be reclaimed from its desolation, becoming once again a land of agricultural abundance (Ezekiel 36:34-35).
5. The Hebrew language will be revived from the dead (Zephaniah 3:9).
6. All the nations of the world will come together against Israel over the issue of the control of Jerusalem (Zechariah 12:1-3). The U.S. recognized Jerusalem as the capital of Israel on December 6, 2017.

PROPHESIES OF ISRAEL YET TO BE FULFILLED IN THE TRIBULATION

1. The Arab nations of the world will attack Israel in a coordinated effort to annihilate the state (Psalm 83).
2. Israel will soundly defeat the Arab alliance (Zechariah 12:6).
3. Israel will dwell in security and prosperity (Ezekiel 38:11).
4. A Russian coalition consisting mainly of Muslim nations will invade Israel (Ezekiel 38:1-17). Russia, Iran, and Turkey are conspiring to do exactly this right now.
5. The Russian coalition will be destroyed supernaturally by God (Ezekiel 38:18-23 & Ezekiel 39:1-8).
6. The Antichrist will intervene and guarantee the security of Israel, enabling the Jews to rebuild their Temple (Daniel 9:27).
7. At the end of three and a half years (halfway through the tribulation), the Antichrist will enter the rebuilt Temple in Jerusalem and declare himself to be God (Daniel 9:27, Matthew 24:15-18, & 2 Thessalonians 2:3-4).
8. The Jews will reject the Antichrist, and he will respond with an attempt to annihilate them, killing two-thirds of them in the process (Revelation 12:13-17 & Zechariah 13:8-9).
9. At the end of the Tribulation, when the Jews have come to the end of themselves, they will turn to God and receive Jesus as their Messiah (Zechariah 12:10, Romans 9:27-28, & Romans 11:25-27).
10. Jesus will return and regather all believing Jews to Israel (Deuteronomy 30:1-9).
11. Israel will be established as the prime nation in the world (Isaiah 2:1-4 & Micah 4:1-7).

12. The Lord will bless the Jewish remnant by fulfilling all the promises He has made to Israel (Isaiah 60:1-62:7).
13. The blessings of God will flow out to all the nations through the Jewish people during the Millennial rule of Jesus (Zechariah 8:22-23).

Israel is clearly at the center of Bible prophesy, and prophesy is being fulfilled so quickly and to such an extent that it is undeniable that we are living in the last days before the rapture.

Just as it was in the days of Noah, so will it be in the days of the Son of Man. They were eating and drinking and marrying and being given in marriage, until the day when Noah entered the ark, and the flood came and destroyed them all. Likewise, just as it was in the days of Lot—they were eating and drinking, buying and selling, planting and building, but on the day when Lot went out from Sodom, fire and sulfur rained from heaven and destroyed them all—so will it be on the day when the Son of Man is revealed. [Luke 17: 26-30]

This describes America now! People are going on with their lives as though nothing is wrong, as though they have forever to live in pleasure and do whatever they want, ignoring God, ignoring history, ignoring the fact that we are nearly out of time, and the rapture could literally occur any day now. This is not my prediction that it will happen within X number of days, because no man knows when the rapture will occur. It could be years. We don't know. But it could also be tonight since God has given us all the signs to put us on notice and warn us. By God's own Word nothing remains undone before the rapture can happen.

You see, what politicians and secular philosophers and economists are all leaving out of their prognostications of the future is God and His sovereign plans. God said judgement is coming. He did not say that everyone lives happily forever after. And He gave us signs to let us know when we are in the last days just prior to His coming wrath and judgment.

We are there today!

Here's what the Bible tells us. God's wrath is coming because of sin in the world. Based on history and Bible prophesy and daily news events that constantly affirm the Bible, we are in the very last days. How many days we have left, no one knows. It could be days, and it could be years.

And let's clear something up about President Trump and all the confusion about where he fits within prophesy, and what his role is in the last days of America and the world. The Bible tells us that God is the one who appoints leaders of nations. We know that from Romans 13:1:

Let every person be subject to the governing authorities. For there is no authority except from God, and those that exist have been instituted by God.

And there are many other verses and stories about God seating and unseating government leaders. In addition, we know that God is not just sovereign in the Universe, he is absolutely sovereign. Nothing is outside his sovereign control and guidance. We also know God is timeless, and he knows the past, the present, and the future.

This means there is no question that President Trump has been put into the American Presidency by God. Was it to save souls or save Christianity? Does his appointment mean he is a Christian? The answers are no, no and no.

Donald Trump was appointed to the Presidency to fulfill America's destiny.

Politicians and government do not have the role that God's Church has on this earth and in the destiny of believers in a nation. It is the role and responsibility of Christians (the body of Christ) to stand against evil and be a light of righteousness in the world, to share the good news, and to lead others into salvation, and toward truth.

In other words, the President's job is to guide America to its destiny, and the job of Christians is to pray, stand against evil, and represent God on this earth.

Unbeknownst to President Trump, he is doing many good things for the Kingdom of God, but that's not because he is a Christian or because he has a personal mission statement to represent Jesus Christ as a Child of God. It is because God has placed this mission in his mind and heart, and God is sovereign.

The Bible tells us much more about the end times and the role many nations will play. Few nations are specifically mentioned. It is clear, however, that Russia, Turkey, and Iran play major roles for evil against Israel. Because Vladimir Putin was placed in his position of leadership in Russia by God, Putin must fulfill this tragic destiny for Russia. One might be prompted to say, "Why don't we tell Putin so he can be saved and change the course of his evil plan for Russia?" Putin cannot deny God's prophesy, and Putin would not comprehend what you are saying. Even if he understood what you were saying, he would not believe it. He would probably laugh and mock you. He is most likely one of the "vessels of wrath" that God will use in the last days to fulfill his prophesies, which also means that Putin, like so many others of this day, has been blinded and cannot see these spiritual truths. It is impossible for him to see them.

The Bible says Israel will be attacked and taken over by an evil leader, someone the Jews will worship, thinking he is the coming Messiah. While the U.S. has been a staunch ally of Israel for decades, with the U.S. being the most powerful military force in the world helping to defend Israel, which is surrounded by enemies intent on wiping Israel and it's people off the map, there is no mention of America anywhere in the last days.

America is conspicuously missing in Bible prophesy in the last days of Israel's defeat, survival, and the return of the King to save Israel and defeat the anti-Christ.

Perhaps it would be best if I gave you the exact Biblical description of the future of the world and of America. It's not pretty, and it certainly isn't the claim of so many today that America's future is bright and we will all live happily forever after. Here it is, but I recommend you sit down as you read the actual future of America and the world.

The True Future of America

We start this Biblical prophesy after the rapture and as the tribulation begins. This end times prophetic vision is taken from my book, *The End of All Things is at Hand*.

Peace will be taken from the whole earth and replaced with chaos and hate and violence, and it will be so bad people will be killing each other. The way the verse explains this, people will be forced to kill each other. This is hard to believe, so let's look at the verse:

> ***Then another horse came out, a fiery red one. Its rider was given power to take peace from the earth and to make people kill each other. To him was given a large sword. [Revelation 6:4]***

Then another wave of destruction comes and kills more people by sword, famine, and plague. Based on the numbers of people dying after the opening of the other seals, it would seem likely that millions die this time also. [Revelation 6:5-6]

One-fourth of the people on the earth will die in the war,

which based on today's population, will be about one and a half billion people. [Revelation 6:7-8]

Massive numbers of believers will be martyred. [Revelation 6:9-11]

There will be an earthquake like no one has ever seen on the earth, resulting in massive numbers of deaths. The sun will turn black, the moon will turn red, and stars will fall to the earth. Every mountain and island will be "removed from its place." People will be suffering so terribly, they will call out for the rocks to fall on them and kill them:

> *Then the kings of the earth and the great ones and the generals and the rich and the powerful, and everyone, slave and free, hid themselves in the caves and among the rocks of the mountains, calling to the mountains and rocks, "Fall on us and hide us from the face of him who is seated on the throne, and from the wrath of the Lamb, for the great day of their wrath has come, and who can stand?" [Revelation 6:12-17]*

And then we learn that:

> *A third of the earth was burned up, a third of the trees were burned up, and all the green grass was burned up. [Revelation 8:7] A third of the sea turned into blood, a third of the living creatures in the sea died, and a third of the ships were destroyed. [Revelation 8:8]*

A star called Wormwood will collide with the earth, and one third of all the rivers of the world turn bitter and many more will die. [Revelations 8:10-11]

> *A third of the sun was struck, a third of the moon, and a third of the stars, so that a third of them turned dark. A third of the*

day was without light, and also a third of the night. [Revelation 8:12]

And out of the smoke locusts came down on the earth and were given power like that of scorpions of the earth. They were told not to harm the grass of the earth or any plant or tree, but only those people who did not have the seal of God on their foreheads. They were not allowed to kill them but only to torture them for five months. And the agony they suffered was like that of the sting of a scorpion when it strikes. During those days people will seek death but will not find it; they will long to die, but death will elude them. [Revelation 9:3-6]

And the four angels who had been kept ready for this very hour and day and month and year were released to kill a third of mankind. The number of the mounted troops was twice ten thousand times ten thousand. I heard their number. [Revelation 9:15-16]

A third of mankind was killed by the three plagues of fire, smoke and sulfur that came out of their mouths. [Revelation 9:18]

Even after all the starvation, war, plagues, slaughters, murder, and death,

The rest of mankind who were not killed by these plagues still did not repent of the work of their hands; they did not stop worshiping demons, and idols of gold, silver, bronze, stone and wood—idols that cannot see or hear or walk. Nor did they repent of their murders, their magic arts, their sexual immorality or their thefts. [Revelation 9:20-21]

Is that not astonishing? It's hard to imagine how cold their hearts will be if after all that they have seen and experienced, and all the wrath of God pouring out on them, that they would still want to reject God and worship demons. This is another huge piece of evidence that unless God loves you first, and unless he "predestines" you for salvation, you are lost forever. In other words, man cannot out of his own righteous purposes be saved. We are saved by faith, but even our faith is a gift from God. Yet, God has not chosen to bestow the gift of faith on everyone. If he has given you saving faith, you ought to praise Him forever and ever.

You can't even begin to imagine what this world will be like when the Holy Spirit no longer restrains evil, and when evil is allowed to come up and out of the bowels of the earth to wreak havoc and chaos and evil on the earth. Who will stop them from smashing down the door to your home and plundering and slaughtering everyone in your home? The Holy Spirit is not restraining them anymore. The police? I don't think so. There may not even be any police.

Thank God that as believers we will be saved by the rapture before the tribulation. But there will be three categories of people who will miss the rapture and will suffer and die in the tribulation —those who are not saved and openly reject God, and those who think they are saved, but are not. The third category is those who are not saved at the time of the Rapture, but become part of the saved remnant during the tribulation but must die a horrible death because of their faith.

We are living in a time when millions claim to be Christians. Watered down Christianity is no Christianity at all. When people live for fame and fortune and have made money their God, the God of Salvation is not their God. Their salvation is their money, but that won't save them from the tribulation.

When people say the path is wide and there are many ways to come to God, like Ophra Winfrey and Joel Osteen, they are proclaiming a gospel other than the gospel of Jesus Christ, and they will be in the tribulation. So will millions of their followers who believed them and relied on them instead of the Word of God.

Can you comprehend how bad the tribulation will be? It will be the worst seven years in the history of the entire world. It will be a time of human slaughter by demons and wicked people. The Holy Spirit will no longer protect you from evil. It will be a time of lawlessness, and there will be no police officers to protect you and your home, and there will be no one to protect your wife and your daughters. There will be a war in which over a billion people die. There will be an earthquake that is worse than any in all of world history, and millions will die. It appears a meteor hits the earth and burns up a third of the world, and a third of all the people die. 200 million demons kill another third of all the people on earth.

Your home will not be a safe place. There will be no safe haven for you or your sons or daughters. You cannot even imagine how horrendous it will be during the tribulation, and I'm holding back here, because I'm not comfortable using explicit language to describe in detail the rest of what will happen.

Now is the time to be absolutely certain about your salvation. You do not want to find yourself in the tribulation. Now is the time of salvation, because if you find yourself in the tribulation, it will be too late. Prepare yourself for the rapture now. Make absolutely certain your spouse and your children know Jesus Christ and are themselves saved. Get serious about these things like you've never been serious about anything in your life.

Torture and death are coming in the tribulation. Hell and the Lake of Fire are real. Eternal condemnation will be forever. Do not delay your decision to repent and trust Christ as your savior, and make absolutely certain those you love do not delay. The rapture will happen when no one expects it, and that could be today or any day, and then it will be too late.

And get your priorities right. You still have to work to take care of your family, and you have responsibilities, but keep the right priorities and prepare for the Lord's return, which could come any day now.

Now do you understand the difference between an exclusively worldly or secular interpretation of world events and the same knowledge but with spiritual wisdom included in the interpretation?

The former claims America will be great again and ignores Bible prophesy totally, placing trust in mankind's technological genius, artificial intelligence, and an evolutionary perspective that we are all happenstance and there is little we can do but seek to save ourselves.

The later acknowledges God and His Bible, which has never been wrong in the hundreds of prophesies that have been fulfilled over thousands of years, and applies the prophetic events and current events to read the signs and watch for the return of Jesus Christ in the rapture. The Bible tells us the world comes to a violent end because of God's wrath against sin.

Since America is not mentioned at all in the war to protect Israel, and the Bible says no nation stands with Israel, either America is already destroyed, or America is so weak it cannot stand with Israel in the great war. Regardless, as you can see from the Bible prophesies, God's wrath is coming upon all the world.

Which worldview will you believe? Choose wisely, because the destiny of your soul for eternity is at stake.

CHAPTER 17
DEFENDING AMERICA AGAINST LIBERALISM
A STRATEGY FOR THE 11TH HOUR

Defending America against these deranged radical liberals and their demons isn't really very complicated, but it does take courage and perseverance, both of which seem to be in short supply in America.

Here's a short laundry list of what it takes to defend America. It takes a person who possesses these things, and unless you possess these, you cannot pass them on to the next generation. You cannot impart what you do not first possess.

The answer to all of the radical liberalism being pressed upon our nation and upon our families every day is included in this short list of values and beliefs. You could also say these are the qualities and virtues of a good American patriot:

1. A minimum knowledge of relevant history, and don't simply accept the history that our liberal educators have prepared for us. Seek out long lost history that has been hidden from us.
2. Common Sense.

3. A love of the truth with a passion to pursue truth as long as you live, not just an ephemeral interest in learning the truth on one minor topic.
4. An aversion for lies, distortions, manipulation, and deception (hatred would be a better word here).
5. A genuine desire to do good and help your fellow man with a spirit of service as opposed to an entitlement and victimhood mentality.
6. An appreciation for freedom and political liberty, and a desire to contribute to your nation.
7. A love for free enterprise.
8. An understanding of the dangers of big government.
9. A discernment that does not run from so-called conspiracies, but examines all things from a lens of wisdom.
10. Remember, truth finds its source in God, so pursuing truth ultimately means pursuing God and aligning your life to God's truths.

You may be thinking, "Wow, 16 chapters on the destructive evil power of radical democrats, and one short chapter at the end about how to combat this evil?" Yes, that's correct. You must first understand how prevalent evil is, its source, the history, and how you have been deceived before you can come to the realization that you need to turn away from all those false beliefs and seek the truth.

Comprehending the problem is the greatest challenge, and realizing you've been deceived your whole life is the highest hurdle you can face. That's the hard part, and it's what takes so long. Once you realize the extent of the deception, you will naturally turn to seek out truth and live accordingly.

Once you comprehend what I've shared in the previous 16 chapters, this short chapter flows naturally, and I really didn't need to explain it to you. You would have already figured this out, and could have made this bullet list yourself. I just wanted to help you with this summary to get you headed in the right direction.

What you'll realize, if you haven't already, is that radical democrats don't have the capacity to believe or practice these values and attributes. Remember what I said at the beginning of this chapter? "You cannot impart what you do not first possess."

Democrats cannot impart these righteous values, because they do not possess them. But you and I can share these values with our children and friends, because we do possess them.

I hope and pray you will be a light in the world and a person who spreads the truth and exposes the lies with boldness and courage.

SPIRITUAL WAR
TRUMPS EVERYTHING

and POLITICIANS ARE NOT YOUR SAVIOR

Chuck Marunde, J.D.

INTRODUCTION

I hope to persuade you of a life altering proposition, and I'll tell you upfront what that proposition is:

> *The real war today is not political, not economic, not military, not social, not philosophical, and not scientific. The real war that is driving everything else is a spiritual war that is thousands of years old. I call this war the War of the Ages.*

We are living in the midst of a war between God and Satan that has been raging forever as we know time. Understanding this reality will change everything about how you see the world and interpret current events. When the deep reality of this war becomes your reality, your perception of this world, current events, and politics will dramatically change.

All those unanswered questions everyone keeps asking will begin to have answers for you. Just realizing there is a War of the Ages beneath everything we see on this planet will change your reality.

Knowing this is much more profound than you may realize at

INTRODUCTION

this moment. You'll begin to understand, for example, why almost nothing politicians ever propose, and almost nothing they ever implement, actually improves the lives of the citizens. In fact, the more politicians promise and the more they do, the more damage they do. Why?

Because the sincere politicians are fighting the wrong enemies in the wrong battlefields. The evil politicians are actually fighting the enemy they intend to fight—you and all your friends and family members. The astonishing and incredibly naïve citizen thinks the government is their friend, but in the midst of this spiritual war, government is our enemy, and that has been proven over and over and over again.

I'll show you in this book exactly why the battle is spiritual first and foremost, and why even good conservatives (and Christians) are blinded and fighting the wrong battles with the wrong strategies. They cannot win the war as they are fighting it, and I'll show you precisely why.

Many will say, "Oh, I know there's a spiritual war. Everyone knows that." That's not at all the point of this book. The proposition of this book goes much further by painting an accurate picture of how evil strategically conducts the war against us, how we can defend ourselves, and finally we'll look at exactly how this *War of the Ages* ends. The Bible tells us how it ends, so we don't have to guess.

> The key is knowing who your real enemies are, where the battlefields are, what their weapons are and how they use them, and becoming an expert with your weapons of war.

What compelled me to write this book? I'm tired of hearing good intelligent people make arguments that we need to do this, or we need to do that, when all those efforts are turned on the wrong enemies in the wrong arenas. They argue we need to stand

INTRODUCTION

up for ourselves, and that we need to call or write our congressman. We need to sign a petition, we need to join a political action committee, we need to volunteer at local political events, and we need to stand on the street corners waiving signs.

You can do those things if you want to, and there's nothing wrong with doing them, but 99% of those efforts are totally wasted effort in this kind of spiritual war.

It is incredibly naive to completely ignore the spiritual war that rages beneath all earthly battles. Bless the well-intentioned efforts of so many, including the few Christian politicians, but they are fighting the wrong battles.

To the radical liberals in control, the facts don't matter. The consequences of the failure of their policies doesn't matter to them. Not even remotely.

Understand this: They don't care about truth or justice, and they have no moral compass. It is unbelievably naive to make arguments that call upon their sense of justice or patriotism. They have none. It does no good to argue facts with them, or to try to persuade them of what is good and righteous. You might as well smash your forehead on a concrete wall.

They are motivated by something far different than you or I. They are motivated by a force that the vast majority of Americans, including most Christians do not comprehend. What is that motivation and what is that force?

It is spiritual warfare on a level that few people comprehend. I'll explain exactly how understanding spiritual warfare is the real key to victoriously handling the battles we face today. If you don't understand spiritual warfare at this deep level, you've already lost the battle, because your enemy will drag you into a battlefield that is outside the real battlefield, and will have you fighting proxies who are puppets in a much bigger war.

The very first task we have is to clearly see the *War of the Ages* that has lasted thousands of years. We'll look at what kind of

INTRODUCTION

battles that war has seen, and who the soldiers and commanders are. We'll also look at their strategies, because believe it or not, we know exactly what their war strategies are.

Now, let's get to it. We have a lot of work to do, and God willing, your eyes will be opened to a world you've never seen clearly.

PART 1

The War of The Ages
The Enemy & His Strategies
The Armies of God & His Victories

CHAPTER 1
THE WAR OF THE AGES
THE WAR THAT LASTS FOR THOUSANDS OF YEARS

There was a time when there was peace in the Universe. God ruled as the Almighty Creator, and He was worshipped by all the angels. God's power and authority were unquestioned. The Heavens resounded with the deep and awesome resonance of innumerable angels singing beautiful praises to the King. Never have such amazing sounds echoed so loudly throughout the Heavens night and day.

Then I looked, and I heard the voices of many angels around the throne and the living creatures and the elders; and the number of them was myriads of myriads, and thousands of thousands. Revelation 5:11 (NASB 2020). The original language indicates that the number of angels cannot be counted they are so innumerable. This is the meaning of myriads and thousands upon thousands.

One angel was the most beautiful of all angels in God's Kingdom. This angel was also the most powerful of all created beings in all of Heaven, and he was given great authority by God. This angel's name was Lucifer.

The other angels looked up to Lucifer, not only for his beauty and power, but for the favor that God bestowed upon him in Heaven. Lucifer was the greatest of all created beings.

Then a most extraordinary event occurred. Lucifer betrayed God.

> *But you said in your heart,*
> *"I will ascend to heaven;*
> *I will raise my throne above the stars of God,*
> *And I will sit on the mount of assembly*
> *In the recesses of the north.*
> *I will ascend above the heights of the clouds;*
> *I will make myself like the Most High." Isaiah 14:13-14*
>   *(NASB 2020)*

Lucifer recruited a third of the angels to join him in the rebellion. He became proud, and he wanted to be like God, and he aspired to rule the Heavens and the earth.

This was perhaps Lucifer's first act of rebellion, and he surely used deception upon the angels who joined him. These were angels who knew God intimately and lived in the Heavens. One cannot imagine what kind of sales pitch it must have taken to persuade one-third of all the angels to rebel against God, but whatever it was, it was Lucifer's first great deception. You can be sure the fallen angels hate Satan now and feel betrayed by him. They know God's power and they know much about his wrath, and worst of all, every one of those angels know that they are condemned to eternity in the Lake of Fire. You think you have some difficult challenges in this life. Imagine being a fallen angel, deceived by Satan and as a result you have no hope of salvation, and you know that your destiny is suffering and damnation for all of eternity!

For his sin and for leading the rebellion, God cast Lucifer and a third of the treasonous angels out of Heaven. They became condemned creatures, condemned to eternal damnation for their rebellion against God.

One third of a myriad of angels is a very large number. Since we know a myriad or an innumerable number of angels were in Heaven, one third could still be millions of fallen angels or demons, or possibly billions.

Lucifer, who became known as Satan on earth, commenced his war against God and against the entire Kingdom of God. The fallen angels became known as demons, and Satan created an entire military command structure to rule the earth and to fight God in the physical and spiritual realms.

> *As part of their war against God, Satan and his demon hosts also battle the holy angels. That is not surprising, since Scripture describes the devil as "the prince of the power of the air" (Eph. 2:2), as well as "the ruler of this world" (John 12:31; 14:30; 16:11). His theater of operations thus includes both the heavens and the earth, and the war of the ages is being fought at every conceivable level—moral, ideological, philosophical, theological, and supernatural. [Revelation 12-22 MacArthur New Testament Commentary]*

In God's infinite wisdom, after evicting Satan from Heaven, God made Satan the God of the earth. In their case the god of this world has blinded the minds of the unbelievers, to keep them from seeing the light of the gospel of the glory of Christ, who is the image of God. [2 Corinthians 4:4 (ESV)] Satan had great authority to do as he willed on earth.

As the world population grew, Satan made necessary improvements to his military command structure. His demons were assigned roles as rulers over nations, over governments, and over geographic areas. Higher ranking demons were appointed as authorities over ruling demons, and a lesser number of demons with great cosmic powers were placed over those with much authority. Finally, Satan appointed the highest rank to demons who would answer directly to him and are referred to as spiritual forces of evil in the heavenly places.

For we do not wrestle against flesh and blood, but against the rulers, against the authorities, against the cosmic powers over this present darkness, against the spiritual forces of evil in the heavenly places. Ephesians 6:12 (ESV)

For our struggle is not against flesh and blood, but against the rulers, against the powers, against the world forces of this darkness, against the spiritual forces of wickedness in the heavenly places. Ephesians 6:12 (NASB 2020)

Young's Literal Translation includes the phrase, "the world-rulers of the darkness of this age."

As far as humans are concerned, this great war began when Satan attacked God's first created humans in the Garden of Eden. When Adam and Eve plummeted into corruption by choosing to listen to Satan's lies and disobey God, the human race became embroiled in the cosmic war of the ages. In fact, since the Fall the earth has been the primary theater in which that war has been fought. Though already fallen, every member of the human race faces the same choice as the angels did in eternity past: to fight on God's side or on Satan's. Remaining neutral is not an option, for in Matthew 12:30 Jesus declared, "He who is not with Me is against Me; and he who does not gather with Me scatters." (Revelation 12-22 MacArthur New Testament Commentary)

Satan implemented his strategy to destroy all of God's creation at the beginning when he deceived Eve. When the woman saw that the tree was good for food, and that it was a delight to the eyes, and that the tree was desirable to make one wise, she took some of its fruit and ate; and she also gave some to her husband with her, and he ate. Genesis 3:6 (NASB 2020)

So sin, which was first conceived in the Heavens and the earth in the mind of Satan, entered the human race, and from that point forward every human would be born into sin. Satan's first military attack was to trap humans into a permanent state of sin, thereby achieving a victory of epic proportions.

Now the earth over which he ruled as the god of this world, had a fallen human race. This fallen race of God's creation would now by default be born into Satan's family of sinners condemned to eternal damnation.

"For all have sinned and fall short of the glory of God." Romans 3:23 (NASB 2020) "Therefore, just as through one man sin entered into the world, and death through sin, and so death spread to all mankind, because all sinned." Romans 5:12 (NASB 2020)

Let there be no doubt what Satan's objective is when it come to us. He wants to kill us, destroy us, humiliate us, and devour us like a lion devours its prey. We are told:

> *Be of sober spirit, be on the alert. Your adversary, the devil, prowls around like a roaring lion, seeking someone to devour. 1 Peter 5:8 (NASB 2020)*

But when Satan was making all these war plans in the beginning of time as we know it, God was not asleep, and because God is Omniscient and Omnipotent, He not only knew what Satan had planned, God's absolute sovereignty set Satan up from the very beginning to play his role and implement a strategy, in this case a war that would last for thousands of years.

We must not reject what God has done because we do not understand it. "For My thoughts are not your thoughts, Nor are your ways My ways," declares the LORD. For as the heavens are higher than the earth, So are My ways higher than your ways and My thoughts than your thoughts." Isaiah 55:8-9 (NASB 2020)

God knew sin would enter the human race through Satan's deception, and that sin would condemn mankind to hell. God also knew precisely how he would defeat Satan's attempt to drag the entire human race into hell with him, and God knew how to save his chosen ones from the consequences of sin.

At no point did Satan stump God, or surprise God, or catch God off balance. We must never forget that God is the Creator of the Heavens and the earth, and of hell and of the Lake of Fire, and everything created, and of every created being. Satan is one of God's creations. God is absolutely sovereign and infinitely in control of the Universe and all who live in it. Satan's challenge to God and his attempted overthrow of God's throne will go down as the greatest epic miscalculation in all of eternity.

God's plan, which Satan did not know before the fall and did not fully comprehend until much later, was to send his only son, Jesus Christ, who was perfectly righteous, to earth to live without sin and to die on a cross as the one and only sacrificial lamb for the sins of all God's chosen ones.

Satan was defeated at the cross, but the War of the Ages must finish its full purpose at the end of thousands of years. Satan is powerful, but there is one who is far more powerful beyond comparison.

> *On earth, among mortals, Satan has no equal, but in the heavenly realms he is far exceeded by the Triune God. The great Colossian hymn of the Incarnation reveals that Satan, and in fact the entire invisible spiritual realm, owes his existence to Christ: "For by him all things were created: things in heaven and on earth, visible and invisible, whether thrones or powers or rulers or authorities; all things were created by him and for him" (Colossians 1:16; cf. Colossians 2:10). There is no dualism here. Satan is not the counterpart of God. Because Satan is finite and God is infinite, our enemy is infinitely inferior! Satan's power is overwhelmed by that of God. (Preaching the Word Commentary Series, Eph 6 (41 Vols.) - PTW)*

CHAPTER 2
SATAN'S WAR STRATEGY
NO EVIL TOO EVIL

Satan, being the smartest (and most evil) creature on the earth, schemed to defeat God's plan to have a savior born through the human race who would have a pure line of inheritance.

In battle after battle Satan has failed to stop the savior from coming to earth, from being born, from surviving childhood, and from accomplishing his mission on earth. This has been a raging spiritual battle, and some of that battle has played out on the earth for humans to witness.

Satan tried to end the seed of Adam and Eve by deceiving Cain into murdering Abel. Satan deceived generations of people from many tribes and nations to serve evil rather than good. These nations' kings continually sought to destroy God's chosen people, the Jews.

During this great war God raised Prophets to reveal God's plans to reconcile man unto Himself. Almost 3,000 years ago Prophets told of the coming Savior, Jesus Christ, that He would suffer and die on a cross as the perfect sacrificial lamb for the sins of man.

Satan was determined to stop God's plans to send the perfect savior who could snatch God's chosen people out of Satan's grip of evil. Satan's war council implemented strategy after strategy for thousands of years, a non-stop evil war machine.

Early in the great war, Satan commanded 200 fallen angels (demons) to go into the world and procreate with human women in order to pollute human DNA so that the genetic line that would ultimately lead to Jesus' earthly mother, Mary, would be poisoned with Satan's seed.

Satan thought that if he could have his demon soldiers giving birth to a whole new generation of hybrids before the world was heavily populated, he could pollute the human race with his seed and somehow derail God's plans to have a pure inherited seed all the way to Abraham, Isaac, Jacob, and down to Mary. This was a major military strategy, one Satan hoped would be successful in stopping God's plans to save God's chosen ones.

That battle lasted for about a thousand years, but Satan's efforts ultimately failed. We know how this all happened, because the Bible tells us. The fallen angels were somehow able to mate with human women, and their offspring were called Nephilim. NEPH'ILIM (nef'i-lim; Gen. 6:4; Num. 13:33). See also Giant. The Nephilim are considered by many to be giant demigods, the unnatural offspring of the "daughters of men" (mortal women) in cohabitation with the "sons of God" (angels; cf. Gen. 6:1-4). This utterly unnatural union, violating God's created order of being, was such a shocking abnormality as to necessitate the worldwide judgment of the Flood. Another view of the Nephilim is that they were particularly violent (the name is from a root, "to fall," i.e., on other people), strong ("mighty"), and infamous ("men of renown") people who predated the marriages of v. 2. This viewpoint often explains the unions as intermarriage of the godly line of Seth (described in 4:25—5:32) with the ungodly line of Cain (4:1-24). (The New Unger's Bible Dictionary) So egregious was this horrendous sin of mating with humans by these fallen angels God bound them to this day.

And angels who did not keep their own domain but abandoned their proper dwelling place, these He has kept in eternal restraints under darkness for the judgment of the great day. Jude 1:6 (NASB 2020)

> *The Nephilim were on the earth in those days, and also afterward, when the sons of God came in to the daughters of mankind, and they bore children to them. Those were the mighty men who were of old, men of renown. Genesis 6:4 (NASB 2020)*
>
> *We also saw the Nephilim there (the sons of Anak are part of the Nephilim); and we were like grasshoppers in our own sight, and so we were in their sight. Numbers 13:33 (NASB 2020)*

Goliath was likely the offspring of Nephilim. There were giants, and they killed, plundered, and apparently ate great quantities of food, attacking villages and stealing the food and murdering people. It is even said they turned to cannibalism and ate humans for food. It has also been suggested that these Nephilim learned how to mix DNA with animals, and this may account for the many half human half animal creatures in mythology.

"And their judges and rulers went to the daughters of men and took their wives by force from their husbands according to their choice, and the sons of men in those days took from the cattle of the earth, the beasts of the field and the fowls of the air, and taught the mixture of animals of one species with the other, in order therewith to provoke the Lord; and God saw the whole earth and it was corrupt, for all flesh had corrupted its ways upon earth, all men and all animals." (The Book of Jasher 4:18 7:33)

Of this latter speculation, we cannot be sure, but we do know the earth was full of these giants, heirs of demon warriors. Their history is expanded in extra-biblical sources, such as the book of Enoch, which itself is credible because it is quoted in the Bible. The book of Jasher is another extra-biblical source with history of the Nephilim.

The giants' skeletal remains have been documented all over the world, although Satan has tried to hide that history, primarily through the Catholic Church, which for hundreds of years has confiscated all giants' skeletal remains immediately upon discovery in what could only be called a massive cover-up. All of this is well documented, but very mysterious. Old newspaper accounts from the early 1900s still have photos and testimonials of people like the farmers who found remains and took photos.

So populated did the earth become with Nephilim, and so evil did the people of the world become, God destroyed the world with the flood. In fact, God killed everyone on earth except eight people, Noah and his wife, and his three sons and their wives.

So we have Noah's birth, which occurred about 1,059 years after the creation of Adam. Then, in Genesis 7:11, we are told that the flood came in the 600th year of Noah's life, so that would mean the Great Flood came approximately 1,659 years after Adam was created in Eden. Using those same numbers places the creation of Adam and Eve at around 4,004 BC. So, doing the math, Noah's flood occurred in approximately 2,345 BC.

How many people did God kill in the Great Flood?

If the growth rate in the pre-Flood world was equal to the growth rate in 2000 (0.012), there could have been about 750 million people at the time of the Flood. However, given the extremely long lifespans prior to the Flood, the growth rate could have been much higher. Increasing the rate by just 0.001 would put the population at close to four billion at the Flood.

Whether there were 750 million or 4 billion people on earth,

God drowned them all, except eight. Many believe this was primarily because of the Nephilim who had populated the earth and were killing off humans, polluting their DNA, and were demonically evil.

The Nephilim were one of the primary reasons for the great flood in Noah's time. Immediately after the mention of Nephilim, God's Word says, "The LORD saw how great man's wickedness on the earth had become, and that every inclination of the thoughts of his heart was only evil all the time. The LORD was grieved that he had made man on the earth, and his heart was filled with pain. So the LORD said, 'I will wipe mankind, whom I have created, from the face of the earth—men and animals, and creatures that move along the ground, and birds of the air—for I am grieved that I have made them'".

While we have no definitive evidence to help us know if this is why God flooded the earth, one thing we can be sure the world was full of wickedness, and God had had enough of it:

> *Then the LORD saw that the wickedness of mankind was great on the earth, and that every intent of the thoughts of their hearts was only evil continually. Genesis 6:5 (NASB 2020)*

The War of the Ages has raged with a violence few among us can comprehend.

We are all but oblivious to this war, and even most Christians don't truly believe in their hearts that the Great Flood really happened. It feels more like a myth or story tale to people. But it did happen, and as big as it was, it was just one battle in the War of the Ages.

Consider the implications for us if the entire world were destroyed by a nuclear bomb, or multiple nuclear bombs, and everyone on the earth was killed except eight people, including you and seven of your family members. For generations afterward, the story would be passed on for all to know and remember. But after about 5,000 years, much would be forgotten, and most would consider it all a myth.

Is there any doubt that such a worldwide event killing as many as four billion people would be considered part of a war? Yet today, people are oblivious to the fact that we are living in a war that dwarfs all other wars in the history of the world.

CHAPTER 3
SATAN'S WAR AGAINST GOD
NO STRONGER HATRED EXISTS

For thousands of years Satan has continually tried to destroy God's chosen people, through whom the savior would come. Evil king after evil king tried to wipe out the nation Israel. Satan's efforts included many military campaigns, and these are only some of them:

- Nero killed Jews and Christians with a vengeance during his reign. Yet God protected them. [Nero became emperor of Rome when he was about seventeen years of age AD (Dan 5), and soon began to exhibit the character of a cruel tyrant and heathen debauchee. In May A.D. 64, a terrible conflagration broke out in Rome, which raged for six days and seven nights, and totally destroyed a great part of the city. The guilt of this fire was attached to him at the time, and the general verdict of history accuses him of the crime. "Hence, to suppress the rumour," says Tacitus (Annals, xv. 44), "he falsely charged with the guilt, and punished with the most exquisite tortures, the persons commonly called Christians, who are hated for their enormities. Christus, the founder of that name, was put to death as a criminal by Pontius Pilate, procurator of Judea, in the reign of Tiberius; but the pernicious superstition, repressed for a time, broke out again, not only throughout Judea, where the mischief originated, but through the city of Rome also, whither all things horrible and disgraceful flow, from all quarters, as to a common receptacle, and where they are encouraged. Accordingly, first three were seized, who confessed they were Christians. Next, on their information, a vast multitude were convicted, not so much on the charge of burning the city as of hating the human race. And in their deaths they were also made the subjects of sport; for they were covered with the hides of wild beasts and worried to death by dogs, or nailed to crosses, or set fire to, and, when day declined, burned to serve for nocturnal lights. Nero offered his own gardens for that spectacle, and exhibited a Circensian game, indiscriminately mingling with the common people in the habit of a charioteer, or else standing in his chariot; whence a feeling of compassion arose toward the sufferers, though guilty and deserving to be made examples of by capital punishment, because they seemed not to be cut off for the public good, but victims to the ferocity of one man." Another Roman historian, Suetonius (Nero, xvi.), says of him: "He likewise inflicted punishments on the Christians, a sort of people who hold a new and impious superstition" (Forbes's Footsteps of St. Paul, p. 60). [Easton's Bible Dictionary)]

- Titus destroyed Jerusalem and scattered the Jews in 70 A.D. Yet God protected the remnant and brought the

Jews back home to Israel. The Jewish Wars began in 66 A.D. and they were a direct revolt by the Jews against Rome's authority. Titus with his Roman legions arrived at the outermost northern Wall of Jerusalem, the Passover of 70 A.D. The Romans built embankments of earthenwork, they placed battering rams and the siege began. The Roman army numbered 30,000; while the Jewish army numbered 24,000. According to Tacitus they were 600,000 visitors crowding the streets of Jerusalem for the Passover. After five months the walls were battered down, the great Temple was burned down, and the city was left ruined and desolate, except for Herod's three great towers at the northwest corner of the city. These served as a memorial of the massive strength of Jerusalem's fortifications which Titus of Rome had brought to rubble. The legions of Rome brought the captives to Caesarea and after over one million Jews were killed, 95,000 captives were taken as prisoners, and among them was Josephus, the ancient Jewish historian. According to Eusebius, the Christians saw the might of the Roman army and through prophetic warning, fled to Pella.

- King Ahasuerus tried to kill all the Jews. Yet God didn't let him. Letters were sent by couriers to all the king's provinces to annihilate, kill, and destroy all the Jews, both young and old, women and children, in one day, the thirteenth day of the twelfth month, which is the month Adar, and to seize their possessions as plunder. Esther 3:13 (NASB 2020)
- Dimitian tried to wipe out all Christians and expunge all Christian writings. Yet God protected believers and made sure Bible manuscripts survived it all.

- The Pharaoh of Egypt enslaved the Jews for 400 years, and tried to kill them during their exodus. Yet God protected His people and killed all the Egyptian soldiers in the crossing of the Red Sea. "Then God said to Abram, "Know for certain that your descendants will be strangers in a land that is not theirs, where they will be enslaved and oppressed for four hundred years." Genesis 15:13 (NASB 2020)
- Satan infiltrated city after city with sexual immorality and sin, like Sodom and Gomorrah, doing his best to alienate humans from God. Yet God brought out Lot and his family, and protected the lineage of Abraham.
- To kill Jesus as an infant, King Herod issued an order to kill all boys two years old and younger in Bethlehem. Yet God protected the baby Jesus. "Then when Herod saw that he had been tricked by the magi, he became very enraged, and sent men and killed all the boys who were in Bethlehem and all its vicinity who were two years old or under, according to the time which he had determined from the magi." Matthew 2:16 (NASB 2020)
- Satan tried to convert Jesus away from being the Savior on a mountain top by tempting him three times, but Jesus refused. Yet Jesus rebuked Satan with the Word of God each time.
- Pilate held a trial and although Jesus was innocent of all charges, convicted and sentenced him to death anyway. Yet Jesus fulfilled his purpose as planned.
- Satan succeeded in having Jesus hung on a cross until he was dead. Yet Jesus was victorious and Satan defeated at the cross.
- Satan has used hundreds of empires and governments to destroy Jews and kill Christians,

including the ancient Egyptian Empire, the Babylonian Empire, the Phillistines, the Persian Empire, the Assyria Empire, the Roman Empire, the Greek Empire, the Byzantine Empire, the Spanish Empire, the Crusaders, Nazi Germany, and Russia. Yet God's people are alive and well, and a remnant is standing firm until the end.

There have been thousands of major earthly battles over the millennia that humans have not recognized as having been coordinated on a spiritual level. Humans tend to rely totally upon what they see, hear, touch, taste and smell, but beyond that their perception of reality ends. The truth is, Satan has been at work for thousands of years, and we are not only living in the battleground, our minds are a battleground.

Thirteen of God's greatest warriors on earth all suffered tremendously as soldiers for Christ, and all but one was martyred.

- Matthew was killed with a sword.
- Mark was dragged by horses until he was dead.
- Luke was hanged in Greece.
- John was thrown into a pot of boiling oil, but miraculously survived and later was taken to Heaven and given a vision in order to pen the book of Revelation.
- Peter was crucified upside down.
- James, the church leader in Jerusalem, was thrown over a hundred feet from the southeast pinnacle of the Temple, but he survived only to be beaten to death with a club.
- James, the son of Zebedee, was beheaded in Jerusalem.
- Bartholomew, aka Nathaniel, was flayed to death by a whip.

- Andrew was whipped and then crucified on an x-shaped cross in Patras, Greece.
- Thomas was stabbed with a spear.
- Jude was killed with arrows.
- Matthias, who replaced Judas, was stoned and then beheaded.
- The Apostle Paul was tortured and then beheaded by Nero in Rome.

These were all soldiers on the front lines of the battle in their times. Satan has fought God constantly from the Garden of Eden to the days when Jesus walked the earth all the way to today, and the war will continue until its prophetic end.

We gain insight into Satan and his powers in the book of Job. Satan has access to God and can enter Heaven to approach God. Satan has this kind of access until Revelation 12 when God evicts Satan permanently from Heaven.

CHAPTER 4

DEMONS VS. ANGELS

THE INVISIBLE RAGING WAR AROUND US

There are untold numbers of battles between God's angel warriors and Satan's demon warriors. ["Demons can cause dumbness (Mat 9:32-33), and blindness (Mat 12:22), and insanity (Luk 8:26-35), and the suicidal mania (Mar 9:22), and personal injuries (Mar 9:18), and impart supernatural strength (Luk 8:29) and inflict physical defects and deformities. Luk 13:11-17. Once they have got control over a human body they can come and go at will." Luk 11:24-26. Larkin, Clarence. The Spirit World (Illustrated) (p. 38). Kindle Edition.]

We are privy only to a few of those battles. As far as we know from what the scriptures reveal, angels, including the fallen angels, cannot be killed, do not ever sleep, and do not have to eat for sustenance. They are so powerful that if it were not for God's protection, they could easily wipe every human off the face of the earth.

We get a glimpse of angelic battles when the Prophet Daniel spent three weeks in prayer and fasting and an angel (perhaps Gabriel) appeared to him and said:

Do not be afraid, Daniel, for from the first day that you set your heart on understanding this and on humbling yourself before your God, your words were heard, and I have come in response to your words. But the prince of the kingdom of Persia was standing in my way for twenty-one days; then behold, Michael, one of the chief princes, came to help me, for I had been left there with the kings of Persia. Daniel 10:12-13 (NASB 2020)

God sent an angel to Daniel, but the prince of the kingdom of Persia held him back for 21 days. The prince of the kingdom of Persia is a demon with great power, enough to hinder an angel sent from God for 21 days, and this demon prince has been assigned a specific geographic or spiritual authority, just as any military commander is assigned a geographic area or a type of command.

"What a dreadful thought … the government offices of a nation occupied by the forces of anti-God!' We don't usually think this way. We have no trouble believing that incompetence and bungling are endemic to governments and political machinery, but we don't as easily think of suave and sinister spirits of evil lurking in the corridors of our congresses or shaping the policies of our parliaments. Veldkamp speaks of any number of Satanic assistants who are 'far more cunning than even the most clever human diplomats' and each is assigned to be an evil influence on the people of a country 'through lies, propaganda, and other means, with the overall goal of stirring up hatred of the church of the Lord'." (Bible Speaks Today (BST): Old Testament Set (33 Vols.)

The angel doesn't go into detail with Daniel about that 21 day battle. We are bound to be curious, but we do not know the details. One cannot help but wonder. In that spiritual dimension, which we cannot see with our eyes, how did the demon prince stop the angel warrior? Did they fight as with swords? When they fight do they have physical characteristics that enable them to fight as soldiers on earth fight? Or is it all spiritual power like a force field that one can send against the other with a verbal command? We do not know, but we know it was an intense 21 day battle night and day. Perhaps in that realm, such a battle is loud and violent and visibly dramatic like any violent war to the death. In the case of an angelic battle, they do not die, but there is victory and defeat.

The angel does tell Daniel that he could not overcome the demon prince by himself, so the angel Michael came and helped him to defeat the demon. The angel called Michael is "one of the chief princes," and in some versions the translation is "Archangel." This affirms that there are levels of military command and degrees of power, and this is true on both sides of the war.

Even when the angel leaves Daniel, he reveals that he must fight again:

Then he said, "Do you understand why I came to you? But I shall now return to fight against the prince of Persia; so I am leaving, and behold, the prince of Greece is about to come. Daniel 10:20 (NASB 2020)

The angel knows he must fight the demon prince again, but he also knows that reinforcements are being sent by Satan via the prince of Greece, another demon ruler in Satan's chain of command. How the angel knew that he would face a fight on his return to Heaven, and how he knew the prince of Greece would join the battle against him is not revealed in the text. Clearly there is much we do not know about these battles, and apparently there are not only one on one fights, but there is a communication system and intel and reinforcements when needed. There is a military command structure, and surely it is far advanced over earthly military systems.

There is an interesting argument to be made that the one who comes to Daniel is the second member of the Trinity, and R. Kent Hughes connects many verses that describe this "angel" in the exact same way Jesus is described elsewhere, looking the same and talking the same with the same greeting. If you want to pursue that, I recommend Hughes 41 Volume commentary.

"These verses show us the battle of the army of the Lord. The Second Person of the Trinity was doing battle with the Prince of Persia, probably Satan himself, over the soul of Cyrus, Darius the Mede. This heavenly battle would eventually find its way into the events of world history when Greece, in God's time, would conquer Persia, as we will see in Daniel 11. But the thing that bothers people the most is that the Second Person of the Trinity was delayed about three weeks by the Prince of Persia. If he is God, could he not have destroyed Satan in a moment? Yes, but we don't understand the ways of God. Remember the historical account of the Second Person of the Trinity wrestling with Jacob all night to a draw. How could Jacob have the strength to match God in a wrestling match? I don't know, but that is what God decided should happen." (Preaching the Word Commentary Series (41 Vols.) - PTW)

We also know that the Archangel Michael fought with Satan over the body of Moses.

> But when the archangel Michael, contending with the devil, was disputing about the body of Moses, he did not presume to pronounce a blasphemous judgment, but said, "The Lord rebuke you." Jude 1:9 (ESV)

This is an important disclosure for us, because we can see that as powerful as the Archangel Michael was as he faced Satan, even

Michael did not use all kinds of confrontational victory language that the false teachers and false prophets of today use. Instead, Michael said, "The Lord rebuke you."

Since Michael knows God personally and spends a lot of time in Heaven, we should give him great credibility in knowing how to face Satan in battle. Michael's defense was to point out that it is the Lord who rebukes Satan. The power is not Michael's, just as the power is not mine or yours. The power that defends us from Satan's wily ways is found in tapping into the power in God through Jesus Christ. Whatever power lives within us, whatever power we wield over evil in our battles, finds its source in our God and Savior.

CHAPTER 5

ANGELS FIGHT FOR US AND MINISTER TO US

MIGHTY WARRIORS TO OUR AIDE

W e get a glimpse of angels helping us and protecting us, although we can never see them and do not realize they are here with us.

> *The angel of the LORD encamps around those who fear Him, and rescues them. Psalms 34:7 (NASB 2020)*
>
> *Are they not all ministering spirits, sent out to provide service for the sake of those who will inherit salvation? Hebrews 1:14 (NASB 2020)*
>
> *When morning dawned, the angels urged Lot, saying, "Up, take your wife and your two daughters who are here, or you will be swept away in the punishment of the city." Genesis 19:15 (NASB 2020)*
>
> *Then the devil left Him; and behold, angels came and began to serve Him. Matthew 4:11 (NASB 2020)*
>
> *But the angel of the LORD came back a second time and touched him, and said, "Arise, eat; because the journey is too long for you." 1 Kings 19:7 (NASB 2020)*
>
> *Then the angel of God, who had been going before the camp of*

Israel, moved and went behind them; and the pillar of cloud moved from before them and stood behind them. Exodus 14:19 (NASB 2020)

He responded, "Look! I see four men untied and walking about in the middle of the fire unharmed, and the appearance of the fourth is like a son of the gods!" Daniel 3:25 (NASB 2020) [This third one may have been Jesus rather than an angel, but we do not know.]

Then the angel of the LORD went out and struck 185,000 in the camp of the Assyrians; and when the rest got up early in the morning, behold, all of the 185,000 were dead. Isaiah 37:36 (NASB 2020)

> For He will give His angels orders concerning you,
> To protect you in all your ways.
> On their hands they will lift you up,
> So that you do not strike your foot against a stone.
> You will walk upon the lion and cobra,
> You will trample the young lion and the serpent.
> Psalms 91:11-13 (NASB 2020)

We have no idea how many and how significant are the battles that angels fight on our behalf:

"Behold, I am going to send an angel before you to guard you along the way and to bring you into the place which I have prepared. Be attentive to him and obey his voice; do not be rebellious toward him, for he will not pardon your rebellion, since My name is in him. But if you truly obey his voice and do all that I say, then I will be an enemy to your enemies and an adversary to your adversaries. Exodus 23:20-22 (NASB 2020)

And there was war in heaven, Michael and his angels waging war with the dragon. The dragon and his angels waged war, and they did not prevail, and there was no longer a place found for them in heaven. And the great dragon was thrown down, the serpent of old who is called the devil and Satan, who deceives the whole world; he was

thrown down to the earth, and his angels were thrown down with him.
Revelation 12:7-9 (NASB 2020)

This vignette of angels doing battle for us and against Satan and his princes of evil is another revelation to us of the massive War of the Ages that has been raging and continues to rage.

CHAPTER 6

REWARDS TO THE VICTORS
WHAT A CELEBRATION THERE WILL BE

W e are all in this war, and have been from the day of our birth. It's a spiritual war that drives all other earthly wars, conflicts, and agendas. We have all been drafted into this war, whether we know it or not. Each of us must decide which side we are on. You are either for God or against Him. There are no other sides, and if you do not choose God, you belong to Satan who keeps you in his ranks.

The reality of this war and our role as soldiers has never been hidden from us. It is in the scriptures as obvious as anything:

Who at any time <u>serves as a soldier</u> at his own expense? Who plants a vineyard and does not eat its fruit? Or who tends a flock and does not consume some of the milk of the flock? 1 Corinthians 9:7 (NASB 2020)

But I thought it necessary to send to you Epaphroditus, my brother and fellow worker and <u>fellow soldier</u>, who is also your messenger and minister to my need. Philippians 2:25 (NASB 2020)

Suffer hardship with me, as a <u>good soldier</u> of Christ Jesus. <u>No soldier in active service</u> entangles himself in the affairs of everyday life,

> so that he may please the one who enlisted him. 2 Timothy 2:3-4 (NASB 2020)
>
> To Philemon our beloved brother and fellow worker, and to Apphia our sister, and to Archippus <u>our fellow soldier,</u> and to the church in your house. Philemon 1:1-2 (NASB 2020)

In this war there will be casualties. Many Christians will be killed in service, and many more will be persecuted and suffer greatly. All Christians will suffer, and that is the calling of a good soldier.

> *For to you it has been granted for Christ's sake, not only to believe in Him, but also to suffer on His behalf. Philippians 1:29 (NASB 2020)*
>
> *Therefore, those also who suffer according to the will of God are to entrust their souls to a faithful Creator in doing what is right. 1 Peter 4:19 (NASB 2020)*
>
> *Blessed are those who have been persecuted for the sake of righteousness, for theirs is the kingdom of heaven. Matthew 5:10 (NASB 2020)*

The picture of the good soldier is not one of seeking pleasure in this life. A good soldier serves his King obediently, regardless of the personal cost in this present arena, because the soldier is loyal and knows he will be rewarded.

> *But we have this treasure in earthen containers, so that the extraordinary greatness of the power will be of God and not from ourselves; we are afflicted in every way, but not crushed; perplexed, but not despairing; persecuted, but not abandoned; struck down, but not destroyed; always carrying around in the body the dying of Jesus, so that the life of Jesus may also be revealed in our body. For we who live are constantly being handed over to death because of Jesus, so that the*

life of Jesus may also be revealed in our mortal flesh. So death works in us, but life in you. 2 Corinthians 4:7-12 (NASB 2020)

The entire Bible from Genesis 1 through Revelation 22 is about the War of the Ages and our role in this war. It is in our best interests to figure out our individual roles, and get down to business as good soldiers, because our eternal destiny depends on it.

Ultimately, Heaven itself will be our reward, and even more so being in the presence of our Heavenly Father and our Savior cannot be adequately described from this side of Heaven. The United States Marine Core recognizes outstanding service in the military with medals and ribbons, but our service as soldiers for Christ will be rewarded in at least these five ways:

1. The Crown of Life. This is the "Martyr's" crown, and is mentioned twice. ["Blessed is a man who perseveres under trial; for once he has been approved, he will receive the crown of life which the Lord has promised to those who love Him." James 1:12 (NASB 2020) "Do not fear what you are about to suffer. Behold, the devil is about to throw some of you into prison, so that you will be tested, and you will have tribulation for ten days. Be faithful until death, and I will give you the crown of life." Revelation 2:10 (NASB 2020)]
2. The Crown of Glory. This is the "Elder's" or "Pastor's" crown, given by the Chief Shepherd when He shall appear. ["And when the Chief Shepherd appears, you will receive the unfading crown of glory." 1 Peter 5:4 (NASB 2020)]
3. The Crown of Rejoicing. This is the "Soul Winner's" crown. ["For who is our hope, or joy or crown of pride, in the presence of our Lord Jesus at His coming? Or is it

not indeed you?" 1 Thessalonians 2:19 (NASB 2020) "Therefore, my beloved brothers and sisters, whom I long to see, my joy and crown, stand firm in the Lord in this way, my beloved." Philippians 4:1 (NASB 2020)]

4. <u>The Crown of Righteousness</u>. This is the crown of those who "love His appearing" [the rapture] and will be given in the Day of His Appearing ("that day"). ["In the future there is reserved for me the crown of righteousness, which the Lord, the righteous Judge, will award to me on that day; and not only to me, but also to all who have loved His appearing." 2 Timothy 4:8 (NASB 2020)]

5. <u>The Crown Incorruptible</u>. This is the "Victor's" crown, and is for those who do not yield to their fleshly lusts, and do not permit themselves to be diverted by worldly amusements and pleasure. ["Everyone who competes in the games exercises self-control in all things. So they do it to obtain a perishable wreath, but we an imperishable." 1 Corinthians 9:25 (NASB 2020)]

Soldiers for Christ will serve until the rapture when they will be taken home to Heaven, but the War of the Ages will go on without them, and it will get exceedingly worse during the seven years of tribulation. Jesus told how us bad it will get:

> For then there will be a great tribulation, such as has not occurred since the beginning of the world until now, nor ever will again. And if those days had not been cut short, no life would have been saved; but for the sake of the elect those days will be cut short. Matthew 24:21-22 (NASB 2020)

Those who do not come to Christ by faith before the rapture will find themselves in the tribulation, a nightmare beyond anything imaginable. There will still be many who are saved during the tribulation, but many will have to die for their faith in Christ, and because they refuse to worship the beast and take the mark. [For a definitive biblical analysis of the Mark of the Beast and what it will mean in the tribulation, I urge you to read my book entitled, "Mark of the Beast and The 7 Year Tribulation."]

CHAPTER 7
THE TRIBULATION WAR REACHES AN ETERNAL APEX

"FOR THEN THERE SHALL BE GREAT TRIBULATION."

Satan's war against God and all his creation, including you and me, has yet to reach its apex. It gets worse and reaches its greatest intensity during the Great Tribulation, the latter half of the seven year tribulation.

Considering that this War of the Ages has lasted thousands of years, and considering how violent it has been with astounding forces of nature coming into play, even the destruction of the whole earth, you might expect that the final battle at the very end would present a very dramatic defeat for one and an extraordinary and eternal celebration for the victor. And so it does. Satan's defeat will be epic beyond explanation, and it will be watched by all of Heaven as well as all humans who ever lived.

Yet the victory will be the greatest victory any human or angel has ever seen from the beginning of time. The rejoicing in Heaven by millions upon millions of angels and by millions upon millions of saved children of God is unquestionably going to be the greatest celebration of the ages after the end of the War of the Ages.

The final battles of Satan's long war against God are yet to be fought. They will take place in the future, during the last half of the seven-year tribulation period, the time Jesus called the Great Tribulation (Matt. 24:21). At that time Satan, aided by the absence of the raptured church and the presence of increased demon hordes (9:1-11), will mount his most desperate assaults against God's purposes and His people. But despite the savage fury with which those assaults will be carried out, they will not succeed. The Lord Jesus Christ will effortlessly crush Satan and his forces (19:11-21) and send him to the abyss for the duration of the millennial kingdom (20:1-2). After leading a final rebellion at the close of the Millennium, Satan will be consigned to eternal punishment in the lake of fire (20:3, 7-10). [Source: Revelation 12-22 MacArthur New Testament Commentary]

Ultimately the full evil potential of Satan will be seen during the tribulation. He is evil beyond the comprehension of any human being. What he does below our visible radar, and what he seeks to achieve in the lives of humans is abhorrent to such an extreme degree, the worst we can imagine does not come close. Satan's character is revealed in numerous places throughout the scriptures.

In the book of Job Satan is shown in detail: he is a heavenly being who, at least in OT times, could appear with the angels in God's presence (Job 1:6; 2,1). He can be in only one place at a time (Job 1:7; 2,2), accuses righteous people 1:9-11; see Zech. 3:1), and destroys anything God allows him to destroy 1:12ff; 2:4ff.). These attributes of Satan are reaffirmed in the NT: he is a tempter (1 Cor. 7:5), a liar and murderer (Jn. 8:44), a betrayer (Lk. 22:3), a perpetual sinner (1 Jn. 3:8), an accuser of Christians (Rev. 12:10), full of hate (1 Pet. 5:8; 1 Jn. 3:10), and conceited (1 Tim. 3:6). People who do live that sort of lifestyle—even those who preach a false christ, Spirit, and gospel—are considered Satan's servants (2 Cor. 11:13-15). Satan is also known as the evil one (Mt. 5:37), Beelzebub and the prince of demons 12:24), the dragon and the ancient serpent (Rev. 12:9), the ruler of this world (Jn. 12:31), and the prince of the power of the air (Eph. 2:2). [*Mounce's Complete Expository Dictionary of Old and New Testament Words*]

Leading up to Jesus statement in Luke 21:28 is his explanation of what events will occur just before His return. There are several places in the Bible that tell us what events will occur before His return at the end of the tribulation. When we pull the verses together, here is what we see:

- False Christs and false prophets arise.
- There will be wars and rumors of wars.
- Nation will rise against nation and kingdom against kingdom.
- There will be increases in famines, pestilences and earthquakes.
- Lawlessness and immorality will rule.
- The love of many will grow cold.
- Christians will depart from the faith giving heed to doctrines of demons.
- Men will be lovers of self, lovers of money, unholy, proud, boasters, blasphemers, unloving, disobedient to parents, unforgiving, slanderers, without self-control, brutal, traitors, headstrong, lovers of pleasure rather than lovers of God and unthankful.

We can see these unfolding today at a pace that is shocking, but they pick up the pace dramatically during the tribulation. These are proven signs of the end of days. The end of the War of the Ages is on the horizon.

The war accelerates during the seven year tribulation. The

tribulation will be the most horrendous seven years the world has ever known. In Matthew 24:21 Jesus said:

For then there will be a great tribulation, such as has not occurred since the beginning of the world until now, nor ever will again. Matthew 24:21 (NASB 2020)

Pause on what Jesus said for a moment. Do you realize how bad it will be if there never has been such a time, nor ever will be again for all of eternity? All the wars of the world combined will be nothing compared to the tribulation!

The Holy Spirit, also known as the "Restrainer," will no longer restrain evil during the tribulation, and you and I cannot imagine how bad it will be. You think government despots are bad now? You think the growing power of the American Federal government is a threat now? You think torture, child sacrifice, rape, and murder are bad now?

You can't even begin to imagine what this world will be like when the Holy Spirit no longer restrains evil, and when evil is allowed to come up and out of the bowels of the earth to wreak havoc and chaos and evil on the earth. Demons will be roaming the earth with a vengeance that the world has never seen.

We've only seen shadows of the wickedness to come, like these:

- Mao Zadong (responsible for 26 million deaths)
- Adolf Hitler (responsible for 17 million deaths)
- Leopold II (responsible for 15 million deaths)
- Joseph Stalin (responsible for 10 million deaths)
- Hideki Tojo (responsible for 5 million deaths)
- Nickolas II (responsible for 3 million deaths)
- Saddam Hussein, (responsible for 2 million deaths)

SPIRITUAL WAR TRUMPS EVERYTHING

All of these men and their evil are just previews of the evil that is coming during the tribulation.

The Antichrist will sign a covenant with Israel that purports to create peace for the world, but in his deception, this will commence the worst time in the history of mankind. He will establish a one-world government with himself as dictator of the world. [Daniel 9:27 and Revelation 6:1-2] Then world war will commence. [Revelation 6:3-4]

Peace will be taken from the whole earth and replaced with chaos and hate and violence, and it will be so bad people will be killing each other. The way the verse explains this, people will be forced to kill each other. This is hard to believe, so let's look at the verse:

> *Then another horse came out, a fiery red one. Its rider was given power to take peace from the earth and <u>to make people kill each other</u>. To him was given a large sword.* [Revelation 6:4]

Then another wave of destruction comes and kills more people by sword, famine, and plague. Based on the numbers of people dying after the opening of the other seals, it would seem likely that millions die this time also. [Revelation 6:5-6]

One-fourth of the people on the earth will die in the war, which based on today's population, will be about one and a half billion people. [Revelation 6:7-8]

Massive numbers of believers will be martyred. [Revelation 6:9-11]

There will be an earthquake like no one has ever seen on the earth, resulting in massive numbers of deaths. The sun will turn black, the moon will turn red, and stars will fall to the earth. Every mountain and island will be "removed from its place." People will be suffering so terribly, they will call out for the rocks to fall on them and kill them:

Then the kings of the earth and the great ones and the generals and the rich and the powerful, and everyone, slave and free, hid themselves in the caves and among the rocks of the mountains, calling to the mountains and rocks, "Fall on us and hide us from the face of him who is seated on the throne, and from the wrath of the Lamb, for the great day of their wrath has come, and who can stand?" [Revelation 6:12-17]

And then we learn that:

A third of the earth was burned up, a third of the trees were burned up, and all the green grass was burned up. [Revelation 8:7]
 A third of the sea turned into blood, a third of the living creatures in the sea died, and a third of the ships were destroyed. [Revelation 8:8]

It's hard to comprehend such destruction, but 1/3rd of the earth will be burned up, and 1/3rd of the sea creatures and 1/3rd of all ships at sea will be destroyed.

You and I cannot imagine what that will be like, because the worst we have ever seen or heard of or read about in history is the two nuclear bombs that were dropped on Hiroshima and Nagasaki in which 214,000 people died, and the Indonesian tsunami of 2004 that killed at least 225,000 people across a dozen countries. According to the CDC in 1918 the deaths from the Flu pandemic were estimated to be at least 50 million worldwide with about 675,000 occurring in the United States.

Now imagine over four billion killed during the tribulation, and then the rest who are not saved condemned to hell at the end of the tribulation. This will be the culmination of a war so big we cannot even begin to capture it in our minds.

This is the War of the Ages that started in the Garden of Eden with Satan attacking God's creation, and has continued for thousands of years without pausing, but during the tribulation picks up a momentum that tears the earth apart and kills billions of humans.

A star called Wormwood will collide with the earth, and one third of all the rivers of the world turn bitter and many more will die. [Revelations 8:10-11]

> *A third of the sun was struck, a third of the moon, and a third of the stars, so that a third of them turned dark. A third of the day was without light, and also a third of the night.* [Revelation 8:12]

> *And out of the smoke locusts came down on the earth and were given power like that of scorpions of the earth. They were told not to harm the grass of the earth or any plant or tree, but only those people who did not have the seal of God on their foreheads. They were not allowed to kill them but only to torture them for five months. And the agony they suffered was like that of the sting of a scorpion when it strikes. During those days people will seek death but will not find it; they will long to die, but death will elude them.* [Revelation 9:3-6]

> *And the four angels who had been kept ready for this very hour and day and month and year were released to kill a third of mankind. The number of the mounted troops was twice ten thousand times ten thousand. I heard their number.* [Revelation 9:15-16]

> *A third of mankind was killed by the three plagues of fire, smoke and sulfur that came out of their mouths.* [Revelation 9:18]

Even after all the starvation, war, plagues, slaughters, murder, and death,

> *The rest of mankind who were not killed by these plagues still did not repent of the work of their hands; they did not stop worshiping*

demons, and idols of gold, silver, bronze, stone and wood—idols that cannot see or hear or walk. Nor did they repent of their murders, their magic arts, their sexual immorality or their thefts. [Revelation 9:20-21]

Is that not astonishing? It's hard to imagine how cold their hearts will be if after all that they have seen and experienced, and all the wrath of God pouring out on them, that they would still want to reject God and worship Satan and the Beast.

All of this is demonstrative of the reality of a War of the Ages, a war above all wars, a war of eternal significance that is still playing out.

It is this eternal war that is over and above all earthly wars. Everything that happens on the earth is part of a bigger picture, and Satan is the god of this world.

What does it mean to be god of this world? Here's a brief synopsis of Satan's power and influence as the god of this world.

- He is the ruler of the earth.
- He has all authority on earth, except that which God has retained.
- He has an army of rulers, authorities, and principalities, a massive invisible army, that works to achieve his evil goals, and no one in his army sleeps.
- He had thousands of years to build governments in every nation that would serve his purpose.
- He structured governments to accomplish his long range plans, and that included the creation of departments, divisions, agencies, and even national security agencies.
- He influenced relationships, hiring, and favors to accomplish his agenda without any of the puppets

knowing they were being used. In other words, Satan had the power to staff the governments he built.
- He has had all the time he needed to build nations and evil alliances.
- He has had plenty of time to build cults, to develop false teachers, and to infiltrate churches.
- He was the founder of all false religions, including, but not limited to, Baha'i, Muslim, Buddhism, Free Masonry, Hinduism, Jehovah's Witnesses, Mormonism, Roman Catholicism, Scientology, Seventh-Day Adventist, Unitarian Universalism, and Satanism. [Roman Catholicism alone claims 1.2 billion Roman Catholics in the world, according to Vatican figures.]
- At his leisure he built entire national education systems, curriculum, universities, and he expunged history in school textbooks, and developed a master plan to re-educate children starting in kindergarten.
- He built an entire central banking system in every country, and coordinated all of it with an International banking system.
- He built financial systems and investment systems, like Wall Street, to facilitate the control of people's money and finances and even their retirement accounts (which he can make go away).
- Satan got deeply into every branch of government in America, including the structure of the executive, legislative, and judicial branches, and today, Satan owns all three branches. There is nothing he cannot make each branch do, and we are witnesses to the evil of each branch today.
- He was always into politics, because that is how he controls governments and laws and courts. Satan's

total domination of politics in almost every nation on earth testifies to this reality.
- He took control of media and put it to work to promote his evil agenda in each nation. Even in America, the obvious lies, distortions, manipulation, and fraud in the mainstream media testify to Satan's total control, fulfilling his need to control the narrative, manipulate people, and brainwash the weak minded.
- While America's founding was a set back for Satan, he recovered by destroying America from within during his two centuries' assault.

There is one big agenda Satan has, but he has not been able to achieve it, and he never will. Satan has worked for literally thousands of years to destroy the nation of Israel and the Jewish people. That hasn't worked out for him, because God's chosen people are the Jews and the nation Israel. Many times Satan thought he had won the victory to kill and scatter the Jews, and destroy them as a nation, and many times God brings the Jews back, and God did restore the nation Israel in 1948.

The last battle in this War of The Ages will be Satan's attempt to wipe Israel off the earth, but when it seems hopeless, God intervenes and destroys all 10 nations attacking Israel. In a matter of minutes, it will be over.

Near the end of this War, it gets extremely intense. As already mentioned billions of people are killed, earthquakes cause mountains to fall into the ocean, volcanoes erupt, a third of all the ocean life is killed, a planet or meteor hits the earth, and most of the earth burns up.

And then Jesus kills the beast with his breath alone.

Then that lawless one will be revealed, whom the Lord will eliminate with the breath of His mouth and bring to an end by the appearance of His coming. 2 Thessalonians 2:8 (NASB 2020)

What Satan and his demons never seem to fully comprehend is the power that Jesus has over them. There's no comparison. God is infinitely more powerful than Satan, and even though this War of The Ages has been extremely hard on the human race, and we even wonder sometimes what will happen, be assured God wins in the end, and it's not even a close contest.

PART II

The Weapons of War
Defensive & Offensive

CHAPTER 8

PREPARING OUR WEAPONS OF WAR

THE ULTIMATE AND ONLY SOURCE OF TRUE POWER

We are living through the War of The Ages, the war of all wars, the war to end all wars. It is a massive war of epic proportions, although we only see the visible battles on earth, perhaps representing less than 1/100th of 1% of all the battles in the spiritual realm.

It is a raging war, violent, without boundaries of any kind for our enemy, and eternal life for everyone who lives and whoever has lived depends upon the outcome of this War of The Ages. Not a single living soul is exempt from the final judgment that is to come.

Since God is absolutely sovereign, and since He is Omnipresent, Omnipotent, and Omniscient, He is the mastermind behind all that we see and all we cannot see in the natural and spiritual realms. He placed us in this war with a purpose, and He knows how we must suffer, be persecuted, and how some must be killed.

But God has not sent us into battle defenseless and without weapons of warfare.

In fact, God has equipped all of us with everything we need to be victorious, yet most Christians are either unaware of these powerful defensive weapons, or they don't take them seriously.

You've read these verses from Ephesians a hundred times before, but this time let's examine the defensive weapons God has given you in the context of this massive War of The Ages that we are living through, and especially so in these last days before the rapture.

> *Finally, be strong in the Lord and in the strength of His might. Put on the full armor of God, so that you will be able to stand firm against the schemes of the devil. For our struggle is not against flesh and blood, but against the rulers, against the powers, against the world forces of this darkness, against the spiritual forces of wickedness in the heavenly places. Therefore, take up the full armor of God, so that you will be able to resist on the evil day, and having done everything, to stand firm. Stand firm therefore, having belted your waist with truth, and having put on the breastplate of righteousness, and having strapped on your feet the preparation of the gospel of peace; in addition to all, taking up the shield of faith with which you will be able to extinguish all the flaming arrows of the evil one. And take the helmet of salvation and the sword of the Spirit, which is the word of God. With every prayer and request, pray at all times in the Spirit, and with this in view, be alert with all perseverance and every request for all the saints. Ephesians 6:10-18 (NASB 2020)*

We must not miss the Apostle Paul's emphasis that he has written in the prior five chapters of Ephesians, because all that he just told us is summed up for this closure when he says, "Finally" in 6:10. He wrote "Finally" to make the point that our defense against Satan and his demons is not a simple formula that we can adopt and be all done. It is not a mechanical strategy that you can sell people, and all are guaranteed to be safe and happy forever.

SPIRITUAL WAR TRUMPS EVERYTHING

Paul wrote "Finally" because he wanted us to know that all he said before must be a part of our defense in this spiritual war. You see, our very first weapon of self-defense is submission to Jesus Christ. Let's expand on this.

There is a logical sequence that unfolds for the genuine believer. First, unless a person repents of their sin and places their faith in Christ alone, they will not be saved, which means they are still on the wrong side of the war and do not have God's protection.

Second, having been saved by the Savior and his death on the cross to atone the believer's sins, there are a number of spiritual transactions that take place in the believer that changes everything about the war we find ourselves in now.

When we are saved in Christ, we are baptized into his death. This means we are dead to sin and alive to Christ. Just as Jesus died once on the cross for our sins, upon our salvation we died once to sin forever, and we have been transferred from the kingdom of darkness to the Kingdom of Light.

> *And you were dead in your offenses and sins, in which you previously walked according to the course of this world, according to the prince of the power of the air, of the spirit that is now working in the sons of disobedience. Ephesians 2:1-2 (NASB 2020)*

Paul clearly connected this spiritual transaction of our souls with spiritual warfare, and he even mentions Satan as the "prince of the power of the air."

Paul also wrote to the Colossians and wanted them to know this powerful truth:

> *For He rescued us from the domain of darkness, and transferred us to the kingdom of His beloved Son. Colossians 1:13 (NASB 2020)*

The genuine Christian no longer belongs to the world and to Satan. He belongs to God, who paid an infinite price for his soul, the death of God's only son, Jesus Christ.

> *Or do you not know that your body is a temple of the Holy Spirit within you, whom you have from God? You are not your own, for you were <u>bought with a price</u>. So glorify God in your body. 1 Corinthians 6:19-20 (ESV)*

This is the first challenge most Christians have when they are babes in Christ. They do not comprehend the extraordinary transaction that has taken place in them. If you don't understand you no longer belong to the kingdom of darkness, and you don't realize how much of God's power lives in you, you will be timid in war, and even though you have an arsenal at your disposal, you won't touch any of the weapons.

Satan absolutely loves the naive Christian who doesn't defend himself. Satan's victories are daily events, precisely because the vast majority of Christians have no armor on and no defense whatsoever!

At the moment of your salvation, you belong to God and Satan cannot touch you . . . unless God allows it.

> *We know that no one who has been born of God sins; but He who was born of God keeps him, and the evil one does not touch him. We know that we are of God, and that the whole world lies in the power of the evil one. 1 John 5:18-19 (NASB 2020)*

Now, having an understanding of the pretext of Ephesians 6 and the power we already have in Christ, let's look specifically at what Paul then assures us we can do defensively against Satan's attacks.

"*Finally, be strong in the Lord and in the strength of His might. Put on the full armor of God.*"

In other words, do not leave an opening for Satan. Do not give him an easy way of attacking you. You wouldn't go outside on a cold winter day in snow at -40 degrees Fahrenheit fully dressed in winter gear but barefoot. You would go outside fully clothed to face the cold weather. Do not be naive with Satan and his demons. Arm yourself with the full armor of god.

To put on the full armor is both a command and a promise. The promise is if we properly put on the full armor, we will be protected.

"*So that you will be able to stand firm against the schemes of the devil. For our struggle is not against flesh and blood.*"

The War of the Ages is not a visible war on this earth, although some of it takes the form of things we can see obviously. The bigger war that rages between God and Satan is the unseen war, and our enemies in this war are not flesh and blood. It is not the politicians or the Wall Street barons or the bankers or the drug traffickers who are our real enemies.

"*But against the rulers, against the powers, against the world forces of this darkness, against the spiritual forces of wickedness in the heavenly places.*"

Here is the list of the ranking forces of Satan's army. There are many, and they are organized into a finely tuned military machine. This is who we face.

"*Therefore, take up the full armor of God.*"

I cannot resist emphasizing that we are called to put on the full armor of defensive weapons, not just some of them or all of them except one. You cannot leave an opening for Satan or his demons, or they will take advantage of it and infiltrate your life.

Such has been the cause of great chaos and harm in many a Christian's life. The implications are many: falling to sexual temptation, adultery, homosexuality, drug use, alcohol addiction, violent behavior, assaults, stealing and lying, misrepresentations, financial fraud, divorce, and the list goes on. How do you avoid going down that long path of destruction? You put on the whole armor of God.

"<u>So that you will be able to resist on the evil day, and having done everything, to stand firm.</u>"

The battles we face in the spiritual realm, which often happen most intensely in the mind and heart, are not like worldly skirmishes where you pull out a gun or a knife to defend yourself as a special forces soldier would do in a close fight. Our fight is not with flesh and blood. This is why we are told to "resist," because resisting evil in all its forms is placing our total confidence in the one who does have all the power and authority over evil. The battle is not for you and me to fight either physically or in our own spiritual might. We must draw upon the power within us, the Holy Spirit who resides in us, upon our Lord and Savior because he already fought the great battle and achieved victory for all of us and because "we have the mind of Christ." When our eyes are opened and we are searching for answers, it is amazing how many places in the scriptures, we see the truth reminding us how we are to conduct ourselves as good soldiers.

> *But a natural person does not accept the things of the Spirit of God, for they are foolishness to him; and he cannot understand them, because they are spiritually discerned. But the one who is spiritual discerns all things, yet he himself is discerned by no one. For who has known the mind of the Lord, that he will instruct him? <u>But we have the mind of Christ</u>. 1 Corinthians 2:14-16 (NASB 2020)*

Having considered the defensive weapons, or at least the weapons that prepare us for battle and tap into God's power and authority, next we'll look at the balance of weapons at our disposal.

CHAPTER 9
HOW TO USE WEAPONS OF WAR
THE VICTORIOUS SOLDIER FOR CHRIST

As soldiers for Christ, we cannot imagine ourselves fighting as though soldiers in an earthly arena.

> *The struggle is futile if fought in and by our own flesh. As Calvin said:*
> *He means that our difficulties are far greater than if we had to fight against men. Where we resist human strength, sword is opposed to sword, man contends with man, force is met by force, and skill by skill; but here the case is very different, for our enemies are such as no human power can withstand. (Preaching the Word Commentary Series, Eph 6 (41 Vols.) - PTW)*

We must prepare ourselves for a different kind of warfare than we are used to seeing on earth. Two of my sons became professional athletes. My oldest son, Jesse Marunde, became the second strongest man in the world in Chengdu, China in the World's Strongest Man Competition in 2005. Jesse's strength was nothing less than phenomenal, but all his power and strength was worthless against the spiritual forces of darkness. Jesse understood that.

My son, Bristol Marunde, became a professional mixed

martial artists, and in the gym behind the scenes in training was good enough to beat world champions, like Randy Courture and Vitor Belfort. He was incredibly strong for his 205 pounds, and his submissions and technique were world class, making him one of the most dangerous men alive. But all his speed, all his technique, and all his power were useless in fighting demonic forces. Bristol fully understands this.

Power in the spiritual realm for the Christian is on a different level altogether. Offensively, we are given powerful weapons for war, starting in verse 14 of Ephesians 6:

> *Stand firm therefore, having belted your waist with truth, and having put on the breastplate of righteousness, and having strapped on your feet the preparation of the gospel of peace; in addition to all, taking up the shield of faith with which you will be able to extinguish all the flaming arrows of the evil one. And take the helmet of salvation and the sword of the Spirit, which is the word of God. With every prayer and request, pray at all times in the Spirit, and with this in view, be alert with all perseverance and every request for all the saints. Ephesians 6:14-18 (NASB 2020)*

Stand Firm Belted With Truth

"<u>Stand firm therefore, having belted your waist with truth.</u>"

The Apostle Paul was in prison and probably chained to a Roman soldier, so one can imagine he was looking at the soldier's armor as he described our spiritual armor. When a soldier tightened his belt he was ready for combat, because in the process of tightening he drew up his tunic and cinched it so it could not impede him as he charged into battle. It also firmly fixed his sword in place.

But the key to "having belted your waist with truth" is that the truth is the foundation upon which all else is established.

Truth holds the spiritual armor in place, and assures that none of the armor gets entangled.

The truth is everything when it comes to spiritual warfare. Jesus said, "I am the truth, the way, and the life." The Apostle John wrote, "You will know the truth, and the truth will set you free." (John 8:32) And John wrote, "Sanctify them by the truth; your word is truth." (John 17:17)

Not only is Jesus the Truth, and the Word of God is true, but all objective truth belongs to God, so we must build our beliefs, our thoughts, our reason, and our behavior on what is true. This is the beginning of all spiritual warfare as it is here when putting on the full armor of God.

The Breastplate of Righteousness

"And having put on the breastplate of righteousness."
When we become Christians, God gives us his own righteousness, so it is not something we earn by ourselves, but a gift from God through the sacrifice of Jesus on the cross. The point of the breastplate is that it protects the vital organs, including the heart, without which you cannot survive. Without God's imputed righteousness to us who believe, we would not survive either. We would be condemned to eternal damnation, since unrighteousness cannot exist in the presence of a God who is Holy Holy Holy.

The Gospel of Peace

"And having strapped on your feet the preparation of the gospel of peace."
Roman soldiers wore boots with nail studded heels so they could stand firm in battle against an enemy. Their feet had traction and they could stand firm without unstable or being pushed back. This is what peace does for the believer. We have peace with

God because we are saved, but we also have peace with ourselves, too. "Therefore, since we have been justified through faith, we have peace with God through our Lord Jesus Christ." (Rom 5:1)

Jesus told us, "Peace I leave with you; my peace I give you." (John 14:27) We can even have peace in the midst of our struggles and daily challenges. There's nothing like being at peace and standing firm in wicked times like these.

The Shield of Faith

<u>"In addition to all, taking up the shield of faith with which you will be able to extinguish all the flaming arrows of the evil one."</u>

The shield Paul must have had in mind was a large shield about four feet high and two and a half feet wide, and the Roman soldier used the shield to stop all kinds of attacks that could come from arrows, stones, spears, and any other dangerous objects that could come out of nowhere at any time while in battle.

As Christians, we are attacked regularly, and the attacks come in various forms, including temptations, an image that incites sexual thoughts, sweet persuasive words from a tempter in business, daily decisions involving money, a moment that presses one to exaggerate or be dishonest about a small issue, and any number of flaming arrows.

We must be constantly ready to raise that shield to protect ourselves, or we can be seriously wounded. In other words, we could fall to sin of various kinds, be shamed as Christians, and even be taken out of Christian service in some cases. The importance of the shield of faith cannot be overemphasized.

<u>"And take the helmet of salvation."</u>

The helmet was a metaphor for salvation, so when we know we are saved, we have the confidence of a believer who is well protected for battle. You wouldn't go into a football game without a well fitted helmet, and we dare not go into the War of the Ages without salvation as our helmet.

Paul wrote, "Being confident of this, that he who began a good work in you will carry it on to completion until the day of Christ Jesus" (Philippians 1:6), and "The hope of salvation as a helmet." (1 Thessalonians 5:8)

God's choosing of us and our salvation is such an incredible confidence builder that gives us tremendous hope and encouragement throughout difficult times, and we see this in one of the most amazing portions of the scriptures:

Blessed be the God and Father of our Lord Jesus Christ, who has blessed us with every spiritual blessing in the heavenly places in Christ, just as He chose us in Him before the foundation of the world, that we would be holy and blameless before Him. In love He predestined us to adoption as sons and daughters through Jesus Christ to Himself, according to the good pleasure of His will, to the praise of the glory of His grace, with which He favored us in the Beloved. In Him we have redemption through His blood, the forgiveness of our wrongdoings, according to the riches of His grace which He lavished on us. In all wisdom and insight He made known to us the mystery of His will, according to His good pleasure which He set forth in Him, regarding His plan of the fullness of the times, to bring all things together in Christ, things in the heavens and things on the earth. In Him we also have obtained an inheritance, having been predestined according to the purpose of Him who works all things in accordance with the plan of His will, to the end that we who were the first to hope in the Christ would be to the praise of His glory. In Him, you also, after listening to the message of truth, the gospel of your salvation--having also believed, you were sealed in Him with the Holy Spirit of the promise, who is a first installment of our inheritance, in regard to the redemption of God's own possession, to the praise of His glory. Ephesians 1:3-14 (NASB 2020)

There's no doubt that the helmet of salvation is a major critical piece of the believer's armor.

The Sword of the Spirit

<u>"And the sword of the Spirit, which is the word of God."</u>
God reveals himself, his truths, salvation, doctrine, history, and the future through his Word, the Bible. This is how he speaks to us in these last days. So the power of the Word as our source of truth and the power we can tap into, is nothing short of astonishing. In the natural world of battles, there is nothing like the Word of God.

When Satan tempted Jesus three times in the desert, Jesus fought each of the three temptations with quotations from the Bible (Deuteronomy 8:3, 6:16, 6:13). If Jesus, the Son of God and second person of the Trinity would battle Satan by using the Word of God from the Bible, then we ought to take a big hint that should be our weapon of choice, too.

The Bible is a powerful weapon against temptation and sin in this raging war. "I have hidden your word in my heart that I might not sin against you" (Psalm 119:11).

The more you read the Bible, the more it transforms your life, and the more you grow to love it more than anything else on earth. And do not underestimate the life changing power of truth in doctrine. The title of one of my books emphasizes the value of doctrine: The 9 Most Controversial Christian Issues Answered: Doctrine to Empower Your Life.

How do we take "the sword of the Spirit?" We read the Bible regularly, hopefully daily. We carefully examine verses, parables, and doctrine. We learn the fundamental principles of Bible study, hermeneutics, to correctly divide the Word of Truth. We learn to use good dictionaries, commentaries, and discern good translations from less reliable ones. We mediate and pray about verses we study. We memorize scripture. And we discuss interpretations with a best friend who also is on the same road of serious Bible study in pursuit of an intimate relationship with God.

Learn to love the Word of God more than anything on earth.

With Every Prayer

"<u>With every prayer and request, pray at all times in the Spirit.</u>"

Paul does not include prayer as one of the weapons he lists, but prayer must infuse all else. After listing all the spiritual weapons, he then says that all of these weapons are to be used prayerfully. Pray is to precede our actions, continue as we take action, and follow all that we do.

Prayer is almost like blood in the veins. It's important to take care of your body, to get good nutrition and to exercise regularly. Blood is not an additional bodily organ, or another strategy to keep your body functioning. Blood is what keeps it all going night and day. Consider what blood does for the whole body:

- Delivers O_2 from the lungs to the cells
- Removes waste CO_2 from the cells
- Responds to injury by clotting
- Carries multiple types of nutrients by various means (free-floating, carrier protein-associated, lipid particles)
- Provides transport for the immune system, which in itself has diverse functions
- Transports waste products to the liver and kidneys
- Moves regulatory molecules around the body (hormones, chemokines, cytokines, antibodies)
- Regulates heat in the body
- Regulates pH and CO_2

Blood carries nutrients and oxygen throughout the body and regulates many critical functions. Likewise, our time in reading the Word ought to be bathed in prayer. Resisting temptation ought to always be covered by prayer. How we study and implement doctrine ought to be embedded in prayer.

The lack of a good prayer life has serious spiritual health consequences, just as the lack of good blood flow throughout your body causes all kinds of problems. Sleep apnea is a condition that interferes with breathing at night, so the lungs aren't getting enough oxygen, which means the blood, which carries oxygen throughout the body is not getting enough oxygen to feed the body. The implications in the short term include insufficient sleep, especially deep sleep, which means healing and reproduction at the cellular level is not happening as it should. The body is not recovering from the exertion of each day's activities. Insufficient sleep means grogginess during the day, and the mind is not clear or performing at its best. In the long term, sleep apnea, if not properly treated, can contribute to heart disease and many other diseases.

Another common condition is high blood pressure, and if it is high enough (hypertension), it can also inhibit good sleep at night. While you might think high blood pressure would increase blood flow and improve oxygen to the whole body, it does the opposite. You wake up at night gasping for breath, but unlike sleep apnea, this time its not because you aren't breathing. You are breathing, and your lungs are working properly, but blood circulation is impeded and there isn't enough oxygen feeding your body. Your body keeps waking you up as part of it's automatic alert system, because you feel like you can't breath. The negative health implications include heart disease, heart attack, stroke, and a long list of short term and long term conditions and diseases.

If you do not pray, or you do not pray much, or your prayer life is weak, you will experience all kinds of negative consequences in your life, some of which can be devastating. Depending upon your personal spiritual condition, and everything else about you that makes you unique, and depending upon your worldly circumstances in life, depending on the rest of your Christian life and the intimacy and genuiness of your life with God (Bible reading, study, mediation, memorization, accountability, and Christian fellowship), you can experience a potentially long list of short term and long term negative consequences.

Prayer is your life blood, and you cannot survive without it, especially in the evil of these last days.

But notice that we are to "pray at all times in the spirit." Again we are to do so all the time as though prayer was spiritual sustenance for us, which it is, and there is an intimacy with the Holy Spirit in prayer, even in knowing what to pray.

As believers who have been baptized into Jesus Christ and into his death, we are filled with the Holy Spirit, who has an entire ministry in our lives, one of which is softly speaking to us and helping us know what we should pray for and how to pray. So prayer ought to be done "in the spirit" and not as an act of our own or in the flesh as though our words had power. Apart from belonging to Christ, being baptized in his death and alive to Christ, and being filled with the Holy Spirit, our prayers have no power.

Prayer is not a strategy—it is how we live and breath in Christ. If you want to starve your spirit, stop praying or pray hardly. A weak prayer life will mean weakness in all areas of your spiritual life. Try reading the Bible without prayer, and you might as well read some great literary work dead to the spirit, although God's Word will always have its intended affect.

The vast majority of Christians in America do not pray much. Many rarely pray. Without daily prayer, random prayer, a variety of prayer, constant prayer, desperate prayer, joyful prayer, pleading prayer, hopeful prayer, prayer in tears, prayer through verses, prayer about doctrine, prayer for the lost, prayer for loved ones, prayer for the persecuted, prayer for our government, prayer for your Christian leaders and church, and random prayer for those who are in need, your life as a Christian will be nothing compared to what it could be.

Are you serious about being a good and effective soldier for Christ? Then pray.

CHAPTER 10
WRONG WEAPONS & WRONG BATTLEFIELDS
POLITICIANS FAIL US BECAUSE THEY ARE FIGHTING THE WRONG ENEMIES IN THE WRONG ARENAS

If a person does not understand that there is a War of The Ages, a powerful and massive spiritual war raging all around us in the world, a War that encompasses this earth, the Heavens, and the entire Universe, a war that every single baby has been born into since the Garden of Eden, a war that drafts every human being whether they know it or not, a war that engulfs every nation on earth and effects every living creature, a war that includes innumerable angel warriors and demons—if a person is unaware of this war of all wars—they will chase the wrong solutions and fight the wrong battles with the wrong enemies.

The answers you get in life are only as good as the questions you ask. Who among the leaders of America today, even in the churches, is asking the right questions so as to address the real war?

Politicians in America are fighting the wrong battles in the wrong arenas. Satan is laughing as hard as a fallen angel can laugh, considering he knows his time is short. On the other hand, knowing his time is short has only made him more vicious and more desperate.

Two Classes of Politicians

There are two classes of politicians controlling America today.

<u>First Class</u>. The first class or group of politicians who dominate American politics today are not believers at all. There's not even a legitimate debate about this. Some of them present themselves as Christians, but they are as phony as a $2 bill. They lie openly, commit fraud openly, and they promote policies that are blatantly evil.

They promote policies that are clearly identified in the Bible as evil or sinful, or at a minimum contrary to God's principles for living, including, but certainly not limited to:

- Abortion
- Homosexuality
- Class warfare
- Voter fraud (illegal aliens and dead people welcomed)
- The Federal government as a replacement for God
- Marxism and Communism
- The elimination of freedom of speech
- The elimination of freedom of religion
- The elimination of the right to bear arms
- The elimination of the right to privacy
- Teaching children at the youngest ages to be sexually immoral
- Taking away parental rights of their own children
- Placing control of all children under the State
- A One World Agenda
- Federal control of all personal healthcare decisions
- Federal control of ending lives of the elderly

- The elimination of the American form of government
- Central control of the executive, legislative, and judicial branches
- Control of all main stream media to promote an evil agenda
- Abuse of national intelligence agencies to promote their evil agendas
- Affiliate relationships with the largest American tech companies to promote their evil agendas on all these items

This is only a partial list of a much longer list of this horrendous and evil agenda. This agenda is fully embraced by the liberal democrats controlling America today.

Whatever they may claim in public about their "Christianity" or "Muslim" or "Ecumenical" faith, they are clearly beyond a shadow of a doubt serving as soldiers of Satan. Many of them won't even know that, and many are blinded and cannot see this spiritual war, but they are serving evil quite effectively in their roles.

They derive power, wealth, and the fulfillment of their lusts with no limits, so they are on top of the world and winning battle after battle—or so they think. They have no idea what is coming!

The Good But Misguided Politicians

<u>Second Class</u>. The second group of politicians are well intentioned, generally honest and hard working. They are what we often call "good Americans" or "patriots." They want the best for America, and they oppose the liberalism that is destroying America from the left democrat side. Some of them are Christians.

Unfortunately, these good politicians are fighting the wrong enemy in the wrong arena. They do not comprehend the spiritual

War of the Ages. Those who are not Christians are blinded to the spiritual reality, so they naturally focus all their well-intentioned labor to fight battles against their perceived opponents in arenas (subject areas) where they also sincerely think the battle is.

Of course, these good men and women are fighting legitimate battles, and they are doing the best to protect our constitutional rights and all our freedoms, and they are doing all they can humanly do to protect us from tyranny.

But their efforts, as well meaning as they are, are only the human battles on the surface. There is no suggestion here that their efforts are wasted or that they should not fight these battles. Someone has to. If, however, this is deemed as the war to fight, and if liberal politicians are deemed to be the enemies who must be defeated, then all is lost.

All political battles are undergirded by a spiritual war of far more power and far more soldiers, and that is the war that determines ultimate outcomes.

If you are a politician, and you do not comprehend the War of the Ages as the realty behind all skirmishes on this earth, then you will spend a lifetime fighting the wrong battles in the wrong arenas.

Perhaps this is an unfair comparison, but to make the point I will remind you of the story of Don Quixote, who thought that windmills were giants. He charged windmills with his lance, and would fight them until his lance failed to kill the giant and his helmet got turned around.

The politicians in Washington D.C. and in state capitals across America are fighting windmills until their helmets get turned around. And then they give speeches to the people about all the battles they're going to wage, and they go back to fighting windmills. They love to tell their constituents that, "Our greatest days in America are ahead of us, not behind us!" They are so embarrassingly wrong, but they don't know about the real war.

Do not judge these politicians, because they are good people. They just are unaware of the War of the Ages that has already been raging for thousands of years, and it is this War of the Ages that will end everything.

What Are Christian Politicians To Do?

If all of this is true, and there's no question the War of the Ages is real, then what are Christian politicians to do today? How are they to fight our battles?

The battles here must still be fought, but an awareness of the spiritual war changes everything in how we strategize and what weapons of war we rely upon. Instead of Christian politicians going into long harangues about how the democrats need to change the way they think, or that democrats need to realize a certain policy does not work, or trying to educate democrats on an issue, or demanding that democrats do this or that...

These same politicians finally must mature in their thinking and realize that the democrats are not going to do what they want, and they will not cooperate, they won't suddenly see the light of day, and they are not going to repent of their liberal democratic policies. The DNC, the democrat national committee, and the entire democrat party cannot repent, and their organizations won't be saved.

Only individuals called by God will be saved, not organizations and not political parties. The DNC does not have the capacity to repent. It is an impossibility. But a democrat who has been a liberal all their lives can repent and trust Jesus by faith as their one and only Savior.

The reality is that all these radical liberals who hate America with a passion and want to bring democracy and America to an end as we know it, who love Marxism and Communism, who love to abort babies with ecstatic joy, who shut down churches and stomp on free speech, who want a one-world order, who hate all things Christian and love all things Satanic—these people who now control politics in America, are destined for hell and the Lake of Fire, unless they individually come to Christ.

We are talking about the people on earth who are faithful soldiers for Satan. Granted, many of them have so little awareness of the reality of God and Satan, they don't know they serve Satan as loyal soldiers. Many, however, are quite aware, and serve Satan openly and publicly proclaiming Satan's evil policies. Whether they know or don't know, the result is the same.

Today, and this is a very sad commentary on the state of American politics, the democratic party has become irrevocably aligned with the agenda of Satan.

This is the nature of <u>mass deception in the last days</u> that Jesus warned us about in Matthew 24. When Jesus' disciples asked him about the last days, there was an extraordinary conversation worth reviewing now in the context of this War of the Ages and where we are politically today in America:

> Now as He sat on the Mount of Olives, the disciples came to Him privately, saying, "Tell us, when will these things be? And what will be the sign of Your coming, and of the end of the age?"
>
> And Jesus answered and said to them: "Take heed that no one <u>deceives</u> you. For many will come in My name, saying, 'I am the Christ,' and will <u>deceive</u> many. And you will hear of wars and rumors of wars. See that you are not troubled; for all these things must come to pass, but the end is not yet. For nation will rise against nation, and kingdom against kingdom. And there will be famines, pestilences, and earthquakes in various places. All these are the beginning of sorrows.
>
> "Then they will deliver you up to tribulation and kill you, and you will be hated by all nations for My name's sake. And then many will be

offended, will betray one another, and will hate one another. Then many false prophets will rise up and <u>deceive</u> many. And because lawlessness will abound, the love of many will grow cold. But he who endures to the end shall be saved. And this gospel of the kingdom will be preached in all the world as a witness to all the nations, and then the end will come. Matthew 24:3-14 (NKJV)

When your eyes are opened by God, and when you realize all these things Jesus said are true, it is a reality check like nothing else could be. Then when you put your eyes into the Word of God, the Bible, and you devote yourself to prayer and spiritual growth and wisdom, what used to be foggy for you, slowly begins to become clear.

So what is the Christian politician to do today in America? He (or she) is to devote themselves to God, to the Bible, to truth, and never compromise what is true and right. They are to pray always without ceasing for God's guidance and for wisdom. They must commit to faithfulness, sexual purity (Satan's greatest weapon against politicians and religious leaders), and they must persevere. They are to rally Christians in support of their Godly causes, and they are never to be ashamed of the Gospel of Christ. They are to stand firm, put on the whole armor of God, and then they are to do the best they can every single day on specific issues as they fight with demon democrats.

Finally, they are to leave the results to God, who is all-powerful, all-knowing, and always omnipresent, and who holds the future of the world in the palm of his hand.

We have the assurance of our salvation, and we know exactly how the War of the Ages ends.

ABOUT THE AUTHOR

Chuck Marunde grew up in Alaska in a 900 square foot cabin with his parents, two sisters and two brothers. They had no electricity, no running water, and no indoor plumbing. Their cabin was heated with a 55-gallon barrel welded into a wood stove. A single kerosene lantern hanging from a 16-penny nail lit the entire cabin. The outhouse was a lonely walk in the middle of a dark cold winter night. Winters lasted for nine months, and their little cabin burned 10 cords of firewood every winter.

Life in remote Alaska was harsh in the '60s, but it was also rich with experiences and valuable lessons for life. Chuck got through college by working as a forest fire fighter in Alaska for the BLM (Bureau of Land Management). After graduating from the University of Alaska with a B.A. in Economics, Chuck got his teaching credentials and taught high school for two years in a little Alaskan town called Nenana. He married and worked his way through Gonzaga University School of Law in Spokane while raising a family.

Chuck joined the United States Air Force and served four years as a Captain and a JAG, first as a prosecutor and then a defense attorney. It was as a defense attorney that Chuck had the privilege of helping clients learn about how to get past the behaviors that got them into trouble, and he discovered he was experiencing more fulfillment in serving God evangelizing and discipling than he was as an officer in the USAF.

It was at this point that Chuck left the USAF and went to work for Chuck Colson and Prison Fellowship Ministries as Area Director of Nevada and Utah. "I really enjoyed going to different denominations to share the vision of Prison Fellowship Ministries and to recruit volunteers and donors. It was also an amazing experience to go into high security prisons to teach the Word of God to inmates who were killers without the possibility of parole. I grew a lot from that experience."

Chuck also learned something else that was life changing. He learned that you do not have to be in full time ministry within a church or para-church to serve God. Anyone can serve God right where they are.

Realizing he needed to get his children out of the gang and drug infested inner city known as North Las Vegas, Chuck looked for a safe place to raise his children. He found that place on the beautiful Olympic Peninsula in Sequim, Washington. Chuck finished 20 years of law practice in Sequim and lives there today.

But this just opened up another chapter in Chuck's life, because God led Chuck to his next adventure, which is writing books as a ministry to reach people for Christ.

Chuck can be reached at chuckmarunde@gmail.com.

ALSO BY CHUCK MARUNDE, J.D.

Conspiracy Theories, Gaslighting & Cognitive Dissonance

How Narcissists Destroy Companies & Kill Startups

Help God! The Inmates Have Taken The Asylum

Political Narcissism: Why America is Imploding

Spiritual War Trumps Everything

The Greatest Motivational Message

The War for America's Soul

America: The Last Days

The End of All Things is at Hand

The 7th Habits of Godly Christians

Success & Eternity

Destroying Strongholds of The Mind

Living Off The Grid in Alaska

The 9 Most Controversial Christian Issues Answered: Doctrines to Empower Your Life

Is Speaking in Tongues For Today? Answers With Biblical Proof Beyond A Reasonable Doubt

The Pre-Trib Rapture

5 Points of Calvinism

Mark of the Beast and the Tribulation

Are Dreams and Visions for Today?

King James Only: The Argument Refuted by Historical and Biblical Proof

Living For God: Pursuing Christ With Passion

From Prosperity to Hell

Manage Your Energy Not Your Time

Peak Performance: The Zones for Peak Performance in Nutrition, Exercise, Mind & Spirit

The Kavanaugh Hearings: The Tipping Point of America's Soul

Day Trading: The Greatest Con Ever Invented

Sequim Real Estate, A Buyer's Guide

Sequim Real Estate Videos for Buyers

Sequim Real Estate Trilogy

Sequim Real Estate for Buyers with Free eBook Updates

Escaping California to The San Juan Islands

The 24 Secrets of Buying a Country Home

The 7 Myths of Selling Your Home

Real Estate Brokerage from Bricks and Mortar to High Tech Virtuality

The New World of Marketing for Real Estate Agents

Buying Your Retirement Home and How Much to Offer

Printed in Great Britain
by Amazon